LINKING WITH THE 4TH DIMENSION

Dictation from The Great White Brotherhood

Bob Sanders

DISCLAIMERS

This is a free eBook. You are encouraged to share it for free (in unmodified form) to whomever you wish. If you have paid for this eBook, you should request or seek an immediate refund.

The author has made every effort to ensure that the accuracy of the information within this book was correct at the time of publication. The author does not assume and hereby disclaims any liability to any party for any loss, damage, or disruption caused by errors or omissions, whether such errors or omissions result from accident, negligence, or any other cause.

COPYRIGHT

This book was authored by Bob Sanders and dictated to him from The Great White Brotherhood by clairaudience, or as some people call "channeling". It is free for everyone to read and share unmodified for spiritual advancement. Please share this book unmodified with anyone and anywhere you can to help spread the messages it contains. For more information please visit the following internet sites:

https://www.thegreatwhitebrotherhood.org

https://www.thestairwaytofreedom.org

https://www.youtube.com/channel/UC2UDv0r4mtNPEWbve5YHDeg/

First edition – February 2020

Cover Artwork by Paul Saunders

Author – Bob Sanders

TABLE OF CONTENTS

FOREWORD 5
CHAPTER 1 6
CHAPTER 2 13
CHAPTER 3 16
CHAPTER 4 21
CHAPTER 5 27
CHAPTER 6 34
CHAPTER 7 40
CHAPTER 8 48
CHAPTER 9 55
CHAPTER 10 59
CHAPTER 11 70
CHAPTER 12 77
CHAPTER 13 82
CHAPTER 14 89
CHAPTER 15 99
CHAPTER 16 104
CHAPTER 17 117
CHAPTER 18 130
CHAPTER 19 140
CHAPTER 20 147
CHAPTER 21 160
CHAPTER 22 172
CHAPTER 23 183
CHAPTER 24 190
CHAPTER 25 201
CHAPTER 26 209
CHAPTER 27 217
CHAPTER 28 223
CHAPTER 29 228
CHAPTER 30 236
CHAPTER 31 246
CHAPTER 32 253
CHAPTER 33 263

FOREWORD

In the first book on auras that we gave you, it was noticed that there were certain promises made in the Foreword of that book that were not, in fact, kept in the meat of the book.

We like to keep our promises, so this volume will fulfill the promises made and, as the subject of auras is comprehensive and continues beyond what we told you in the first volume, we will add new information above and beyond the information contained in the original book.

In the first book we promised to show you techniques for entering the different dimensions - auras and dimensions being the same thing - and this we will do in this volume.

However, we must add a warning.

We have already, many times, explained how to enter the higher 4th dimension, which is where we are to be found and we will do so again, but the higher 4th contains many levels or layers (we have referred to them as landscapes), so we will explain how to enter some of them that you would not normally be able to enter without this new knowledge. But it is not without difficulty.

To enter spiritual areas requires attuning oneself to those landscapes, adjusting one's frequency.

Therefore, it will require much training to achieve this.

We will teach you how to align yourself to certain landscapes but we cannot do it for you. We will be with you to protect you, but we require you to act in a responsible, adult manner.

What we can teach you is not a game. It is serious spiritual wisdom and must be treated as such.

Further, we have decided to give you new, previously undisclosed information about the auras and, once again, we ask you to treat this information with respect because it will be information never before revealed to man in this cycle of incarnation.

We are treating you as advanced students of cosmic wisdom or consciousness and this wisdom is not given lightly by us.

If you are not prepared to approach this course in cosmic wisdom with total seriousness, it would be better not to read this book.

Only the most conscientious of students will arrive at the end with a mastery of the subjects explained.

However, we will give you the information and leave you to attempt to learn or not.

CHAPTER 1

SUMMERLAND – WELCOME HOME

As we said in the Foreword, we will do two things in this book, which is an update of the book on auras we gave you.
The first will be to give you information on how to enter, safely, the various regions of the upper 4th dimension and the second will be to give you new information about the various auras.

In case you are wondering why we will only be talking about the upper 4th dimension, the answer is that the upper 4th is the only area with life as you would understand it to exist.
All the other dimensions are involved with assisting life but do not contain any complete humans, plants or animals, as you would know them to be.
So, if you were to enter any other dimension, you would be completely lost and, indeed, certain dimensions are dangerous.

So, in order to be able to contact any meaningful landscapes and to contact the beings that live in them, it suffices to learn how to enter the upper 4th dimension.
It is separated into a host of different landscapes or sub-dimensions.
All areas are separated by being of different frequencies, some higher and some lower.
If you have studied all the information we have given you, you should know this.
We will describe the actual technique later but we will describe some of these landscapes first so that you will be prepared to understand what you will be seeing.
After all, if you were going to visit a foreign country, it would make sense to learn something about that country and its population, so it makes sense to be informed about the various areas you may learn to enter in the heavenly spheres.

So, we will describe some of these areas but please do not think that having awareness of them will enable you easily to enter them. It won't.
It will take months, possibly years of training to learn to explore these areas or landscapes.
After all, even to travel from one country to another requires a lot of preparation, so to explore the spiritual realms also requires much preparation.
This is why, in the Foreword, we gave you that warning.

Imagine that you were going to a good university to study a subject.
Before being qualified, it would take a number of years of dedicated study before receiving a diploma.
Now, the actual diploma is a meaningless piece of paper given to the student in order for him to show a future employer that he has an in-depth knowledge of the subject that he studied. It is the in-depth knowledge that is important not the diploma.

Following the spiritual path for a sufficient length of time will give in depth knowledge of spirituality but you will not receive a diploma. Spirituality deals in realities, not in make-believe.

It is possible, in certain universities, for specially selected people to obtain a diploma without having demonstrated an in-depth knowledge on a subject and it is possible to obtain a forged diploma.
But, in either case, the student has not become proficient in the discipline he was supposed to be studying.
The spiritual realms do not work like that. If you have not perfected the techniques for entering the spiritual realms, you cannot do it.

Quite simply, as one applies oneself to the discipline of following the spiritual path, so one's frequency rises.
As the planes or landscapes in the upper 4th dimension vibrate to various frequencies, it is as one's own frequency rises to become compatible with the frequency of a landscape that one is able to transfer one's consciousness into that landscape and observe life at that level.
Until one has achieved that level of advancement, it is not possible to make this shift from 3D reality to one of the planes of the upper 4th.
The higher the frequency that one can vibrate to, the higher the level one can go to.

It is a strange thing that it is possible to go to lower levels but only go to higher levels when one has obtained that skill.
For example, if one considers any skill on Earth; music, art, gymnastics, mathematics or whatever, it is possible to demonstrate at a very basic level a skill but it is only after much study that one can demonstrate higher levels.
In mathematics, it is possible to write that 1+1=2. But it takes a higher skill to do algebra, calculus and so on.
Someone who knows calculus will also be able to show that 1+1=2, but a child only able to show that 1+1=2 would be lost trying to do calculus.
The spiritual path is the same.

As one advances in spirituality, so one's frequency rises and, by the law of mutual attraction, one can see and enter higher landscapes but until one has done the necessary study it is not possible to leave one's Earthly attachment and fly off to other areas of life.

We have warned you that this book is for serious students of spirituality so, unless you are prepared to spend a great deal of time following the path, this book may not be for you.

We wish to describe at least some of the areas you may see, if and when you can raise your frequency sufficiently to leave your body and enter the spiritual realms.
As we said, we will describe the technique required to achieve that later.

We will also say that we have described some of the landscapes of the higher 4th dimension in other works but as we promised to give you a book describing completely all of this discipline, we will repeat much of what we have already told you. For some, at least, it will be new information.

So, assuming that one is meditating and assuming that one has done this sufficiently often and with sufficient dedication so as to have attracted guides, one day one or more guides will assist you to go to the higher 4th dimension.
Now, we must say at this point that guides will vibrate at a higher frequency than you when you first start following the path so, although, from the beginning, if you follow the techniques we will give you, they will be protecting you, they won't be able actually to interact with you until you have raised your frequency to the point that they can so interact.
This may take some time.
Guides are serious people and will only help serious students.
If you try to enter the heavenly spheres for simple curiosity, in all probability you will not be helped but if you genuinely devote your life to the spiritual path, so as to assist all mankind, they will help you all they can.

As we said, guides cannot help you until you have raised your frequency to their level and they will only help you if you have the correct attitude.

Assuming that all this is in place, sooner or later a guide will take you to Summerland.

Now, what happens is that, as the student is deep in meditation, a guide will link with the appropriate aura of the student and "push" him from his physical body into that aura.
Actually, it is the consciousness that moves. The body is sitting on a chair and the student's consciousness is moved into an aura.
It will not be the etheric double but a true aura.

The student may or may not be allowed to observe the transfer.
If it is decided that it would be better for the student not to observe the transfer, the student will experience a feeling as if he is being lifted from his chair. There will be a few seconds of blackness and then the student will be in the beauty of Summerland.

If, however, it is decided that the student should be shown the transfer, he will watch his consciousness floating through space - which may also seem black - until, once again, he arrives at Summerland.
He may even observe orbs floating in the same direction as himself.
These are the consciousnesses of newly deceased people making their way to Summerland.

We should, at this point, question why there appears to be a journey between leaving the earth plane and arriving in the upper 4th.
In fact, it is made so that the student, or the dead person, can adapt to the fact that he is changing dimensions.
With experience, it is possible to make the switch instantaneous.
The student desires to enter the upper 4th dimension and, as he is already vibrating at that frequency, he just arrives.

What does he see or hear?
The first thing is light.

God is pure starlight, pure vibration and so, at the highest, Godlike level, one would observe blinding white light of unbelievable power.
Obviously, for the average person this degree of light would be harmful. But that is because the average person is vibrating to a much lower frequency and one is only comfortable in areas of light, heat or sound commensurate with one's own frequency. There are entities almost at the level of God that live in that area but that is because, being so pure, they are close to God and thus vibrate to the same - or similar - frequency as God.

If one were to meet such a person, we would be blinded by his effulgence, his brightness. If he was to speak to us his voice would sound booming. This is not that he would be shouting. He wouldn't. It would be because sound, like light, is frequency and the purer the sound, the louder it would appear to us.
It would be the audio equivalent of pure starlight.
Unfortunately, we do not have a means of describing "star sound" but that is what it is. Mention has been made in the Bible of powerful angels coming close to man and were observed as blinding light. When they spoke, their voices filled the heavens like thunder. Such is the nature of purity.

However, we are concerned with what you would see if you were to visit Summerland. As we said, you would see light.
If you had not been able to raise your frequency through meditation and other disciplines, you would not have been taken to the higher 4th dimension but, having been taken implies that one has made the grade.

We will break off here to say that all dead people are taken to that area as well but that has to do with the higher self and we will explain that later.

The student, still very much alive and sitting on his chair in his meditation room arrives in Summerland.

He may well find himself alone but his guides will be close by.
He's in no danger but his guides will direct his journey through this experience.
His guides might well be invisible to him but that is because his guides might vibrate at a higher frequency than the student and different vibrations count in the spirit world.
The guides will see the student, vibrating at a lower frequency than them, but the student may not see the guides. But rest assured they are there.

What is Summerland? It has been called Summerland because that is what it is.
If you can imagine an endless landscape of beautiful countryside, that is what you see.
This is not quite true.
It is more like an endless and perfectly kept garden with miles and miles of immaculately manicured lawns, dotted here and there with trees, lakes, flowerbeds and paths.
There are benches should one wish to rest, although one never grows physically tired.
The sky is a deep azure blue.
But there is no visible sun. This is because Summerland is, itself, illuminated by the sun and is part of the sun.
We will explain this fuller another time.

The air is warm.
A gentle music fills the air that comes from the flowers and plants for they are alive.

The colours are much more intense than one would see them on Earth. It is as if a veil has fallen from our eyes.

We will see people strolling about chatting to each other. They may greet us but probably would not question us deeply as to why we are there. We may explain the reason for our presence but they would not question us. To question would be impolite.
We may or may not hear our guides talking to us, explaining things.
This depends, to a certain extent, on whether one has learned telepathy.
But in any case, they will impress their desires for explanation on us so we will understand.

One would, perhaps, question that if all people when their incarnation is finished go to the heavenly spheres (higher 4th) and this has been happening since the dawns of humanity, one would expect the heavenly spheres in general and Summerland - where many of us end up - in particular would be getting a bit crowded by now. But such is not the case.
The reason is simple but takes some explanation.

Our non-physical body is not solid as our physical body appears to be.
Spirit is pure energy. However, people have will, desire - call it what you will.
So, a spirit form can appear physical to other spirit forms if it so desires or it can be invisible.
It can assume a human form or just remain as pure energy. Even in its pure energy form it will retain its identity signature.

So, one person in his energy form can identify and link with another energy form and can exchange information.
If one person in his energy form wishes to contact another, he can but he will instantly know if the second person wishes to be contacted or left alone. They both will know if the communication is to take place while they are both in energy form or whether they want to appear as physical people to exchange information.
Sometimes one form is better than another.
For instance, two people who have been in the heavenly realms for some time will have learnt to operate as pure spirit. It is a skill that has to be learnt.
Others will need to imagine physical bodies.
If you go to Summerland, you, in all probability will need to imagine yourself as physical.
You will observe others in physical form. Those using just energy will remain invisible to you.
So, heaven is not crowded but it does respond to the thought forms being sent from one person to another rather as you can send telephonic messages to each other, or using the internet.

So, you look around you at all the beauty. You will feel peace and love. You will be filled with the joy that is the result of being surrounded with peace and love.

Nothing can go wrong. There is no danger. Accidents cannot happen. There are no criminals.
It compares to the Biblical concept of the Garden of Eden.

Now, we must say the garden you find yourself in is a reflection of your personal frequency in terms of your rise to perfection.
This gives the impression that there is not just the one landscape that you find yourself in.
That is one of many that are a reflection of your state of advancement.
So, if you were of a lesser state of advancement you would be in a place, although extremely beautiful, that would be less magnificent than one that someone of a higher vibration would arrive at.
Equally, of course, someone of a higher vibration would find himself in an area of even greater beauty.
Can you imagine what someone like Jesus would see if he arrived here?

We need to answer the question as to how many levels of Summerland there are.
The answer is one. Actually, it is zero but collective desire of the countless people who finished their incarnations and, having risen to heaven, expected to find themselves in paradise, created with their minds this beautiful place.

But, as it is a reflection of the level of spirituality of the new arrival, what the person sees is a reflection of his degree of perfection.

One could say that it is created from imagination and, to a certain extent it is but the reality is more complicated than that and what we observe in the heavenly spheres are far from imaginary.
It would be better to say that each person who came to Summerland, expecting to see paradise, laid a block more of its creation.
So, Summerland certainly appears real but, we repeat, it is unique to each person.
What one sees is a reflection of the degree of one's personal spiritual frequency.

However, it is more complicated than that, in that, for instance, when one first passes into the afterlife, one is met by a glowing person and one has a one-on-one conversation with that person.
If you think about it, at any moment of time, there must be a considerable number of people dying and going to Summerland. In which case one would think that the reception area would consist of a vast number of newly deceased, battling to be received into heaven.
But such is not the case.
Each new arrival is alone with the person tasked with receiving him.

The reason is simple. It is a question of vibration, frequency.

The newly deceased would vibrate at a certain frequency according to how he is.
Some might be lowly creatures and some might be quite holy so there would be a considerable difference in frequency between the lowest and the highest.
So, what is done is a sort of default frequency is projected to the dead person that enables him to appear to vibrate at a frequency required by the receptionist guide.

This is not complicated but is difficult to describe in earthly terms.

You could imagine people who have to wear certain robes to be admitted to a place or to have a pass badge.
It is not quite like that but the effect is that the newly deceased person is given a sort of covering that enables him to vibrate at a certain frequency.
Each person is given a unique frequency so that each person finds himself isolated from any other new arrival.
His greeting guide would vibrate at the same level so the new arrival and the guide find themselves alone together.
This gives the guide the opportunity to explain to the newly deceased what has happened and where he is.
Then the person would have his life review and his true frequency will be revealed, this default frequency disappears and the person finds himself in one of the areas that corresponds to his spiritual frequency.

But we must say that, although each and every person has a unique frequency that, in effect, isolates him from any other person, with many people their vibrations are sufficiently close as to more or less overlap and so some people can communicate much as people on earth do.
The main difference is that the overlapping is limited and so each person would only find himself with people like him.

In the next chapter we will describe to you the spiritual family (oversoul) that you belong to.

CHAPTER 2

THE OVERSOUL

Having taken you at least in an introductory sort of way into Summerland, let us begin to explore some of the other areas of the higher 4th dimension.
As we have said, that area is the only one in which true, complete humans live. They do so from the moment of their transfer from the 7th dimension until the moment, many years later, when they will blend with God and disappear from our view.
The only interruption to this long sojourn, is when people decide to incarnate on Earth and thus move to the 6th dimension for the duration of that incarnation.
When that finishes, they return to the upper 4th for the rest of eternity.

So, you can see that there is a lot going on in the 4th dimension.
By the way, as we will often be referring to the upper 4th dimension, let us abbreviate it and just call it the 4th. We hope that when, for the rest of this book you'll see us referring to the 4th, you realise that we are referring to the upper or higher 4th dimension, which is everybody's home dimension.

Perhaps we could start at the beginning and examine somewhat, what happens to an embryo spirit when it leaves the 7th dimension and moves to the 4th.

One might question why it is necessary to have a constant supply of new humans descending from the 7th dimension to the 4th?
The answer, quite simply, is that there is always a stream of perfect humans moving into the God sphere and thus they need to be replaced with new humans to keep the supply going.

So, a group of embryo humans decide to move from the 7th to the 4th. No one forces them. The young spirits volunteer and so, always surrounded by angels guiding them, they change dimensions and arrive in the 4th.
Already, at this point, they would have a unique frequency but these frequencies would be sufficiently close so that communication between them can occur.
The angels, by lowering their frequencies, can interact with the young spirits also.

They will be placed in what is called a group spirit or oversoul.
This is to give them a base with which to relate.
All this is, is a group of like-minded individuals. But it is very important. Although any one individual is free to leave his oversoul and join another, in general, close bonds are formed and the people in any oversoul will go through eternity together, sharing triumphs and failures. They will act, eventually, as if they were one person.

Some of the members will, eventually, incarnate and become members of one's family: mother, father, brother, sister and so on but not necessarily.
It is possible for members of another oversoul group to incarnate into a family in order to have experience but, usually, if there is a close bond between family members, it is because of belonging to the same oversoul group.

Let us consider what an oversoul is.
It is not a place or a building of any type.
It is a group of like-minded souls.
When people move down from the 7th dimension to the 4th, they come in groups. Not individually, one by one, but in groups, rather like children starting a new school or soldiers being inducted into the army.
So, any group of souls selected for a human existence at any one time, would be roughly of the same age and would arrive together in the 4th.
So, they would be attached to the same oversoul.
There are exceptions to this but that is the general rule.

Now, all oversouls have existed for a long time and so there would be a large number of people who would belong to the same oversoul (and some new arrivals) but who joined a long time ago.

Imagine, if you can, a school but one in which the pupils remain forever.
This school would be divided into houses.
Certain pupils would be selected to go into certain houses but each year's intake would follow on behind previous intakes.
So, some students would have been in that house for many years, while others would be more recent arrivals.
The older, more experienced members of an oversoul will sometimes take new arrivals under their wing and will nurture them. But not all do this. Some older members concentrate on the subjects that interest them and ignore new arrivals, whereas others will help new arrivals if and when they can.

There are a large number of oversouls depending on the arrival dates of groups from the 7th dimension and also depending on people's individual personalities.

Now, we wish to explain something about oversouls. They are compiled in a pyramid.
If you can imagine a pyramid formed of layers there would be, at the bottom, a large area of whatever the pyramid is made of but at the next level there would be slightly less. At the next level after that there would be even fewer until, at the very top would be a single capstone.

Oversouls follow this format.
At the base level there are a large number corresponding to people's various personalities.
People with similar personalities join one oversoul of many.
But, over time, as people advance spiritually, there might be people of one oversoul who think very much like people from another oversoul and so they leave the first oversoul and join with others in a higher oversoul - the second level of the pyramid.
Then, as time progresses and as some advance, they will move to a yet higher level.
This progresses over vast eons of time until, finally, they join the capstone which represents God - perfection.

However, there is more to this. As people advance so their individual personalities reduce, their ego reduces, their sense of individuality reduces and they start to link into group personalities.

The higher oversouls are there for that purpose.

Finally, very advanced souls think as one, as God, and reach the top of the pyramid at which point they can remain to serve or disappear into the Godhead.

When your incarnation is finished, you will return to your home in the 4th, rejoin your oversoul and continue your long journey to the top of the pyramid. This journey will take a long time.

As you progress, so your frequency will rise and you will move to ever more wondrous areas of the 4th.

We will say at this point that even during your incarnation you will remain attached to your oversoul and are always being cared for by loving family and guides. You are never alone.

One way of looking at this is if you were born into a family and, at some point, a decision was taken that you should go to a boarding school. The boarding school would be your incarnation.

Even though you would be cut off from your family during the time you are at school, your family are still there and their love goes out to you and their help and advice is always available.

Then, once the school time is finished, you would return home to your family and be greeted back into its bosom.

The family is your oversoul group.

So, if we may recapitulate.

You were, at one time in, first, the 8th dimension. Then you moved to the 7th and you stayed there for a long time until, in your and our case, we were selected to become humans.

Then you moved to the 4th and were placed in association with an oversoul and a group of like-minded people.

In your case you took the step to have an incarnation and this is where you are at the moment, having an incarnation in the 6th dimension.

Eventually, when your incarnation ends, you will return to your oversoul in 4th.

For the moment, you are going through your chosen incarnation in the 6th dimension.

However, being separated from your oversoul group by your incarnation does not mean that you are cut off from your oversoul.

Members of your oversoul are constantly with you and, if you take up meditation you can learn to reach out to them and, eventually, return, in your mind, to the 4th and meet again with your oversoul members - or some of them.

That is what this book is about.

So, we will end this chapter here and move on to other areas of the 4th.

CHAPTER 3

GUIDES

You will, we hope, forgive us if we repeat somewhat information that we have given elsewhere but for those who have not followed our previous teachings we feel obliged to give an overview of the basic areas of the 4th before describing areas that we have, as yet, not covered.

Life in the 4th tends to be a series of lessons, one following another, rather like classes in a school so it is important to have an understanding of the basics before advancing to more esoteric lessons or areas.

We got to the point where young spirits arrived in their various oversoul groups and were taken control of by wise guides and also wise angels.
Each young spirit, person, is put into the specific care of at least one guide or angel.

Now, it is important to know that a guide would be a person who has spent many years in the 4th and has an extensive knowledge of many of the landscapes of the 4th.
He would belong to the same oversoul group as his pupil.
He will remain in constant communication with that student and will help guide him for a long time until that student no longer requires his assistance.
Then they will split up and the teacher will link with another new arrival and start the education process again.

That guide will remain in close contact with his student even if and when the student decides to have an earthly incarnation.
He never leaves his student.
These are the people known as Spirit Guides and all people have at least one.

We will mention at this point that all students are different and, according to their interests, they may attract other teachers who can impart specific knowledge on specific subjects.
Equally, there might be students who are not interested in learning in which case there will be one guide who looks after the student but does not push him to learn any specific subjects.

We mentioned angels.
These would be human angels and their interest is spirituality.
Now, very few students are interested at first in spirituality. They might well take an interest in learning subjects very similar to those available for study on Earth but not many would be drawn to study spirituality until they have lived in the spirit world for a long time.
But there are a few who are naturally interested in spirituality and, to help them, human angels come close to them and guide them along the path to perfection.

So, such a student, both while in the 4th and also if he decides to have an incarnation, would have his spirit guide with him but also an angel who will try to open doors to assist the student to advance in spirituality.

This does not imply that the student would start spouting high sounding spiritual phrases or would have a high degree of spiritual wisdom.
The spiritual guidance given by an angel would be more a question of being guided along a path that would enable him to gain access to spiritual knowledge.
The student, in all probability, would have no idea that he has two guides, the first, the friend and helper that all have and the second an angel.

Now, we should ask if the first guide and the angelic guide work in close harmony?
We can say that both individuals would be aware that the other one is there but would not necessarily work together to aid the student.
Each guide has his own mission, his own priorities and will work separately to assist the student.
Certainly, one will never get in the way of the other so if one guide wishes to spend time assisting a student with a project, the other guide will withdraw until the first guide has finished what he wanted to do before entering the fray once more - although it is never a battle. It is each guide assisting the student when it is the appropriate moment.

In principle there is no limit to the number of helpers or guides that a student may draw to him.
The minimum would be one. No one is ever left to his own devices. So, he would always have one.
Equally, depending on what the student does with his life there is no limit to the number of helper guides that he might have.
As his interests grow and expand so, by the law of mutual attraction, the student will attract a larger number of helpers.

Now, these helper guides do not necessarily need to be holy. If the student turns to evil the student will attract a guide or guides that will assist him along the evil path.

No one is judged nor criticized in heaven.
People have free will and if they choose to take the left-hand path, that is their choice.
That does not mean that a guide will actively assist or push someone down the path of evil but they will do their best to help and protect the student that has been placed in their care.

Another point we should mention in relation to spirit guides is that all spirit guides have spirit guides helping them. By which we mean that no one is left on their own.
You may well have a spirit guide who is with you, out of sight but there, 24/7, but that guide also has a guide more advanced than he is that is helping him.
In turn, that guide will also have a guide higher than him that is assisting him.
And so it goes on, guide above guide.

Quite where it all ends; we cannot say because there are so many levels of existence that it seems to go on and on endlessly. Each and every person has someone higher than him that is helping him along the path.

So, this is a magnificent way of living.
Even though we are really talking about spirituality, the same would apply to whatever interests a person.
Suppose, for instance, that someone is interested in any imaginable subject. That person, by the law of mutual attraction would draw towards him at least two guides.
The first would be the guide charged with assisting the person along his basic path. That guide would have a guide helping him just as we described.
But, depending on the discipline that interests a person he will draw a second guide that would assist the person with his chosen subject. That guide, in turn, would have a guide who is also interested in that subject.
So, it goes on.

This is a cleverly thought out way of progressing.

Any one person has a sort of mother/father figure that acts very much like a loving parent on Earth does. They allow the child to experiment with life and make mistakes but is always there to pick up the pieces of any grave errors their child makes.
Then, according to the interests of the child, a tutor will be there to assist in educating the child.
We mention child but, of course, student or chela would be a better description because a guide can and will be with his charge for practically all eternity.

We hope that you can understand that the process of having a guide starts at the moment the student enters the 4th dimension and continues for virtually all eternity.
Actually, the guide is chosen for the student while he, the student, is still in the 7th dimension but contact in earnest starts at the moment when the student enters his oversoul group in 4th. This implies, of course, that as the student and guide will belong to the same oversoul group the decision as to what group the student will link to is taken long before the student moves to the 4th, while he is still in the 7th.

Now, we must consider how the relationship between student and guide develops over time.

Normally, the guide will always be one step more advanced than his student.
As the student advances so, in turn, the guide is advancing and so the guide remains in advance of his charge. However, it can happen that the student might be precocious and catches up or passes his teacher in spiritual wisdom. It is rare but can and does happen.
In this case the guide drops out and is assigned to another newly arrived student while the precocious student is put in the care of a more advanced guide.
There would be no point in having a student more advanced than his guide who also acts as a sort of teacher.
A guide's prime purpose is to act as a loving parent but that also implies guiding the student down the spiritual path to a certain extent or at least to be available to assist the student when he needs help.

All this implies the guide to be ahead of the student in wisdom.

We have used the word student but that is a poor description of the relationship between the guide and his charge.
The guide accepts his charge and spends many, many years - both in the heavenly spheres and during an incarnation - caring for his charge.

The relationship is not so much teacher/student but more parent/beloved child. The relationship is based on total platonic love.

Now, it is not customary for the student to know the name of his guide nor any personal details of that guide.
It has been found best to keep the personal details apart from the student.
He will learn a certain amount about the guide when in the 4th but during an incarnation the guide remains somewhat secret.
He is in close contact with his student but the student is not permitted to have a too close connection to his guide.
This communication can develop but it implies the student taking the necessary steps to develop the ability to communicate spiritually.
Even then the personal guide tends to remain in the background.
It is rare for a student, especially while incarnate, to be able to converse with his personal guide.
If, however, he is able to draw secondary guides to him, if it is appropriate, he may develop telepathy and/or clairsentience and thus be able to talk and/or see these secondary guides.
They make themselves visible or talk so as to impart wisdom to the student. They could not do this if they remained invisible or silent.

So, we have two distinct sorts of guides.
The first is the guide that is selected because he has an affinity to the young student. We should also mention that this guide would have wisdom and infinite patience and is willing to devote a countless amount of time to the care of someone else other than himself.   Not all people have these qualities so we must all be very grateful to our guides because even we in the 4th have guides.

The second sort of guide would be one - or more than one - person attributed to a student if he takes an interest in a subject.
This guide may or may not be of the same oversoul group as the student.
He, too, must have great knowledge of his subject, great patience plus an ability to transfer his knowledge to his student.
If the student loses interest in a subject the guide will drop out and if the student decides to pursue a different subject of interest to him a new guide will be sought to assist him.
But his first guide always remains.

In the case of demonic creatures from the lower 4th exactly the same process obtains.
Each and every evil spirit has a guide - who also has a guide assisting him - and also may draw another guide to assist the evil spirit with any project he may develop. All is one.

It is difficult to imagine that a plant would have a guide or even an animal would have one, but they do. The amount of love, care or information given would be very limited compared to humans but they do have plant or animal guides who would be the same sort of plant or the same sort of animal as the 'student' plant or animal.
This helps plants or animals develop rather in Darwinian fashion.
Humans are not connected to animals and follow a totally different course of development to plants or animals but one could say that even humans follow a course of progress as proposed by Darwin to a certain degree while incarnate.

Obviously, the development of fauna, flora and humans as noted by Darwin and others is not directly connected to survival as he (they) imagined it. We have described at length the actual process but one can appreciate that people observing the way life altered, which enabled them to survive - or not - from a strictly physical point of view, with no knowledge of the esoteric activities, would give the impression that nature favored changes thus enabling life to adapt to changing events.
So, we do not criticise people who follow Darwinism although we look forward to the day when people can regard life with developed vision.
But we must accept people as they are because we, when incarnate, only had limited vision.
As ascension develops so more and more people will start to study and accept expanded wisdom.
Not that it will alter the basic fact that life is constantly changing and developing.
It is understanding the reason behind change that will alter, not change itself.

This change, often linked to Darwinism, is mainly concerned with physicality - the 6th dimension - but change also happens in the 4th.

Our concern in this book will be limited to the 4th and how to navigate around it so we do not wish to become sidetracked in considering physicality.
Also, we are considering in this chapter guides.
So, let us stop here and move on to describe other areas of the 4th.

CHAPTER 4

THE ONENESS PLANE

So, we explained that each and every person has a guide that links with him at the moment of his inception into the 4th and stays with him for virtually all eternity.

This simple statement has greater implications than just writing it would suggest.

To start to understand, one would need to be fully conversant with the contents of book 7 which was entitled Personalities and, as the name suggests, was about personalities!

In order fully to understand this chapter and much that follows requires an understanding of book 7 because it should be obvious that all people have personalities and guides also have personalities.

The reason for book 7 was to bring to your attention the importance of DNA and a multitude of diverse elements that, collectively, we call personality.

We stressed that every aspect, that we described as fully as we could in book 7, needed all to come together before life as we know it could exist. Not one aspect could be missing.

If one aspect was not there all life would disappear in an instant and there would be nothing.

Not just an individual's life but life in a global sense - all life.

What has this got to do with the subject of this book which is about auras but, more importantly, the 4th aura or dimension and how to enter diverse and different areas of it?

Now, at the risk of repeating ourselves, at the end of book 7, which was both long and complex, we suggested that the basis of life (God) was a number of things that have different names but, essentially, mean the same thing.

We proposed that God was consciousness.

We also suggested that God was formed from our individual and collective personalities.

We also said that God was DNA.

So, assuming that God exists it must be the result of at least three above-mentioned things; consciousness, personalities and DNA.

As God is not only prime creator but also all that is, it implies that consciousness, personalities and DNA are one and the same thing.

Of course, we mentioned higher self and the Holy Spirit but we will not get involved with those aspects for the moment.

May we say that if you do not understand what we are talking about you refer to book 7.

What we are implying is that all the eight carrier waves exist in their own right but only as carrier waves.

It is the information that is stored in them that give them any meaning, any value.

As we have said, our focus in this book will be the 4th dimension.

This dimension contains a vast amount of life, for everything is created by God and anything created by God is alive.

That is what God is. God is life and life is God.

But as we said, in order to make sense of life it is divided (if we may use that word) into a number of aspects, some of the most important being consciousness, personality and DNA.

There are a number of sub aspects that support life but it is fair to say that the three words we used above, counting DNA as one word, are the most important.

So, this implies that all life contained in the 4th or indeed the 6th, where incarnation takes place, are created through the life spirit being connected to consciousness, personality and DNA.

At the moment of writing these words it is assumed, generally, that God equates to consciousness but our investigations have demonstrated that personality and DNA play an equally important role in creating life.

So, what does all this mean?
Where does it take us in our investigation of the 4th?
The answer lies in vibration, frequency.

We have all met people with noble, high-ranking thoughts and we have all met people with low, cross thoughts.

This does not mean that one person is less than another. We are all equal. But it does imply a difference in frequency.

This difference in frequency does not play a huge role to those in incarnation in the 6th dimension or aura but it certainly does in the spirit world. It is the prime means of separating good angels from demons, good people from bad people and is the fundamental fashion in which all the non-physical realms are organised.

If you could imagine all the people incarnate having a unique identity number and those people being grouped according to groups of numbers but, for instance, having a letter followed by numbers; A1234 then B1234 then C1234, a similar system is used in non-physicality.

Obviously, it is totally different but the principle is the same.

All those whose spiritual vibrations would be similar would find themselves grouped together. Then those with a slightly different group of vibrations would be grouped but apart from the first group and so on.

It sounds complicated but, in reality, is very simple.

As there are landscapes that also have groups of vibrations, by the law of mutual attraction, people whose vibrations are similar to the vibrations of landscapes are drawn to those landscapes. We have already explained this in detail in other works.

The thing is getting around to explaining how many different areas there are and how many of them someone incarnate would be likely to be able to visit.

We must say that there are so many different areas in the 4th that it would take a large compendium just to list all the areas and, as many of them would be beyond the capabilities of even the most advanced student incarnate to enter we will limit our investigation exclusively to those that you might be able to enter.

We have already mentioned some of them: heaven/hell, the lower 4th, Summerland and, in previous works, the educational areas.
We have also mentioned the akashic record which, although not really part of the 4th nevertheless is used by those in the 4th to investigate and also to obtain personality from.
We also mentioned that there are areas for plants and animals.
We mentioned the oversoul and stated that as one advances so one tends to lose one's sense of individuality and starts to link with other like-minded people to form a collective personality.

In fact, one should consider this the other way around.
Our natural state would be total unity to all life.
We should all feel as one person because that is what we are. Indeed, this one person is God.
But, for various reasons that we have already described, God's archangels created a system of vibrations that enables us all to appear to have separate personalities.
Indeed, when incarnate we all have unique aspects to us; appearance, skin colour, gender and many other aspects that enable both us and our acquaintances to see us as unique individuals.

Many of us feel that this sense of individuality is very important and we would feel lost if we were all just one person.
It is interesting to consider why we feel that we need to have this sense of individuality but the reason is simple and we have already explained this.
God, for some reason, decided that he required us to feel individual so that we could all have experiences.
If we were all one, we would all think and act alike but if we feel separate, we can have a multitude of different experiences but, behind this sense of individuality is an area where we can realise our oneness.

We would like to introduce you to this area because it exists as a real area within the 4th and one can enter this area if one chooses and one knows how to.
So, we need to explain this area carefully because it is quite an important place.

We have explained that there are three basic areas that we are normally drawn to in the 4th according to our frequencies. These areas are hell, Summerland and heaven.

We all, not only are part of an oversoul but are part of the many sub-frequencies or landscapes of hell, Summerland and or heaven and most of us spend virtually all of our time in the area or landscape that corresponds to our frequency.
But there is this other area that we mentioned where we can visit in order to experience what it feels like to be part of the oneness of all life.

Now, this area would include all or most of humanity, many plants and many animals.
But it would not include those from the depths of hell nor would it include any demonic entities from the lower 4th.
The reason for that is that, quite simply, negative beings cannot raise their vibrations to the level of this oneness plane.

But we could consider it to be rather like a holiday area in which people can visit to take a break from their everyday activities.

Not everyone in the non-physical (upper 4th) visits this area because not everyone knows about it. The strange thing is that the various guides and tutors that assist the students on a day-to-day basis do not mention this area because the student needs to mature to the point that he works out for himself that there has to be more than what he is aware of.
In other words, the student has to start to question why all life is separate and why, if God only created one life form, do we all have distinct personalities.
We explained personalities in book 7, called Personalities, and made a case that it was important for us all to have distinct personalities.
However, for those who can think back to the origin of life and learn that we are all one, some, at least, start to question what it would be like to be able to all link back to this oneness.
Then it is considered that they are ready to begin the journey to this oneness place.

We might be giving the idea that the student packs a bag with what he would need for a voyage and sets off into the sunset.
Life in the spirit world is not like that. All is vibration and in the spirit world it is not necessary to journey anywhere. All is done through meditation, adjusting one's frequency until one is compatible with the frequency of the appropriate area. Then one arrives in that area.
So special guides are brought in who assist the student in the special meditative techniques necessary to develop the correct frequency.

We will mention at this point that this area of the upper 4th has never been talked about before so you will be the first group of people incarnate to know about it. However, we will not mention the technique required to be able to enter this place. That will be for future generations to be told.
We will also say that it has been known for some fortunate people to have a Near Death Experience (NDE) and instead of going to Summerland, find themselves in this oneness place and these people have described some of the wonderful experiences.
They are quickly recuperated from that area and are either returned to their body or go to Summerland before returning to their physical body.

As the student adjusts his frequency to that of the oneness area, he can start to visit it. This would be done with guides in exactly the same way that someone on Earth having done sufficient meditation to be able to raise his frequency to the Summerland level would be taken by guides to visit Summerland. In the same manner a student visits the oneness plane with guides who assist the student through the experience.

It will be worth taking a few lines to describe why someone having an NDE and who finds himself in this oneness place is removed as quickly as possible.
When one arrives in this area - and we will say that it is a vast area and anyone having an NDE will only see a small part of it - nevertheless is bombarded with incredible amounts of esoteric knowledge.
He sees, feels, knows all there is to know about any area he might visit.
Now, this can have dramatic results once he returns to his normal life.

Some people have little residue memory of their visit but others retain the ability to know everything about all people he encounters.

Thus, he might enter a busy shopping place and is bombarded with the thoughts, emotions and feelings of all the people in that area.

He would know every detail of their lives, every experience they have had and all their life history.

This can cause great upset for those not able to handle all this information and many a person has either committed suicide or has finished up in a mental institution.

That is why NDE visitors to the oneness plane are removed as quickly as possible.

But for those who are not in incarnation, if they show interest in visiting this oneness area, they are prepared by teachers who know about that area and get the student to the point that it will not come as a shock when he is bombarded with masses of knowledge and wisdom.

This area, this oneness plane, is broken into a number of areas.

There is a place where every detail of human history is contained.

There is another where the equivalent of the akashic record concerning humans is contained by which we refer to the personal lives of people.

Yet another concerning animals, another for plants and yet another concerning the galaxy as a whole.

So, the student is asked what area he would like to visit first and the student makes a choice.

Once that decision taken the student is guided to that area.

So, let us explain a typical visit, a typical experience.

No matter what subject area the student chooses, as soon as he arrives in that area, he is immediately aware that he knows everything that there is to know about that area.

His mind contains everything that exists in that area.

He not only knows everything but can experience it as a living area and every single object contained in that area he feels as being alive, connected and can feel the connection back to prime creator.

It is an experience difficult to describe so we ask you to imagine how you would feel if, suddenly, you knew every aspect of anything; human, animal, plant or mineral?

Imagine, if you can, if you suddenly knew everything about all and every individual animal that had ever lived, is living or will live in the future.

Imagine if you could feel, intimately, every animal's thoughts and reactions to life and of its connection, not only to all other animals, but it's connection to all life and the God force itself.

You would know the life history of every animal from the moment of its conception until the moment of its demise.

You would know all about its parents and its brothers and sisters.

You would know every aspect of its life, others of its own species with whom it mated and about its offspring.

You would appreciate the terrain in which it lived in every aspect of its life in any manner possible to imagine. And this for every animal that ever lived, is living or will live.

To use a modern expression, it would be mind-blowing and it is only because the student has been carefully prepared for the experience that he is able to handle this amount of information.

The student stays with his guides in that area for only a few minutes because all this knowledge is downloaded to the student in a flash so there is no need to remain for long there.
Then the student is returned to his home in the 4th and his guides allow all the time necessary for the student to come to terms with what he experienced.
Eventually, if the student wishes he will be escorted to another area of the oneness plane and will experience all that there is to know about that new area.

Not all students can handle that amount of knowledge and for those who cannot, help is given to reduce or erase the memories.
For those who can handle it, it assists greatly to the rise in wisdom and spirituality for the spiritual aspect is clearly seen when he receives the information. All comes from God and it is the connection to God that can be seen in any area and in any life force.

Can we describe how and why this area exists?
This is simple but not easy to explain or understand.
The simple truth is that all life is one and that one is God.

We have explained in a book entitled Personalities how this one force is split, via the Holy Spirit, into all that we think exists.
Now, this Holy Spirit contains an area where all of creation is contained as a series of 'lumps' if we may use such a crude expression, before being divided into all of creation.
So, what the student does, in effect, is to link to this area and connect to one of the lumps of information.

Quite why God's archangels put this area into place we are not sure but we are grateful that it does exist for much of the information we give you is influenced or inspired by visits to this area and we are able to garner massive amounts of information that would otherwise not be available to us.

We mentioned this place because we were talking about some of the areas of the upper 4th.
Now, we do advise you that, unless an accident happens, you will not be able to visit that area and it would be most inadvisable to try.
You may visit it one day when your incarnation has finished but it is not for now.
We mentioned it because we are describing the upper 4th and this oneness area is an important part of it.
So, we will end this chapter here and move on to other aspects.

CHAPTER 5

NON-PERSONALITY

We have promised in this book to correct two emissions made in the first book about auras, which was to describe the various auras and how to enter them if and when appropriate.
However, we decided that it would be largely sufficient for the purposes of this book to limit ourselves to the upper 4th and only those areas that a student could safely enter.

We considered this idea and decided to change it somewhat.
We felt that if we only described the areas that someone incarnate could enter, it would greatly limit the import and impact of this book because there are many areas of the upper 4th that are interesting but that you, incarnate, could or should not enter.
So, to make this book more complete and more interesting we will describe a number of areas but tell you that you should not attempt to enter some of them.

We have already mentioned one such area in chapter four and we hope you can realise why you should not attempt to enter it. It could destroy your mental equilibrium.
There are other areas that we will discuss but will advise against you trying to contact them.

As we said, the technique for entering the upper 4th we will describe at the end of this book.
First, we wish to describe some, if not all, of the areas of the upper 4th.

We have already stated that the upper 4th is the only dimension that contains life in a complete sense.
Dimensions 8,7,6 and 5 have already been described in other works and although dimension 6 contains physical life, that dimension is a pale shadow of dimension 4.
Also, of course, the fact that you are in incarnation and thus are in the 6th dimension suggests that you would know sufficient about it that we do not need to explain much more about physicality then we already have in other works.
But, of course, your knowledge of the 4th will be limited and we have tasked ourselves with explaining what we can about the 4th and hope to fill in some of the blanks.

So let us examine another area that you may not know much about.

We wish to take you to an area in which life is regarded in another fashion.
This is, once again, the sort of gobbledygook that we often mention so stay with us and we will explain.

If you have read and digested all the information we have so far giving you - and it is more than has ever been given to anyone incarnate - you will have realised that life is amazingly complex and you may have wondered why this is so.
We have often stated that we feel that God dislikes complexity and, through his archangels, tries to keep life simple.

But, at the same time, life as we have so far explained seems to be vastly complicated.
Far more complicated than any logic would suggest is necessary.
We will also state that what we have so far explained is far from all that is and there are countless levels of life that we have so far not touched upon.
So, let us try to describe this new area - new to you, that is.

It is a place that is, in some ways, the opposite to the oneness plane.
In the oneness plane everything about a particular aspect of life is felt as a composite whole.
But to keep life in balance it would not be surprising if there was somewhere where the opposite to this oneness was explored.
So, what is this place and what aspect of life, of personality, is examined?

It is an area where it is possible to experience what it is like not to have any personality.
We must say, straight away, we are not considering the nowhere place where God or higher self is found.
This is a different place.

This area will not be easy to explain because we are all used to having personality.
There are many aspects of personality and we know that we have one main aspect and also a variety of sub aspects that, collectively, make us who we are from a personality point of view.

There are, unfortunately, some people who have mental illnesses and withdraw within themselves to the point that they will just sit for hours without moving, will stay for long periods of time without talking and we could consider that such people have rejected much of their original personalities.
But this area that we will attempt to describe is not an illness.
It is an area that contains a lack of personality.
What does this imply?

If we think about it, virtually everything has personality.
Not only humans but animals and, to a certain extent, plants.
Even buildings have personalities, admittedly created in part by the people that have lived in them but also due to the nature of the buildings themselves.
And not only buildings but open spaces also; parklands, countryside, deserts, seas etc.
That is why people love to visit castles, palaces, parks and even travel to the coastal areas to frolic in the sea.
It is the personalities of these areas that people seek and, for a while, exchange their lives for the life that they sense is being projected to them by the various areas they visit.

So the more we open our minds to the fact that everything has personality in one way or another, the more we realise that we are surrounded (bombarded) by personality from the moment of our birth to the moment of our release from incarnation.
Then we return to our home in the upper 4th and there we sense the vibrant personality of each plane with ever greater force.

Everywhere, that is, except this one area which is completely without personality.

As we have often stated, everything is vibration so this area vibrates to a certain frequency and it is just a question of us being able to adjust our frequency to this plane, this landscape, that permits us to link with it.

We have already stated why this place exists but will do so again.
Life always needs to be kept in balance and so as much of life contains personalities, it is necessary to have a place that does not contain personality in order to keep life in balance.

Of course, it could be argued that a plane that has no personality is a misnomer. We could be trying to describe an area where its personality is not obvious, but that its very lack of personality, in a way that we are familiar with, is just life presenting us with another facet of personality. Rather as if we were trying to describe the opposite of something.
If it is true that virtually everything has personality it would be normal to consider that some aspects would be the negative, the reverse, of others.
For instance, we might have love and hate, light and darkness, heat and cold.
These things might well be the reverse face of something but, we would agree, would have an equal amount of personality.
It is just us observing a different way that life presents itself to us.

So, if we suggest to you that there exists a plane where total lack of personality obtains, would that be correct or is it just that whatever personality this area has, has been incorrectly named by us because apparent lack of personality is this area's way of presenting its personality to us?
This lack of personality is its personality!

We would not argue against this logic except to say that we have been informed that this area does exist and those of us who have visited this area have experienced it first-hand and can confirm that it does seem a place without personality.

So, can we describe this place because if by its very nature it contains no personality, it would suggest that there is not much to go on, not much to describe.

This is not entirely true so let us begin to examine what an area that has no personality might look like.

So, having made the necessary adjustment to link with that plane we automatically find ourselves there.

We have got somewhat ahead of ourselves so let us go back to the point where, having heard about this place, our quest for knowledge prods us to want to investigate it.

We talk to our guides and specialist teachers are introduced to us that have knowledge of this area and they teach us the meditative technique that enables us to develop the frequency that corresponds to this area.
As you might imagine this is not easy because in virtually every aspect of life, meditation enables us to develop a frequency that would correspond to an area that has, according to our explanation given above, personality.
But this time we have to learn to match our frequency to a place that has no personality.

This does not imply that nothing exists, but what it does imply is that in some way we have to match ourselves to a totally unique area in which things exist but these things are without personality.

Can you understand just how difficult this is to do?

For the first and last time in our lives we must try to develop the frequency that would enable us to enter a realm where things exist but those things do not have the concept of personality attached to them.
As we look at the above few words, we do understand that we have done a poor job in explaining the training process due to the simple fact that it is almost impossible to imagine somewhere totally without personality in any way, shape or form.

As we have said previously, we might imagine that there are some things that do not have personality but that is just because of the limited way we have of considering creation. In fact, everything, from the tiniest microbe to the whole galaxy has personality and life could not be if it were not so.

We have explained that personality is an integral part of life - of God - but there is this one area that God's archangels have created that does not contain personality.

We will make an aside here and say that we said that God is created from at least three things; consciousness, DNA and personality.
As everything can be traced back to prime creator - God - is it possible for there to be a part of God's Kingdom that lacks one of the fundamental aspects that created God… personality?
One would have thought not, but either we should not limit the creative power of God or, in this place, personality was replaced by another, equal force.
We will consider these possibilities later.

You may have noticed that we have spent several pages of this chapter so far skirting around the edges of this subject without actually describing it and the reason is that it is not at all easy to describe this area.
A place with a distinct character is relatively easy to describe but a place that has nothing to describe, nothing to cling onto is a different order of complexity.
But we must try, so let us make a start.

It was hard enough to explain what the basic concept of this plane or landscape was and now we must delve into its meaning.
So, let us assume that we have mastered the technique for entering this place and, with our guides, decide so to do.
What do we see, what do we feel?

The first thing is what do we see?
We see an area that is hard to visualise because it is nothing like any area that we have ever seen before so we have nothing with which to compare it.
We can only use an analogy.

Imagine that you had spent your existence up till now in an area that was solid such as under the Earth or under the sea by which we imply being totally surrounded at all times by physical forces; the pressure of Earth or water.
Then imagine that you suddenly found yourself in a vacuum.

As we have explained, "nothing" is itself "something" and those who have had the opportunity to visit the area in which higher self or even God exists will know that this appears to be a completely empty space, totally lacking in anything we could relate to. And yet, this area in which higher self and God is, is the most important aspect of life. Further, we know that higher self and God need personality in order to exist so to be in a place that seems totally devoid of anything is, actually, the creation point of personality. So, we could hardly say that the higher self/God plane is devoid of personality.

The area we are trying to explain is not that area.

But can we describe an area that we know exists but has nothing that we could describe? As personality gives meaning to life, along with consciousness and DNA, to remove personality also, in a way, removes life.
But we know that this is not true.

The problem is that language does not exist to describe anywhere devoid of any form of personality.

What else can we say about this strange place?
When we visit this area, we are bombarded with the frequency of this area and thus we find that our personality no longer exists.
Obviously, this state only continues for as long as we are linked to this place and as soon, with the help of the guides who oversee our visit there, we return to our normal area of the 4th our personality returns.
But for the duration of our visit our personality disappears.

Now, try yourself to imagine that you had no personality!
How would you feel?
The answer is that question would have no meaning, as to ask such a question would imply that we have the curiosity to ask about feelings.
So, straight away we have two aspects of personality. One being curiosity and second, feelings.
If we remove all curiosity, all feeling, all sense of who we are and any other possible aspect we can think of, what we would be left with is what this place is about.

Do we feel that we are still alive? This is a meaningless question in this place.
Do we feel that we are dead? This is a meaningless question in this place.

This is what makes this subject so difficult to describe because it is not that we don't exist in that area but that we cannot ask any questions.
We cannot ask if we do not exist.
We cannot ask if we do not exist because that would imply curiosity which is part of personality.

So, we have the greatest difficulty in describing this area and can really only do it by mentioning all that it isn't because life as we know it is usually linked to us asking questions and seeking answers; all linked to personality.
In this area we do not ask questions and we do not seek answers. We just are.

Now, there is another aspect to life that this area does not have and that is intelligence.
Generally speaking, the more intelligent we are the more we tend to ask questions and the more we seek answers.
Thus, intelligence is linked to personality.
Which brings us to the reason, we think, that this place exists.

You may have noticed that amongst the plethora of personalities and sub-personalities that people may have there are some people who seldom question and seldom try to understand.
These people are very valuable to those who run organizations.

Armies contain vast numbers of people who are content just to obey orders.
Religions are the same.
Many businesses require such people either acting in security positions obeying, without question, the orders from those above them.

Indeed, it would be difficult to run such organizations if people questioned orders and, possibly, refused to implement them if they did not agree with the director's point of view on a subject.

Thus, many organizations actively seek people who do not question.
Other organizations use brainwashing techniques to mould their servants to act automatically and without question.

So, it is our understanding that such people as we have just mentioned link, at least in part, with this non-personality area and incorporate it into what personality they may have been born with.

We said that personality is linked with intelligence and this is true.
And yet there are large numbers of highly qualified people in many domains that do not question.
We find this in many disciplines of life: medicine, science, religion, history in all its connotations and so on.
Thus, we find people, going back over considerable periods of time, that had evidence staring them in their faces that they dismiss.
We find, for example, Egyptologists, when faced with evidence contradicting accepted wisdom, just refuse to consider new evidence and insist that what they expound is correct.
We just mention Egyptology but you can work out for yourself the vast number of highly qualified, highly educated and much respected experts on a variety of subjects that turn a blind eye to anything that disturbs their paradigms.

This, we think, is because they have incorporated at least part of this non-personality area into their personalities thus eliminating, at least, some important aspects of personality such as curiosity.

So, this strange non-personality area turns out to be an important aspect of life and, if it did not exist, life as we know it would be vastly different.
If it were not for people blindly following orders, advice and instructions from manipulative people, armies would not exist.
Politics might not exist and many religions would not exist because they are all based on the concept of a manipulative few directing the actions of many, not to think but just to obey.
This concept has been highly prized by the leaders who realised that they could manipulate people with non-personality active in their makeup.

The good news is that gradually, with ascension, people will realise the choice they have.
They can either remain like sheep or turn into leaders going in the right direction.
Over time, manipulative leaders and sheep like people will fade out to be replaced with more intelligent people and so this non-physicality area will fade from incarnation.
It will take time but will happen.

So, we turn from this strange and unfortunate area and will explore something else.

CHAPTER 6

THE ARTISTIC PLANE

Could there be much more to describe?
We have mentioned heaven/Summerland and hell.
We have mentioned the oneness plane and the plane that has no personality.
In other works, we have mentioned the many educational areas and we have talked about spirit guides, some of which are human as you and we are and some who have become angels.
In another work we described the incredibly difficult and painful process - emotionally painful that is - that a person has to go through to become angelic.

And yet the upper 4th contains many more areas for development, for exploration and for us to describe.
We cannot, unfortunately, describe all these areas for a variety of reasons, the main obstacle being that there are areas that are so bizarre that we could not describe them and even if we could, you would not understand.
God's Kingdom is, indeed, vast and complex.

We will admit that there are areas that even we do not know about or cannot match our frequencies to and, thus, these areas remain out of our reach.
However, there are still areas or landscapes that we can visit and, thus, can describe to you.
One such area is the next one we wish to portray to you.

It is a rather strange area or landscape because it concerns a part of the human psyche that we might or might not be aware of and that is the desire to produce works of art.
Now, this may sound strange, but if one traces humanity back to the point that they start to be aware that they have creative power - and we are referring to children here - a part of them awakens that contains the desire to create a place, a space if you wish, that satisfies their creative desire.
This may not seem at all obvious today and we are sorry to say that modern computer games are having a negative effect on this creative desire.

Before this modern era, it was common for children to sit down, draw something and proudly show their drawing to their parents who were expected to congratulate warmly the child. That is the beginning of the connection to the area we wish to describe.

We wish you to note that in this chapter and the previous one, although there are areas within the upper 4th that can also link to people incarnate because, although incarnate in the 6th dimension, nevertheless, you always retain a connection to your home in the upper 4th and thus can incorporate some of these landscapes into your "physical" life on Earth.

So, we become this mixture of the personalities that we decided to incorporate into our psyche before incarnation plus, sometimes, areas that we might have felt ourselves in harmony with during our journey around the heavenly spheres before incarnating.

There is nothing wrong with this because we are all quite complex beings and thus have multiple facets to our personality.

Therefore, many of us are born with this desire to stand out from the crowd by producing works that are directly ascribed to us and to no one else.

That is why a child proudly shows his latest drawing or model that he might have constructed or little clay statue.

It can be almost anything but it is the desire to create an individual, unique object that is behind this and that comes from an area in the higher 4th that explores this concept.

We will also mention at this point that, although virtually all people incarnate with that desire present in their personality, the family into which people are born can affect the development of this aspect.

Some lucky children are born into families in which the parents, or schools, actively encourage their children to develop their artistic talents and provide their offspring with the materials necessary to explore their artistic desires.

There are other families that the parents have no artistic desires and thus do not encourage their children.

Then there are cases, in some poor places, in which children have to work to help provide financially to the family and thus do not have the opportunity to develop any artistic desires.

This was explored in a poem by a poet, Thomas Gray (1716-1771), in which he sat in a graveyard and wondered if the people buried there, under other circumstances, would have made more of their lives. The poem is entitled 'Elegy written in a country churchyard'. He, clearly, had a privileged upbringing in which he could develop his poetic skills and, from that vantage point, was able to appreciate that poor people had to devote their lives to working, raising their families and surviving.

It is an excellent poem and is a tribute to a great poet and also to the countless people who suppressed any artistic desires in order to feed their families.

Anyone interested in this chapter would do well to read that poem because it describes exactly the plight of talented people who, because of poverty, will never be able to express their talents.

Lastly, we mentioned modern children who, instead of exploring their artistic talents just play computer games. This has been deliberately created by evil people to stifle young people's desire to create art. It is a brainwashing technique to keep this and future generations in a moribund state, mindless slaves, because the creative plane is vital in creating lively, thinking individuals.

The desire to create is a fundamental aspect of humanity.

It is what separates us from animals.

It is what has enabled humanity to develop to the point that it has.

Without this creative plane, humanity would still be in the Stone Age.

Thus, we strongly advise that all people, particularly parents, turn off the TV's and create works of art in their spare time.

We are not suggesting that people should try to become great artists but we are suggesting that using creative aspects of personality will bring happiness into people's lives more than watching TV or playing computer games.

Let us return to the upper 4th (which we will return to calling the 4th) and see what it is like to enter this important plane.
We must explain something at this point.

Some areas of the 4th are actually solid, physical areas landscapes, such as the levels of hell/Summerland/heaven and people can live in these areas, and many do.
But, due to the nature of the 4th, other areas are more just thought created places. Areas of vibration, of frequency where there is nothing physical to see but one enters by adjusting one's frequency to the appropriate area.
There is really nothing on Earth that we can use as an example so we hope that you will just accept our word that these areas exist.
This is the third such area we have mentioned. The first being the oneness plane, the second the non-personality plane and the third, this one, the artistic plane.
Obviously, there are many others.
The rather special feature of these non-physical areas is that they also link to personalities, via DNA, and so they serve a dual purpose. They can be areas one visits out of interest or curiosity but they are also areas that can assist man in his development either in incarnation or through the non-physical dimensions.
Imagine the void in many domains that would be if people did not have the desire to create works of art: no paintings, no sculptures, no books, no architecture, no gardens etc. Life would be very primitive.
Indeed, early caveman explored art and created beautiful paintings on rock walls.
That art plane already existed all those years ago and was influencing primitive man.
People are still influenced today in many domains. We will say that there is not one aspect of life and industry that does not have, behind the scenes, skilled people linking with the art plane to produce all that we see around us.
Do not think that art does not exist in the 4th. It does. Our libraries are full of books and poetry all created by artists in the 4th.

Therefore, to visit these non-physical areas it is a question of learning the frequency of the required area.
This would not be possible on one's own because one needs a teacher who knows of the frequency and is able to teach a student the technique for aligning to that frequency.
Who the first person was that discovered these frequencies we don't know. His or her name is lost in the mists of time but we can say that the technique has been handed down to teachers of this day and will go on being handed down.

Therefore, it is interesting that these areas existed but, we assume, were not known about until someone, somehow, discovered them and then brought them to the attention of interested students. Then, of course, the techniques for entering these areas was handed on ever since.
It begs the question, of course, are there other areas in the 4th that have not yet been discovered?
Obviously, we cannot answer that question but it would not surprise us if there were.

But to return to the subject of this chapter about the artistic plane.
We have mentioned some things about it and have said that it is quite important in the advancement of mankind.

We wish to explore this area a little more although, due to the fact that it is a non-visible area and due to the fact that it is also connected to personality, somewhat limits what we can say about it.
However, let us try.

Now, in these other areas that we previously described, as we entered them, we instantly were filled with the subject of that area. In other words, in the oneness area we were filled with all that existed in that area. In the non-personality area, we were filled with the feeling of non-personality.

This area is slightly different.
We are not filled with every artistic creation ever thought about. But we are filled with an overwhelming desire to create something.
What that something is, is not defined.
It is just the desire to create and the area leaves to us just what we might create.
This, of course, implies that there is a part of us that deals with creating works of imagination, whatever form that creation might take.
However, we will deal with that area later.
Our interest is the area in the 4th that promotes the concept of creation.
As you can imagine, this is not going to be easy to explain as it is one of the invisible areas and thus there is nothing to see, nothing that we can describe in any meaningful fashion. But this area does exist.
We have mentioned that there are often links between the various dimensions and we have further mentioned that DNA plays a role linking parts together.

But, in the case of the artistic plane it starts in the 4th and waits patiently for people to learn to link with it.

In the case of the student of esoterism he has to learn to locate and develop the correct frequency. Then he finds that he can link with that area.

The feeling of linking with the artistic creation area is strange in that it creates almost a feeling of irritation. Anyone who has gone through the intense desire to create something; a work of literature, a painting or any other original or fairly original work will understand the feeling we are trying to describe.
If we were to try to describe it in physical terms, we might feel an itch on the body or a disturbance of the mind and this would continue until the project is clearly defined and then the mind can get on with producing the work which will be achieved with the help of the brain.
So, when we enter this area of the 4th, we are filled with this intense desire to create something, made worse by the fact that we have not decided to create anything. We just have the intense desire.
This is an uncomfortable feeling and one can feel sympathy with the lucky ones that have never had the desire to create anything. For the rest of us, that feeling is well known.

We also understand that for very creative people this feeling can become overwhelming and it is not unknown for some of them to turn to alcohol, drugs, self-mutilation or even suicide to relieve or remove the symptoms.

For those who have finished their incarnations and are now in heaven, the same emotions are felt but we receive special training to be able to create without suffering. For those of you in incarnation who are highly creative, no such training exists. Perhaps, in the future it will become available.

So, what happens is that a creative person is suddenly hit, if we may use that word, with an idea that he feels he must bring into reality - physicality.
The idea, of course, comes from his ID, which is considered to be the personal aspect of who he is: the man looking back in the mirror.
This person, being creative, will tend to be fairly expert in a subject.
This may be almost anything; art in some form or science, philosophy, architecture or any creative skill.
At that point he knows that he cannot rest until he has brought into the light of day that which he imagines in the various aspects of him that are concerned with creation.
This would include his ID, as we mentioned, his higher self, the imagination plane, his mind, his brain and a number of aspects of DNA.
All the while, part of his imagination is in connection with the aspect of the artistic section of the higher 4th which is pouring into him this desire to create.
Thus, in answer to this call, he cannot rest until he has satisfied this urging by creating something.
What area he creates in is decided by his personality so it might be almost anything, any of the multitude of objects, works of art, buildings, chemical processes and on and on that people are involved with.

Virtually everything that exists since the dawns of time have been created by this process because the higher 4th, complete with all its areas - or most of them - has been in existence since the beginning of life on Earth, pushing all life; animal, vegetable, mineral or human to create.
Without this desire to create, all life would be static.
It is true that minerals show no desire to create although you would be surprised to learn that the desire to create is available to them.
Most animals are much the same although some of the higher primates could and do invent to a limited extent.
So, it is left largely to man to make use of the creation area although it is open to all life if it becomes advanced enough to desire to create.

So it is largely thanks to humanity that we have all that we see around us including a few buildings and artifacts left over from previous epochs before the latest elimination level event (ELE) wiped the populations out and life had to start again.

It is interesting that there are quite a variety of artifacts remaining from previous epochs dating from basic work tools that often bear a remarkable similarity to basic work tools used today up to magnificent works of art that people would be hard pressed to produce today.
Of course, many of them are classed as 'anomalies' and are hidden in the storage areas of museums.

However, some are on display and anyone with any psychic abilities developed can link with the people of long ago who produced these anomalies and can appreciate the work of these gifted and talented people from so long ago.

So, it is interesting to note how history tends to repeat itself and the same or similar artifacts are reinvented.

We can easily discover why. In the case of primitive tools; hammers, chisels etc, these are basic tools without which almost nothing could be created.

In the case of a hammer or striking implement we can safely say that it was probably the first implement ever to be invented.

After that came cutting implements; chisels, knives etc, and then, gradually, more sophisticated tools were invented.

But look in almost any workman's toolbox today and you will find hammers and cutting tools.

Primitive cavemen had stone hammers and stone cutting implements which gives some idea of the importance of these basic tools.

So, we can be sure that however far back in the history of mankind we trawl we will find hammers and cutting tools being manufactured.

But the original idea was and is contained in the plane of artistic invention found in the upper 4th dimension.

From these basic inventions all that exists today spring. There is virtually no creation that we can find in the civilized world that does not, at some point, need the use of striking or cutting tools.

For instance, to make a painting it is necessary to create a foundation material; paper, or whatever, on which to paint and that requires cutting and hammering fibers. Then the paint pigments must be crushed into a powder.

The brushes require the use of basic tools in order to create them.

Finally, if a frame made of wood is to be made, cutting tools are required from the moment of chopping the tree down to the manufacturer of the pieces of the frame.

So, you can see that without the basic tools we mentioned there would be no paintings, no statues either for that matter.

And it all starts in this amazing area of the 4th dimension - the artistic plane.

Having given a brief overview of that area let us see what more we can explain to you.

CHAPTER 7

GOING DOWN

We hope that you are finding this book interesting because we are revealing information concerning the 4th dimension that has never been made public before.
As we have said, there are many areas (landscapes) in the 4th and it is our intention to make as many as we can available to you, at least so that you know about them even if you will not be able to enter and experience them whilst incarnate.

We should say that all, or most, of the areas we describe are available for your inspection whilst incarnate but our experience suggests that very few of you will have the time or freedom from your daily duties that would permit you to spend the long hours in meditation necessary to develop the frequencies that would enable you to link with the areas we describe.
But at least you will be aware that these areas exist and when your incarnation ends and you have more freedom from daily tasks, you will be able to develop the frequencies necessary in order to enter these areas and experience for yourselves that which we describe.

So, let us go on and describe another area.
We might call this area the "light plane".
What we mean by this is that as one rises in spirituality (frequency), one can approach the starlight of God more and more.
Light is frequency - vibration - and the higher one rises in frequency, the brighter the areas one can interact with become.

Now, we need to explain how the heavenly spheres operate and to do so we will use an analogy.
Let us assume that you who are reading this chapter have some knowledge of mathematics or physics.
Let us also assume that some of you have more knowledge than others but that even for the most knowledgeable of you, your knowledge ends somewhere.

So, we could start with basic arithmetic, proceed to algebra, calculus and so on until we have the mathematical skills to create mathematical models to describe events in life.
This might include some areas of physics or time/space, gravity or whatever.
But, for most of you, there would be a point where you could not proceed any further.
Although the answers to your questions are out there somewhere, until you develop the skill to proceed, your progress stops.
There have been great mathematicians or scientists that are aware that the answers to their questions must exist but, until they develop the skill to contact those answers, they are obliged to stop.

Progress through the heavenly spheres is a bit like that.
We all have a degree of frequency (of light) that we vibrate to. Actually, we all have two frequencies.

The first is our body that vibrates to the quiescent frequency of planet Earth - and the galaxy - and the second is the spiritual frequency that denotes a person's degree of holiness.
The first frequency is the same for all physical things.
Everything in the entire galaxy vibrates quite slowly like a pulsing heart or the beating of a drum.
You don't notice this pulsing because everything is pulsing to the same frequency.
We will just mention that this frequency will increase somewhat as ascension asserts itself more and more and the quiescent frequency responds to the light pouring into the galaxy.

But, the second frequency is dependent on the degree of holiness of the person.
By holiness, we do not refer to people walking about in fancy robes pretending to represent God on earth. We refer to people's decency, kindness, love for all life and so on.
This is the sort of frequency that increases more and more as a person becomes ever more holy.

So, this second frequency, which is contained in the auras, shines around the body of a person. It can clearly be seen by those with psychic vision and can even be sensed by ordinary people.
This second frequency is personal to all people.
No two people will have exactly the same degree of holiness, so no two people will have their auras vibrating identically.

As we have mentioned before, evil people have very little light emitting from their auras and in the lower 4th dimension, powerful demons actually absorb light. They "glow" (if we can use that word) to a negative light, darker than pitch black. This negative light actually absorbs energy, whereas positive light creates energy.
Fortunately, the great demons tend to remain in the lower 4th and so do not concern us.

We know that it is the desire of many black magicians to summon demons but, fortunately for both them and us, they invariably fail because a really powerful demon summoned into physicality would cause irreparable harm. But, as we said, this has almost never happened and, on the odd occasion when someone was able to summon a really powerful demon, the good forces, who are constantly monitoring life, chase them back to the lower 4th.
Light chases darkness so demons, being made of negative light, fear real light. Thus, the positive angelic forces always win.
Those who practice the black arts, demonology, would do well to realise that they are chasing shadows and by following these black arts, will never gain the power they seek.
Negativity is always destructive so those who hope to gain power in any fashion by practicing evil will only ever reap negativity.
Demons are cunning. Cunning is a negative act so demons are well versed in producing cunning.
Thus, a black magician who contacts a demon will be promised many things but, at the end of the day, demons, who can only produce negativity, will always only create emptiness.

Many black magicians have fallen into this trap.
They are willing to do the most horrendous acts in the hopes of gaining power, fortune or success, but once the person's personal money or talent exhausted, he or she will be abandoned by the demon because the demon's aim was always to produce negativity.
A demon might seem to befriend a black magician but the end result will always be the destruction of the magician.

It might seem strange to positive people that black magicians cannot see that to get involved with negative creatures will result in negativity but there are enormous numbers of people throughout time and into the present that are willing to do anything in the vain hopes of getting a positive result for themselves.
Life, however, does not work like that.
Interactions with negative entities only ever results in negative results for the person concerned.
This will become ever more evident as we move into positivity, called ascension.
Then, of course, once a person's incarnation ends, the unfortunate magician finds himself in the depths of hell repaying the debt he incurred whilst incarnate and causing harm to God's creatures, humans or animals.
But people have free will and if someone chooses to follow black magic, he is free to do so.
He should realize, however, that there is a price for everything and the price for harming life is high indeed.

You may wonder why, if we are going to describe the light planes, we should mention the lower 4th?
The answer, as you may well have realized, is that the 4th dimension is one area divided into two by light or lack of light.
Light or its lack are, of course, connected. There can only be darkness where there is lack of light but they are two aspects of the same force.
Darkness can only exist where there is lack of light because light chases darkness rather as day chases night.
But light starts somewhere and the foundation point of light has to start at the point where there is lack of light.
So, the 4th dimension, which is really one dimension, starts at the point where there is total darkness, which we could describe as lack of frequency.
Then, as soon as the first glimmer of light appears, a change occurs and we move from the lower 4th to the upper 4th and the upper 4th continues with ever increasing frequency until we reach star light which is considered to be as bright as light can get.
But the origin has to be a zero frequency which is total lack of light.

Let us now go on into the upper or higher 4th and start to examine the light planes from that first glimmer up to pure star light which is considered to be equal to God.
We have already, in previous chapters, mentioned a few areas of the upper 4th (which we will just call the 4th) but they all required degrees of illumination before they could be examined or experienced.
However, as all is vibration (frequency), there are many areas in the 4th that have more or less illumination.

There is a point where the first, the faintest glimmer of light starts.

Obviously, this is not a very spiritually advanced area but it is the foundation point on which all the higher levels of light are based.

If we were to visit this area, what would we see?

First of all, it must be obvious that there would be very little to see as there is so little light but this area does exist and is a solid area (as opposed to a thought area like some we have mentioned) but looks rather like the surface of the moon, just a barren wasteland.

For things to grow, for life to exist, light is usually needed so this area, being so dim, has nothing growing in it.

On Earth, there are a number of plants, fungi and some primitive creatures that can grow in a lightless situation but in the heavenly spheres light is nearly always a prerequisite to life.

As this is a heavenly sphere and as there is so little light, there is no life as we would know it.

Now, we have stated many times that all is frequency (vibration) and the greater or higher the frequency, the brighter the light and thus the more that intelligent life can be housed.

We break off in our discussion of light planes to mention how one can visit these areas.

There are basically two ways.

The first is to learn to adjust one's quiescent frequency to that of the plane one wishes to visit in which case as soon as one starts to vibrate to that frequency one arrives in the desired area (landscape or plane).

But there is another technique.

Imagine that one has already arrived in an area of the 4th and one wishes to move to a higher or lower plane in terms of frequency.

In the heavenly spheres we can create things with our imagination so we create in our mind the desire to visit a higher or lower area and we suddenly see a path in front of us. We start to walk along this path and, after a few minutes, we notice that the light is either getting brighter or dimmer according to which direction we choose to travel.

You may remember that in another chapter we mentioned mathematics. We did this for a reason and that reason becomes relevant now.

If you have some knowledge of mathematics, it would be fairly easy for you to trace the path back to ever more simple calculations but, going forward, you would eventually reach a point where you could not go on.

Following these paths follows a similar format.

In theory, it would be possible to go to areas of ever less frequency.

In the heavenly spheres, frequency equates to spiritual advancement so to reduce frequency equates to passing through areas of lower and lower holiness.

Eventually, the path would take us into the hell regions although, as we have said elsewhere, that would be ill advisable as our natural brightness would tend to frighten the denizens of those regions.

But, in theory, we could go on and on, down and down through hell until we reached the point where there is only the faintest glimmer of light, that we mentioned.

But, going forward into ever higher regions, one quickly comes to the point where our level of holiness stops. Then we can go no further.

It is the equivalent of coming to the limit of our mathematical knowledge.

In fact, as we walk the path towards the light, we are aware that the landscape becomes brighter and more beautiful. But sooner or later we reach a point where there seems to be a fog and we find that we cannot proceed any more.

That is the limit of our spirituality.

However, there is another way of advancing a bit further.

Imagine, to use mathematics again as an example, one had a good teacher. That teacher would locate our natural limit in mathematical knowledge but he could explain, to a certain extent, more advanced techniques and so, whilst the teacher was with us, we could enter areas of mathematics that we could not do on our own.

It is similar with the spiritual path.

With a guide, using his advanced level of spirituality, we can progress a bit further down the positive path than if we were on our own.

Once the guide leaves us, we of course, return to our previous limit.

So, we hope that you can imagine that the light plane has a virtually unlimited number of landscapes that are also very much connected to hell/Summerland and true heaven, starting at the depths of hell where there is just the faintest glimmer of light up to the God plane itself.

This darkest area that just contains the merest glimmer of light is actually very important for it is that glimmer of light that is the hope for all of those sad people in that area of eventually rising to ever higher landscapes should they choose to do so.

That glimmer, faint though it is, contains the God Spirit, so even the worst criminal is never abandoned.

It is that faint light that affords his connection to God and to salvation, should he choose to follow it.

Without that light there would be no hope for him.

But God is ever merciful and always makes his bounty, his forgiveness available to even the most abject sinner.

It is that faint glimmer of light that is the source of his salvation.

We should say that on very rare occasions, some people in that bottom level of hell choose to abandon life altogether and they reject that faint light and, at that point, their life essence is snuffed out and they cease to be. Fortunately, this is very rare and, generally, even the greatest sinner clings to some hope of redemption. Thus, he clings to the light.

It is interesting to note that a person who rejects the light would not go down to the lower 4th and join the ranks of the demons.

He was formed as a positive human and should he reject his humanity, he just ceases to be.

The lack of energy caused by his disappearance is compensated for by another human being created, for life must always be kept in balance and if the loss of one person was not compensated for, all life would cease.

As we said, fortunately, someone giving up life is very rare but it does happen so we must mention it.

We have spoken about hell in other works and we do not wish to bore you by repeating ourselves but for those who are not familiar with this area, we will repeat it.
Those who are familiar with what we have said about hell could skip this section if they wish.
We will not add very much new to the topic.

Before we begin our trip into hell, we would like to make a few introductory remarks.
First, we assume that all who read these books we give you are decent people. If you are not you probably would not be drawn to this information.
So, we are going to assume that you have been to one of the landscapes of Summerland but, desirous of visiting hell, have created the path that will lead you there.
At the moment you are in Summerland and can see and appreciate the beauty of that area and can feel the happiness of the people you might meet there.
But, with your guides you set off down the path that will lead you to the landscapes of hell - and they are many.
Let us also assume that you would be invisible to the people living in hell due to the fact that your quiescent frequency is higher than theirs.
As you walk, you will notice that the light becomes dimmer.
You will notice that the temperature becomes cooler and the people there seem less happy.
But you would not notice much difference except that the vegetation becomes less beautiful.
As you proceed, so this effect becomes more and more marked.

We will notice groups of people earnestly discussing various topics.
Let us, invisibly, listen in on their conversations. We would find them rather unpleasant.
We would hear groups discussing the pleasures of hunting - killing God's creatures.
We would hear others discussing the pleasures of raping men, women, children and even animals.
We would hear groups of once professional soldiers discussing the pleasures of shooting or destroying enemy soldiers or civilians.
We would see people discussing robbery and all sorts of antisocial activities.
As we proceed along the path and as the landscapes become more sombre and barren, we would meet people who thought it correct to torture other humans or animals, those who thought the inquisition correct, those who thought that slavery was a good idea and so on.
There is almost no limit to the iniquities to which some can stoop and these people with similar penchants tend to draw together and discuss, reinforce and justify their points of view on any subject.

It might seem unthinkable to normal, decent people that to harm God's creatures - human or animal - is justifiable but you would be surprised to see how many people there are in different areas of hell that are there because they thought that they had the right to inflict harm on others.
Some of these people have been in the hell areas for centuries and some are recent arrivals.

Many you would not recognise but there are a huge number of kings and queens, princes and princesses, politicians, army generals and soldiers, church people of all denominations and religions, all convinced that the dreadful harm they caused was justified.
They are all at varying levels of hell depending on the degree of their crimes and of their unwillingness to repent the harm they caused.

It is fair to say that there is not one level of the power structures of virtually every country that is not represented in the hellish regions, huge numbers of people that had power over people and animals and abused that power in contradiction to the oaths that they took to protect all life.
Indeed, it would be a good lesson to many who rise to positions of power if they could visit hell and see where they might end up if they abused their positions.
But, unfortunately, they do not visit these areas.
In fact, the opposite obtains.
Many who rise up through the stages of power end up living in magnificent homes with servants waiting on them hand and foot and, gradually, divorce themselves from the people they swore to serve.
There is an old expression: All power corrupts and absolute power corrupts absolutely!
This saying tends to be true.
Very few resist the temptation of power and so find themselves in hell repaying their debts to life.

Of course, hell contains many more people than just powerful people.
There are vast numbers of ordinary people who were unkind and thus are in one of the levels of hell but it is fair to say that the deepest levels tend to be occupied by those who were the most powerful when on Earth.
The reason is simple.
Ordinary people may have power over their spouses or their children but their power stops there.
More powerful people have much greater scope for manipulating large numbers of people to their evil intentions so their degree of crime is greater.

Of course, please do not think that we are globally criticizing all powerful people - we are not.
But there are, unfortunately, a large number who did and do abuse their authority over others and thus the degree of harm they have to pay back is greater.

As we progress along this sad path, we notice that the light glows less and less. The landscapes appear more and more barren until we reach levels of staggering unpleasantness.
There would be no point in describing graphically these areas because we do not want to be too dramatic.
Suffice to say that there are levels for really evil people that would almost defy description until we arrive at the last level where there is just the glimmer of light that we mentioned.

Before we return to Summerland let us say that there are brave souls that go down into these areas and try to persuade the occupants to repent, which would give them the chance to rise to lighter planes but, unfortunately, many of them in hell reject any offer of help and so they remain for long ages. That is their free will.

So, we will end this chapter here and return to Summerland.

CHAPTER 8

SUMMERLAND – IN GREATER DEPTH

So, we retrace our steps and we enter the glorious landscapes known to you as
Summerland. We just refer to it as home as most of you will come to know it when you
return there.
We have described Summerland many times but, for those who do not know the area, we
will describe it one more time.
Once again, we will not add much new information so this chapter, which we will keep
short, will give a brief overview because much more in depth descriptions have already
been provided elsewhere in other books, videos and lessons.

So, we return to the beautiful gardens of Summerland. We are surrounded by the beauty
of the lawns, flower beds, paths and lakes that constitute this area.
We see birds of the most colorful plumage flying around. We see butterflies of similar
staggering colours.
We see people walking and talking, each one as happy as it is possible to be in that area.
We see animals - beloved pets - of all types following their friends that you would call
owners. Not just dogs and cats but lions, tigers and all sorts of animals and birds that
were loved by their owners and, in turn, were loved by these pets.
In Summerland, where there is love there can never be separation.

We apologise to those who are familiar with Summerland but, to help those who are not
familiar, we feel obliged to repeat the information.
Summerland is not just one area or landscape. There are many levels of Summerland.
According to one's spiritual frequency, one goes to a level of Summerland that
corresponds to that level of spirituality.
Thus, there are an infinite number of landscapes that we call Summerland.
The first or lowest level starts where the highest level of hell leaves off. So, this first or
lowest level would not be very beautiful and would correspond, roughly, to the sorts of
parks that one would see on Earth.
Obviously, we exclude desert areas and we just apply this lowest area to the sorts of
parks one would find in areas of Earth where it rains sufficiently to promote flora of all
sorts.
The people one would find there would be kind, decent (ordinary) people who did little
harm during their incarnation on Earth but did not do much to help their fellow man
either. Just ordinary people.

Let us go on walking along the path towards the light that we described in the last
chapter.
If we listened to the conversations of these people, they would just be talking about
families they had on Earth, their jobs, the sorts of houses and cars they had and just
everyday subjects that ordinary people talk about whilst incarnate.
These people are happy and contented. They appreciate the place they are in and ask for
no more.

They are in this fairly low level of Summerland because their ability to love is not very developed.
There is nothing wrong with this. It takes all sorts to make a world, as the saying goes and these are just ordinary, decent people but with their level of spirituality not very developed.

As we proceed along the path, the light grows stronger, the landscapes more beautiful and we start to see people with levels of spirituality more developed.

You may ask why people in any one area do not walk to higher or lower levels but remain in their one Summerland?
This question was answered in the last chapter.
They could easily go to a lower landscape but ask yourself, if you were in their situation would you choose to move to a colder, dimmer, bleak or barren area or would you remain in a sunny, warm and beautiful place?
Equally, if they tried to move to higher landscapes, they would find their paths blocked by this fog we described. They could not surpass their level of spirituality.
We, of course, being more developed have greater freedom to move to higher areas!

So, we progress along the path and the landscapes become ever more sunny, warm and beautiful. The flowers start to 'sing' if we may use that term. This is not really singing as we would know a song to sound but it is a mixture of bell-like sounds and other very musical tones coming from the flowers and plants.
Why should this be?
The answer is that flora that is full of love needs to express that love.
They do this in a number of ways: beautiful colours, wonderful perfumes and, finally, by emitting musical sounds.
This may seem improbable but is so.

The people who live in these landscapes start to glow with light, spiritual light.
This light may be of many colours. They would all be beautiful colours which are, actually, the reflection of the love contained in their auras.
At the highest end of Summerland, the people would have white light surrounding them.
It is interesting to note that the pets that some might have also reflect the love given by their human friends so these animals also would have their auras glow to the same colour as their friends.
Animals are quite capable of love and if their friend or master has such a degree of love that his auras shine with colour or white light, their pets also absorb that love and shine with the same frequency as their human friends.

So, as we progress further we, in effect, leave Summerland and enter the true heavenly planes.
However, the change is gradual and there is no landmark or barrier dividing Summerland from true heaven. We just see things getting ever brighter and more beautiful. Eventually, it would be obvious that we have entered the true heavenly planes but one just blends into the other.

We should also say that, at the opposite end, we leave the highest level of hell and enter
the lowest region of Summerland.
Once again, there is no barrier between the states.
They just blend from one to another.

Thus, it would be possible to start at the lowest level of hell, walk towards the light and
pass from hell into Summerland, cross Summerland and enter true heaven.
If our level of spirituality permitted, we could continue along the path until we arrived at
the God plane. It would all be one path.
Thus, in theory, it could be possible for someone who is in the depths of hell, by
repenting of his sins and by following the spiritual path, to progress from the deepest
depths of hell, through Summerland into true heaven and finally end up in the arms of
God.
Although this does not seem very likely, it does happen and, although it might take
millions of years, is the path that all take.
No one is left out. No one is abandoned so all are encouraged and tutored to become
better people in the hopes that they will progress towards God.
With many it is hard going at first as the worst criminals reject any help but brave souls
persist until, one by one, the poor wretches see the light, so to speak, and proceed towards
that light.
So, to repeat, no one is abandoned. Even the most abject criminal is shown love.
Eventually, they all respond to this love and climb slowly back to the light which is God's
love.

Now let us mention the newly deceased.
Once again, we have mentioned this but for those who have not followed our books we
will repeat.

When a person 'dies', in effect the link between his spiritual aspect and his physical body
dissolves and the person is freed from incarnation.
He may look from his spiritual body down upon his physical body which is lying inert.
This will be the last time he sees his physical body because for all eternity he will live in
his spiritual body. Reincarnation is not true.

In reality, his physical body was never alive and only appeared alive because of the
energy that flowed from his spiritual body into his physical body by an umbilical cord
which attached the two.
This umbilical cord is sometimes referred to as the silver cord.
This cord is very flexible and can be short when the spiritual and physical bodies are
close together but can stretch for great distances if the person is doing Astral Projection.
At the moment of death, this cord dissolves and the link between the two bodies ceases,
at which point the physical body dies.
The spiritual body is free at that point.

At this moment the spiritual body needs to go to Summerland.
This happens in one of two ways.
Either a close member of the family arrives in astral form and guides the person to
Summerland or a portal opens between the higher self and Summerland that is called the

tunnel of light and the person proceeds along the tunnel until he sees a bright light which is the entry point into Summerland.

We should just mention at this point that there are a number of evil or misguided people who are advocating not going down the tunnel.
This is very stupid and dangerous advice because, after death, the spirit body must go somewhere and if it does not go to Summerland it will go to a place called limbo.
Limbo is in the etheric planes and there are quite a large number of lost souls who are in that area because for one reason or another, they did not go to the heavenly spheres.
Limbo is not a nice place to be and can be avoided by the simple process of either following the guide that arrives to take them to heaven or by going down the tunnel of light.
So, we repeat, when your time comes to leave incarnation either follow the person that comes to collect you or go down the tunnel of light.
Do not end up in limbo. It takes a long time to get from limbo to Summerland and limbo is very unpleasant.

Assuming that one arrived safely in Summerland, one will be met by someone. This person will seem very bright to the new arrival but that is his degree of spirituality shining.
Now, as you can imagine, there are a large number of newly 'dead' people arriving in Summerland each and every minute of the day or night, but each person is met by someone completely alone.
Further, each newly deceased person, regardless of whether he was a horrible person or an extremely nice person arrives in Summerland and is met by someone.
Tales of people having a near death experience (NDE) and finding themselves in a burning hell surrounded by imps who torture them is imagination. The burning pit of hell does not exist. It is an Archon invention to scare people.

What happens is that there is a large group of advanced spiritual humans that have chosen to welcome newly deceased people.
When they are alerted that someone is on his way to Summerland, one of these advanced humans volunteers to greet the person.
So, he or she does a couple of things.
First, he or she creates a place with a unique vibration for the deceased person to arrive in.
Second, at the moment of arrival, a sort of shield or cloak is placed around the new arrival that corresponds to the frequency of the area of arrival.
In that way, no matter how noble or how crass the person is, he or she arrives at this particular spot.
The person concerned is met by the human who is charged with greeting the newly deceased and explains that the person's incarnation is finished and he is now back home in the heavenly spheres.
We will drop the modern he/she concept and return to the classical convention of calling all people "he". For "he", please assume that we include "she" also. No insult is intended.

Obviously, for each nationality of deceased person, there is a guide (if we can thus describe the welcoming spirit) of that nationality so there is no barrier of language or culture.

The deceased person is introduced to his loved ones who are already in Summerland and allowed to acclimate to his new home.

Eventually, he has his life review.
This consists of him viewing every moment of his entire life and he sees all the good that he did and also all the harm he caused.
Not only does he see it from his point of view but sees it also from the point of view of those who were affected by his actions.
This gives the person concerned the opportunity to repent - or not - the harm he might have caused.

Now, the person has a quiescent frequency which is masked by the cloak or shield that was placed around him when he arrived.
As he watches his life review, his shield is gradually removed and his true frequency is revealed.
So, for every good action taken the frequency rises somewhat.
But for every bad action, one of two things can occur.
Either the person was glad of the harm he caused, in which case his frequency drops or he is sorry for the harm he caused and wished he had not done the misdeed, in which case he forgives himself and the misdeed is forgiven.

All this results, ultimately, in him having a certain frequency, and by the law of mutual attraction, the person is drawn to a level of hell / Summerland / heaven that corresponds to his new frequency.
So, you see that no one judges you. It is all quite natural and is the result of the way you led your life and your reaction to the life review.

This is an important aspect of life in heaven.
It is the desire of all noble spirits in the higher regions, that all people, once their incarnation finished and having nothing to regret, having led a peaceful and love filled existence but, unfortunately, such is not the case at the moment. Deception and falsehood is rife in all sections of parliamentary, business, religious and family life at the moment. Eventually, as we move into ascension, these acts will stop but, at the moment, it is not the case and is not helped by the fact that our leaders in politics, business and religion do not hesitate to spread falsehoods in the vain hopes of improving their personal situation. However, heaven is not fooled, and at the life review, the full extent of the deceptions perpetrated by such people is revealed to the perpetrators.
We, who once had an incarnation and some of whom were guilty of such duplicity are very anxious that all people going through their incarnation should be aware that one day these people will have to face the consequences of their acts just as we had to.
However, having said that, we must also say that it is possible to repent for one's actions and thus can progress through the heavenly spheres.
But how much better it would be if people were honest and did not try to present false images to our fellow man.

We may rest assured that duplicity will be revealed sooner or later and how much better it would be if those in our soul groups could pat us on the backs for an incarnation well lived instead of watching some of us descend to hell to repay for a life of crime.

Perhaps not crime as contained in the statute books but crime as observed from the spiritual realms.

Love is the rule by which we should all live.

Love for all of God's creatures; human or animal.

No spiritual person would do any action to put himself above any other human.

Jesus summed it up by saying that we should love our neighbour as ourselves.

We should also mention that, as all is one, to harm animals through hunting, animal farms and by eating animals is also considered a sin in heaven, and although people that do not know that to kill God's creatures is a sin cannot be held accountable, once they are aware that killing or eating animals is a sin and carry on doing it, they are considered accountable under God's laws.

How much better would it be if the life review was just an account of a life spent helping all other life, human or animal, and not an endless tale of crime against God?

We can take our lead from young children, who have recently arrived from the heavenly spheres and thus are filled with love.

Can you imagine the effect on a child if he was taken into an abattoir and was shown the slaughter (murder) of beautiful animals?

Also, can you imagine the effect on a child if he was taken hunting and watched people kill animals or birds?

Lastly, what would be the effect on a child if he was taken into the death cell of a prison that has the death penalty and watches some poor wretch have his life terminated?

We can learn a lot from children, as Jesus noted. 'Suffer the little children to come unto me.'

Jesus understood the purity of children, and those who claim to be followers of Jesus would do well to think of this when they sit down to a meal containing meat, fowl or fish.

It is not sufficient to say that it is mentioned in the Bible that Jesus ate meat.

The Bible often contains half-truths at best and often downright falsehoods.

We will also say that the old Greek term for food and for meat was the same word and so, when the Bible was translated into english, the translators could not imagine anyone surviving on a vegan diet, despite many Indian people having done so for ages, and so they attributed a carnivorous diet to Jesus.

The views of Jesus are known to us and if he was incarnate today, he would be a strict vegan.

So, can we say that the followers of Jesus are really walking in his footsteps if they hunt, fish or eat anything other than vegetables?

In an ideal sense, people incarnate would not eat anything - not even vegetables - and there are a gifted and blessed few that do not eat but get their sustenance from the ether as we do in heaven, but for the rest of those incarnate, it is considered acceptable to eat vegetables as they contain so little consciousness that they do not suffer when eaten.

It should be spiritual law for anyone wishing to lead a holy life that they should banish any animal product; meat, fish, eggs, milk and cheese from their diets.

To eat anything other than vegetables, fruit etc., involves suffering of sentient entities and is a crime. A crime that must be repaid at some point.

However, we have strayed somewhat from our discussion of Summerland.
But be aware that if you have led a life of sin in any fashion, through your personal and business activities or through your diet and even the clothes you wore, if they contain animal fur, leather, wool or silk, this will lower your vibration. We suggest that you banish any clothes that contain fur, wool, silk or leather - including shoes - and only purchase garments made from vegetable fibers.
Thus, if you pay attention to this advice, your vibration will rise and, at the end of your incarnation, you will find yourself in one of the higher levels of heaven instead of one of the lower.
The choice is yours, but life's incarnation is short compared to the eternity we spend in the heavenly spheres and to follow the spiritual path involves making a few sacrifices that we will list below.

1. Do not take any action that will benefit only you.
2. Always compare how any action you might take will affect others.
3. Do not take any action that will harm any person or animal.
4. Do not hunt or fish.
5. Do not eat anything other than fruit, nuts, pulses and vegetables.
6. Do not wear anything of animal origin.
7. Do your best to act in a kind and loving fashion to all life.

To sum it up.
(A) Do unto others as you would have them do unto you.
(B) Never do to others that which you would not like done to you.

These simple suggestions will take you into the upper reaches of Summerland or even the true levels of heaven, which will be the subject of the next chapter.

CHAPTER 9

THE TRUE HEAVENLY SPHERES

So, as we continue to walk along the path and start to leave Summerland, we notice that the physical landscape alters in that it becomes ever more beautiful but, more importantly, it is the atmosphere that alters and becomes increasingly peaceful and loving.

This is an atmosphere that fills our hearts with joy as the atmosphere enters our auras.

We are visitors to this area. Our normal level of development would not permit us to be here but we have been granted permission by noble people who live here and that have taken us under their wings, so to speak, and are helping us along the path.

Just how far we can progress, even with their help, remains to be seen because we only have a limited level of spirituality and even with the help of these high beings that are boosting our level of spirituality for the moment, we will only be able to go so far.

After that we must rely on what these people can tell us to complete the trip.

First, let us describe these high beings.

Normally, they would just be orbs of light because they have long since passed the need to take physical form - in an astral sense.

However, for the purposes of this book they have agreed to take physical form in order that we might describe them.

Now, race has no meaning in the heavenly spheres but these people, most of whom had an incarnation on Earth at one point long ago, still retain the memories of what country they lived in and to what race they belonged.

Thus, they would appear to us, when they take physical form, to be of a variety of skin colours.

Skin colour is no barrier in heaven.

So, some would be white, others brown skinned, others black or yellow skinned. Yet others would have the colour of Native Americans and so on.

The only thing that counts in heaven is the level of spirituality.

We see some of them laughing as they look at their friends, appearing for the first time as physical people as opposed to orbs of light and they see each other with various skin colours, tall or short, men or women.

In their world they would have long passed any sense of physicality or gender. They all interact as spheres of spiritual light so they find it highly amusing to observe each other as they appeared whilst in incarnation.

They tend to talk telepathically but we can pick up some of their thoughts as they joke to each other about how they look in physicality. This is all good-natured banter and they take advantage of appearing in physical form to joke to each other about their appearance.

They all wear long, thin robes of dazzling white material.

They all glow - indeed, blaze - with pure white light radiating from them.

This light, as you should know, is the starlight of God that fills these people.

However, they are anxious to assure us that they are far from the top of the tree in terms of spiritual advancement and that there are others, far more advanced than themselves, who would be too remote from us to be able to communicate with us.

These are extremely powerful people in terms of spirituality.
There may well be others more advanced than them but, as their auras blend with ours, we feel almost overwhelmed by their power.
Goodness knows what it would feel like if we contacted even more powerful people.
We must reinforce the fact that these people are not angels. They are people who were, at one stage, just ordinary people like you and us but that have advanced to a higher spiritual state.
We notice how happy they seem to be. They have a serious side to them but there is no trace of aggressivity. They seem to be full of joy, of bliss and as their auras overpower us we, too, feel the joy that they have. It is a wonderful feeling, and we must say, is a little strange to us.
We tend to take life seriously and often have meetings for instance to decide what books to present to you.
These people can decide serious matters but the seriousness of the issues they deal with in no way affects their emotions.
They act quite impartially, deciding serious events, but what they talk about remains remote from the joy that they live in at all times.

It must be good to be able to take life changing decisions, being absolutely sure of their decisions, but what they are dealing with remains remote from their sentiments of joy.
This is the nature of life in the heavenly spheres, to be able to deal with problems in an intelligent fashion but any negotiation they might have amongst themselves or with other groups does not affect the love they have for all life, which is the source of their joy.

When one considers the matter, if it is true that the theme of our God is love and that everything is affected by this love, it would be foolish to do anything else but love all life, yet how many of us spend our lives living in opposition to that emotion.
We can, to a certain extent, understand and excuse those who live without love if they have fallen under the influence of negative beings; Archons and negative Reptilians, but we all have free will and do not have to draw these entities to us.
Many do so by trying to gain money or power.
Money is not used in heaven but power certainly is and the power of these great beings that are helping us is immense, but it is a positive power.

This should be obvious to you because, if it is true that the theme of our God is love, that love is a real and vibrant force.
The more someone incorporates that power of love into his being, the more powerful he becomes.
We can assure you all that a few minutes spent in the company and under the influence of one of the more powerful of these advanced beings would change one's life forever.
One could never go back to being a negative person again.

So, to return to the theme of this chapter which is a description of the heavenly spheres, we walk this path for as long as we can, going in the direction of the starlight of God.

As we walk, beauty grows ever greater, joy grows ever more, and if we could follow the path to its conclusion, we would enter the God sphere.

Obviously, that place is far away both in terms of the distance the path would need to go and also in terms of the degree of spirituality we would need to develop.

So, we hope that you will forgive us if we can only go so far. After that we can only speculate or relate what higher beings than us explain to us.

Now, what do we see in terms of the ever unfolding landscapes?

This is a bit difficult to describe because there is nothing revolutionary to describe.

As you can imagine, the landscapes grow ever more beautiful in terms of the Flora but we cannot really describe anything extraordinary.

Beautiful flowers, parkland, lakes and so on are much the same wherever one is in heaven. There are no cities that we could see, though we were told that they, like Summerland, have libraries, schools and study areas, no doubt, far in advance of those we might have in Summerland but a school is a school.

We were not shown any but accept that they exist.

The reason we were not shown any is twofold.

1. They would be incomprehensible to us, being so far in advance to anything we would understand, and
2. They would only exist in orb form and thus would be invisible to our eyes.

But, as we advance, so the feelings of bliss overwhelm us and we have this great desire to remain forever in this emotion of total peace and joy.

We understand that people who have a near death experience often want to remain in Summerland as opposed to returning to incarnation.

We have the same feeling - the great desire to remain in this area - although we do realise that we are only visitors and sooner or later we must return to our level of Summerland.

But the feeling of being ever more at home as we approach the God sphere grows stronger and helps us realise that God is our home.

We are all on a long journey, having been created by God, and have been sent out on a long voyage to perfect ourselves and when this is done, we return home to our Father, God.

But we are not there yet.

We have eons of time before us, before that happy day arrives when we will return to our maker.

Joy increases with every step we take but the ultimate joy of returning to source - God - must wait until we have perfected ourselves.

This is the main message of visiting the heavenly spheres.

We must do all that we can to perfect ourselves.

We must learn to love all life, help and assist all life and always keep our focus on the goal which is to incorporate all life into us so that we become one with all life and thus with God.

So, reluctantly, we say goodbye to our advanced friends who assure us that we will meet again when we advance sufficiently to be able to live in the heavenly spheres, and we retrace our steps to our level of Summerland.

This chapter is short because there is not much to describe in physical terms.

Everything happens in an emotional sense and that emotion is an ever-increasing sense of love.
Love for all life.
Total understanding and forgiveness for all that are less than we are because we, too, had to progress from lower thoughts.

The heavenly spheres project ever increasing levels of joy, of bliss, of understanding and of truly comprehending the meaning of oneness. The oneness of being close to the God plane which is where we came from initially.

CHAPTER 10

NATURE SPIRITS

Many people are interested in the various small creatures that share the planet with us.
We are not sure that we can describe them all fully in one chapter.
It would take a complete book to give a detailed description of all of them, and even then,
it would be difficult because there are so many, and without having visual depictions,
mere words would hardly describe them.
If you take, for example, describing in just words all of the animals in the world, the book
would not only be enormous but would be meaningless using just words - a written
description of each and every animal that populates the animal kingdom.
There may not be quite as many nature spirits - if we can thus call them - as animals, but
there are a large number. Some are known to you and some you may well never have
heard of.
So, you can understand how difficult our task is going to be.
We have promised to try to explain all life that inhabits the various dimensions, and
certainly, nature spirits fall into this category, so we will do our best to describe at least
some of the more well-known ones to you.

Before we start, we must advise you not to interfere with nature spirits. Many are
peaceful but some can be aggressive if they feel threatened, just as most animals can
defend themselves.
The main difference between wild animals and nature spirits is that animals, if cornered,
will attack physically whereas nature spirits, usually being of astral or etheric origin, have
a mastery of manipulating the etheric realms. By which we mean their defense
mechanisms will affect your mind.
This can have dramatic effects on a person so attacked, ranging from feeling lost or
confused to putting themselves actually in physical danger. For instance, crossing a busy
thoroughfare and not seeing the traffic passing. Or walking off the edge of a high cliff,
not seeing the edge but just thinking a field goes on further.
These are extreme cases but have happened.
Our advice to you is to leave nature spirits alone, and if seen, do not try to interact with
them.
They can play tricks with your mind and thus put you in danger.
The way they do this is as follows.
All people not only have an etheric form that extends from their bodies as a sort of cloud
around a person but also have auras which extend for a considerable distance from the
body.
You may not see your etheric double nor your auras but nature spirits can see them.
From their minds they can project images that interact with either your etheric double or
your auras and these images pass into your mind and brain and thus affect what you are
seeing or feeling. In that manner they can cause you to have illusions that can be
dangerous to you.

It may not be that these nature spirits mean to cause you harm. It is a defense mechanism at work but the effect on the mind can be similar to if someone took hallucinogenic drugs and can distort reality.

Therein lies the danger.

So, if by chance you come across any nature spirits, do not interfere with them. They distrust most humans and have a variety of methods of breaking contact with humans. Some can be dangerous.

We hope that you will bear this in mind because, if by chance you spot one or a group of nature spirits, natural curiosity pushes you to observe them and the antics they get up to. But if they spot you, you may be in trouble.

Having given that warning, let us begin to describe at least some of the better known ones.

First of all, let us say that nature spirits, as the name suggests, tend to be found in the countryside. There are some that inhibit towns and cities but the majority prefer to live in places where humans do not live.

This implies that the more remote an area is the more chance you have of seeing one.

The majority are etheric but there are a small number that are physical but generally have developed an ability to move into the etheric realm at will and, thus, will be invisible to all unless that person has developed psychic skills.

The first group you may find strange for us to mention.

It is Bigfoot (Sasquatch).

Now the majority of nature spirits are quite small but Bigfoot is huge.

We are sure that you are all familiar with Bigfoot.

Some believe they exist and some don't but we assure you that they do exist.

We include them in the nature spirit category because, although they are not true nature spirits, they exhibit the mannerisms of nature spirits.

They are physical but can move into the etheric realms.

Bigfoot, as we said, is not a true nature spirit. It is actually a close relative of humanity but they are so similar in their abilities to move into the etheric or to play games with people's thoughts that they exhibit many of the mannerisms of nature spirits.

They are shy and avoid contact with humans but they are huge and immensely strong. If cornered they will either project horrible smells or strange thoughts. As a last resort they will attack.

They can only move into the etheric if they are calm.

If they are alarmed by finding themselves close to an armed human, they lose the ability to move into the etheric and thus resort to the tactics we described above.

We will now attempt to describe true nature spirits.

The most well-known, perhaps, is the group you call fairies. The spelling can alter (faerie) but we are sure that you have an image in your mind of a fairy.

Actually, there are a number of different sorts and sizes of beings that come under the fairy heading.

They are etheric. They always remain in the etheric realms but can come so close to physicality that they can often be seen by ordinary people.

The first group are generally small, about a foot tall, although there are some who are a bit larger.

Like all true nature spirits, they do not eat or drink. Nor do they breathe.

They do not live eternally but do have very long lives, living for hundreds of years in some cases.

In the etheric realm they do not have gender but they spend a lot of their time at play and they ape the human form and human activities.

Very few people see them but they can see into our physical realm and often spy on humans as they perform what, to the fairies, seems like games; working, feasting, holding marriage services etc.

Then they incorporate these activities into their games.

That is the origin of the little creatures that make shoes, for instance. They would have spied on a cobbler making or mending shoes, or indeed, people making or mending clothes and they will copy these acts in a play situation.

Of course, fairies are not the only nature spirits that do this. Gnomes will also copy human work activities, especially ancient crafts.

It is the same with marriages, feasts or parties.

The fairies will have observed marriage ceremonies, or people sitting around a table eating and drinking or people dancing at a festivity. They spy on these activities but having no understanding of what is going on, copy these activities and hold fairy weddings, feasts or they dance in circles.

It is just these delightful and fun-filled fairies copying human behavior.

For those who have been lucky enough to see these little creatures enjoying themselves, it is a fascinating experience, especially when one sees them copying the types of things we humans get up to but realizing that they have no concept of the true meanings of what we do. They copy the form but not the fact.

Before we continue it might be worth us taking a few lines to discuss the origins of nature spirits because, like all life, they were created by God's archangels and thus have a place in existence.

The archangels decided, when they were organizing life forms, that there should be a group of beings bridging the gap between flora (plants) and fauna (animals).

As you should know by now, humans were never intended to incarnate to planet earth but it was noted that there was a large gap between plants, which are sedentary and comparatively 'lifeless' entities in terms of mobility and communication, and animals which, it was hoped, would develop to the point of being able to send spiritual power back to the God Force.

So, nature spirits were created as a sort of bridge between plants and animals.

The aim was to take the peaceful and loving aspect of most plants and communicate that love to animals to help them develop the skill to project love back to God. As you should be aware, animals did not develop this skill so humans were encouraged to fulfil this function.

But the nature spirits remain and still, to a certain extent, fulfill their function of taking the peace and love of plants and trying to transmit it to animals.

Obviously, over the vast amount of time that this has been going on, the situation has altered somewhat and nature spirits have developed to the point that they stand apart as a distinct and solo group, neither plant nor animal.
They make a distinct group in isolation from plants and animals and have developed distinct personalities both in a group sense and in an individual sense.
Thus it is that we have a number of distinct groups with distinct names that have little contact with their former role in a two way sense.
But this role, particularly in relation to plants, remains and nature spirits have been seen caring for and nurturing plants. However, the relationship with animals has dwindled somewhat and the relationship with their original function tends to stop just at caring for plants.
This, of course, is partly the fault of animals that failed to fulfil their functions of sending spiritual power back to God.
Equally, the gap between nature spirits and us humans is great and also our aggressive nature has not encouraged any real contact between nature spirits and humans.
This, we feel, is a pity because we look forward to the day that all sentient entities can live in trust, friendship and harmony together.
Can you imagine how delightful it would be to have fairy folk sharing your homes and your lives with you?
But, of course, that would require that a number of things alter.
Man would have to give up his aggressive nature and learn to live in peace with nature.
Then man would have to learn telepathy to be able to talk to nature spirits for virtually all of them communicate telepathically.

We have mentioned fairies, the ones typically described in children's fairy tales although we assure you that they are real and pass most of their time in the etheric realms.
When seen by humans they tend to appear to be clothed in white but this is just because the etheric realms, when seen by human's naked eye, tends to be white.
We will say, before we move on, that they do not have wings. As they are etheric creatures living in the etheric realms, they can move by thought and thus can seem to fly through the air like birds, which is why people depict them with wings.
By changing frequency they can blink in and out of our sight as can all entities with a mastery of the etheric.

So, to round up this brief description of typical fairies. When seen, they appear very much like tiny humans but that is when they are playing at aping human activities. In their natural state they would just be orbs, which is the natural state of all life.
When seen aping human activities, they would be quite beautiful, foot high creatures with human form. They nearly always seem happy and they are because they cannot be harmed, never require food or drink and they just fill their time, when they are not fulfilling their primary function which is to care for plants, in play like small children.

We should say that their size and their dress can alter somewhat according to the dress of inhabitants of certain countries that may wear different types of garments.
But when they are concentrating on play activities such as dances, banquets, marriages etc, they tend to remain in their etheric colour which is whitish.

The fairy population is vast. Apart from the small ones that we have described, there are others that remain in close contact with water, particularly streams and cascades, others with seas, others with clouds and yet others that are attracted to mountain tops.

We do not know why these diverse groups of fairies are attracted to these areas but it is so.

Like all fairies, they tend to avoid areas where humans congregate but can be seen in remote areas.

Being etheric, they cannot be harmed by extreme weather conditions.

Those drawn to running water, for instance, love to dive in and out of waterfalls and cascades.

These sorts of fairies can be very large and are quite often translucent, aping the environment they are interacting with.

For instance, a typical fairy playing with a waterfall would be perhaps 6 or 7 ft tall, once again vaguely human in appearance but with a translucent body and he would be seen diving in and out of the foamy water of a waterfall.

Sometimes he would be seen diving from the top of the waterfall to the bottom and sometimes doing the reverse rather as one sees salmon leaping up a waterfall. They will do this for hours on end, never seeming to grow tired of this game.

Why they do it, we cannot say.

But we must say that it is not easy to spot these fairies as their bodies mirror sunlight on cascading water and so blend with the water.

They are almost never seen in still water and slow running rivers. It is tumbling water making lots of splashing that attracts them.

We mentioned size and it is fair to say that these fairies will always be bigger than the typical woodland fairy but they can change size according to the size of the cascade. The greater the waterfall, the larger the fairies tend to be.

It may well be that a small water fairy in a huge waterfall would find it difficult to control his movements in really aggressive cascades, so he takes a larger form in order to be able to control his actions within really dynamic waterfalls.

We should mention something that we forgot to mention earlier.

Gender plays no role in their makeup. If they are playing at a wedding scenario, one will pretend to be the groom and one the bride but it is just play acting as children might. In reality they have no gender and would certainly have no knowledge of human sexual behavior.

To go back to water fairies, in seas, fairies also appear and the rougher the sea the happier the fairy appears to be, diving in and out of huge waves.

Like river fairies, they dress, if we can use that word, very much like the waves and so are difficult to spot as they plunge in and out of the waves. They are often far out to sea which makes them even harder to spot.

They avoid calm water and only appear during storms. The rougher the sea, the more they seem pleased.

Then there are those that are seen in the sky.

Once again, they ape clouds and can be really huge, the size of a typical cloud.

They also tend to take on the appearance of clouds and so would be virtually indistinguishable from a rolling cloud.

These fairies also love stormy weather and the rougher the weather the more they delight in rolling and tumbling through the windswept skies.

Yet again, we can offer no explanation as to why they do this.

The last group of fairies we will mention are those that live on mountain tops.

The higher the mountain, the more fairies are drawn to them. This may be because of the extremes of weather in mountainous regions and also because of the paucity of humans.

These fairies can be quite large and often blend in with the snow usually found at extreme altitudes.

Once again, they prefer inclement weather, enjoying the storms that frequently occur at high altitudes.

With all these nature fairies we have described it appears that action is what draws them and the more violent a cascade or a storm, the more these fairies seemed to enjoy taking part in the action.

They seemed quickly to grow bored with calm water or calm weather but love to be involved in the sorts of conditions that we humans tend to avoid.

Obviously, humans can be harmed in violent water or atmospheric conditions whereas fairies cannot and thus they enjoy being tossed around in helter-skelter conditions.

Of course, even humans like to put themselves into mock peril when they go to fairgrounds and ride on these helter-skelter events. The adrenaline rush is what is being sought in the case of humans. What thrills nature spirits get from what they do we can only guess at.

The small fairies tend to engage in peaceful events just aping what activities humans get up to but there are others who get pleasure from playing in rushing water or storms.

Let us now turn to cousins of the fairies because all the nature spirits are related.

Let us look at gnomes.

These beings are, of course, etheric but like fairies can come close to physicality and can thus be seen or photographed with digital cameras, as can fairies.

They tend to be slightly larger than fairies, perhaps 2 feet tall and tend to dress in autumnal colours; green, brown etc.

They ape humans, particularly humans that lived a while ago and thus wear hats, have beards and old-fashioned clothes.

Of course, their clothes are not real. They are etheric matter modified by the gnome's minds to look like clothes.

It is interesting that they seem to prefer climates in which greenery flourishes. No doubt, there might be some in hot, dry climates but the majority tend to live in countries where it rains regularly and thus vegetation grows more readily.

This may be, of course, so that they can blend into foliage easily and avoid being seen.

The small fairies we mentioned earlier are communal entities and are usually seen in groups whereas gnomes tend to be solitary creatures although pairs are sometimes seen.

We have the impression that their function was to care for trees, particularly forest trees, whereas the fairies tend to care for wild flowers.

So, gnomes are often associated with trees and when seen, it is often in association with forest trees although, of course, they might be seen around fruit trees.

They tend to be associated with the country of Ireland but this may be for a few reasons.

Ireland is a country where it rains a lot and gnomes are often found in temperate areas where it rains frequently.

They do not like hot, dry, desertic landscapes.

Lush forest is their preferred habitat.

It must be said that, years ago, the population of the country of Ireland were mainly agricultural people and obviously the more time someone spends outdoors, particularly if the person roams around seeking wild fruit in forests, the greater the chance he would have of seeing a gnome.

As we said, the cool, damp climate of Ireland particularly suits them although they are seen in many countries where there are forests and where it frequently rains.

They do not like countries where it gets very cold in winter.

They try to avoid snow and so, once again, in countries where it remains not too hot in summer nor too cold in winter and where trees readily grow, suits them.

We mentioned the country of Ireland but there are other places with similar atmospheres and seasons where gnomes are to be found.

We should, perhaps, mention that Irish people have very lively imaginations and there are wonderful myths - often based on fact - that have grown up concerning the existence of fairy folk.

But we must stress that gnomes are seen in many countries where the climate and the vegetation suits them.

No talk concerning nature spirits would be complete if we failed to mention the country of Iceland which, although perhaps not ideal in all senses due to the extremes of temperature, nevertheless has a very adult attitude to the existence of nature spirits and takes into consideration their habitats when planning urban development.

We applaud their attitude and look forward to the day when all countries take into consideration the requirements of the life forms that share the planet with us, including endangered species of plants, animals and nature spirits.

Although nature spirits are not endangered as such, they live in particular areas and we should not bulldoze their habitats mindlessly just to build more houses or roads.

Nature spirits are sensitive creatures and do not appreciate areas where they have lived for thousands of years being covered in concrete.

Gnomes are often associated with rocks but from our understanding, as they are etheric, they do not need to hide in rocks. They can easily disappear, if they are frightened, by the simple expedient of moving into higher etheric frequencies.

It may be that they have been observed sitting on rocks and thus have become associated with rocks, but they spend most of their time in forests.

When one considers how rare sightings of such huge creatures as bigfoot occur, a small gnome hiding amidst the foliage of a tree would be a very rare sight. Thus, if one is sitting on a rock it would be easier to see which might account for them being associated with rocks.

We hope that you can appreciate that in one chapter about nature spirits we can only give a brief outline of their main characteristics.

But let us move on to look at elves.
This is a race that a lot of fantasy has been built up around. They are often portrayed as very beautiful, highly intelligent, almost human creatures.
In fact, they are etheric, like all nature spirits but, once again, they like to ape human behavior.
They tend to be almost human size when seen and dress in pale colours of white or pale grey.
This dress is, of course, fabricated by their minds.
They live in deep forests, avoiding human contact as much as possible and are almost never seen.
The stories built up around them come down today through folklore when, perhaps, they were occasionally seen. Today, it would be a very rare event to see one as they live in the remotest forested areas of the world, once again, in areas of temperate climate.
They like neither heat nor great cold. We have never heard of any being seen in deserts nor the North or South poles.

Not much is known about them except what comes down to us through folklore, but from what is known about them, we can say that they are gregarious (living in groups) and are peaceful.
We do not think that they are particularly wise and intelligent but, as we said, so little is truly known about them that it is hard to tell.
What their functions in the fairy kingdom is we are not sure but it has been suggested that they play a coordinating role between other groups of nature spirits and plants, animals and even humans.
If this is so, that would account for the concept of wisdom attached to them.
So, unfortunately, we cannot say much about this group, the elves, because so little is known.
This is a shame because if we were able to contact them, we are sure that they would prove to be a fascinating group to study.
But, even we know very little about them as they are such a shy and reclusive group of spirits.

We will just repeat the main points that we are sure of.
They are etheric nature spirits that, as is so often the case, like to ape the human form.
They are about human height, can take on the form of either male or female although, of course, they do not have a gender.
They form garments either of white or pale grey.
They are very shy and timid and, living deep in the largest forests, they can avoid contact with man.
We are not sure but we feel that their function is to oversee and coordinate reactions between other nature spirits and the fauna and flora of Earth.
To our knowledge, in modern times they are never seen, but they do exist. It is the fact that they live so far from man that makes them almost mythical.
That is all we can say about elves without entering the realms of myth and fantasy.

We turn to goblins.

Once again, most people are familiar with the name goblin and they are generally considered today not only to be mythical creatures but are usually associated with evil. In fact, there is a group of etheric entities to which we can attribute the name goblin.

Up till now, in our description of nature spirits we have tried to give the impression that what we have described tend to be peaceful, calm and even loving creatures, many of whom it would be a pleasure and even an honour to know and to befriend.

However, as we have often mentioned, nurturing living flora is all very well but we also need destructive entities that help dispose of flora that has come to the end of its incarnation.

Much as it displeases us to talk about negative entities, they do exist and play an essential role in the balance of life and death in incarnation.

The goblins are one such group and exist to help dispose of dead plants.

Their appearance is rather unpleasant and bears no resemblance to the mythical descriptions of goblins.

Once again, and we apologise for repeating this, they are etheric beings.

In form, they tend to resemble humans but no human would resemble a goblin.

It is true that they have a head, body, two arms and two legs, but they appear, when they are seen, as naked, deathly white skinned entities and we can truly use the word hideous to describe their appearance.

Fortunately, they only appear at night when life is at its lowest ebb and their function is to withdraw the remaining life force from dying plants.

They tend to crawl about on all fours searching for dying plants and when they find one or more such dying plants, they project negative energy towards the plant thus lowering its frequency until the plant dies.

They are never seen during the daylight hours and they avoid humanity when they can which is just as well because, if you were to see one of these creatures, you would find it a traumatic experience.

As we said, they are seldom seen but we understand that they have been captured on digital trail cameras, at night, crawling about in their search for dying plants.

We seem to give the impression that we are against goblins but this would not be true. We accept that negative creatures must exist to help keep nature in balance but we cannot help feeling revolted by the appearance of goblins as they crawl about in forests in the dead of night dealing the death knell to beautiful plants.

But goblins play an essential role in the balance of life and we must accept this.

In size, they would be - if they stood upright - the size of a small human but they remain crouched on all fours like most animals, with their heads close to the ground searching for dying plants.

When they find one, they project negative energy at the plant, which has the effect of reducing its life force. Thus, the plant has its life-force reduced and its incarnation shortly after comes to an end.

The lifespan of these creatures is virtually endless and, if it has a home at all, it would be in the lower fourth dimension where the demonic forces reside.

Why it chooses to look human, but hideous, we cannot say but we notice that most of the nature spirits take a human form of sorts. In the case of a goblin, it looks horrible to us as it is projecting the negative attributes it contains.
Fortunately, not many people roam about in the dark, so goblins are rarely seen.

Mythology usually portrays them in a rather Hollywood style. Why this should be rather baffles us because the true image of a goblin, as we said, is a fairly large, naked creature with skin the white colour of a European corpse.
It has a round head and is usually crawling about on all fours as an animal might walk, but with its face close to the ground either sniffing or looking for dying plants.
From our description you can see that it bears no resemblance to the creatures pictured in mythology.
We suppose that it could stand up and walk like a man, but it tends to concentrate on its function which is to lower the frequency of dying plants to remove the last vestige of life. Thus, it creeps about on all fours.

The only link between a real goblin and a mythical one is that they are all pictured as negative creatures.
But, we repeat, like all negative entities; demons, sprites and djinns, they play an important role in keeping life in balance by helping in the never-ending cycle of birth, growth, decline and death.
Goblins act on the last two parts of this cycle, whereas the other nature spirits we have mentioned act on the first two parts of the cycle.

We are drawing this chapter to a close because we have described a few of the many nature spirits that share planet earth with us.
There are many names given to nature spirits that are just other names for the same creatures that we have described.
Equally, there are a few nature spirits that are close cousins to the entities that we have mentioned and understanding what we have said will give an understanding of the form and function of these others.
Before we finish, we will mention a few that do not exist but that are in folklore.

Dwarves. These are considered to be small human looking creatures that live underground and mine for gold and jewels. Unfortunately, they do not exist and any sightings of such beings would probably be gnomes.

Trolls do not exist either. What the mythical creature called a troll is based on is hard to say. It might be a type of bigfoot that has whitish fur, for there are not many nature spirits that are enormous.

We have described sufficient nature spirits for you to have an overview.

We must say that the rather scary stories of babies being stolen or replacements left where the original baby was, can be attributed to human activity. People have been known to steal babies, and a family that gave birth to a defective baby might attribute its condition to nature spirit activity but, generally, nature spirits do not concern themselves with humanity unless interfered with by people.

As we said at the beginning of this chapter, our advice is not to interfere with nature spirits as they have the ability to play tricks with one's mind, the effect being rather as if one had taken hallucinatory drugs.

People under the influence of these drugs sometimes claim to see nature spirits. This is the result of opening the mind into areas where nature spirits reside and thus, they are seen.
Unless you are very lucky and can befriend a nature spirit, they are best left alone.

We will end this chapter here which we hope you have found both interesting and informative and will turn to another subject to be found in the astral dimensions.

CHAPTER 11

THE ABSTRACT THOUGHT PLANE

We have, so far in this book, drawn on events found in the upper 4th dimension, with the exception of the last chapter, because we are interested in describing to you, areas - landscapes - that concern humanity.

Even the last chapter, which was about nature spirits, nevertheless had links to humanity because many humans have been interested in and have reacted with nature spirits for many hundreds of years.

As we mentioned, we look forward to the day that positive nature spirits lose their fear of man and openly share their lives with us.

But the other chapters, by and large, concerned delving into descriptions of places - landscapes - within the vast dimension which is the upper 4th.

Of course, the lower 4th also concerns us because the various demonic forces play a role in balancing physical life.

However, once incarnation finished, the role of the creatures in the lower 4th have less significance because demonic forces cannot raise their frequency sufficient to enter the upper 4th.

They do play a significant role in acting as the trashmen in physicality, which is part of the 6th dimension, but providing man follows the holy path, demons cannot interfere with him.

They can only influence those who choose to follow the left-hand path or who actively seek to be negative.

But the upper 4th, which we will return to just calling the 4th, contains a multitude of landscapes.

It might be fair to say that there are areas that we do not yet know about although we have a comprehensive knowledge of most of it. The idea that there might be yet more to be discovered enthralls and interests us and keeps us on our toes, so to speak, always on the lookout for areas new to us.

So far, we have not found any but we keep an open mind and hope to find new areas one day.

But let us look at an area or landscape that we do know about and describe this area to you.

It is a place, if we can thus call it, that deals with life in an abstract sense.

What do we mean by this?

Generally speaking, if you read our books, lessons or watch the videos we make, we are dealing with fairly concrete concepts.

Even what we might consider to be somewhat abstract concepts, such as art in all its various forms, usually has a concrete form. For instance, a painting ends up with a physical work of art, even for us in the astral realms.

Writing gives us books which we store in our libraries - the akashic record.

We could go on and describe virtually any concept thought about by man because they usually end up with a physical object of some sort.

To make this perfectly clear. If we have the desire to create a picture, a statue, a building, cook a dish, make a garment and so on, whatever we think about and have the desire to make, if that desire is pushed to its conclusion, we finish with a physical object being produced.
Do not think that just because we live in an astral plane - the 4th - that we cannot create physical objects. We can.
Our dimension seems to us to be as real and as solid as your dimension appears to you.
So, we can create things in exactly the same way that you can, the only difference being that we can create mental thought form tools to help us create as opposed to you who have to create tools and machines in solid form to translate your thoughts into reality.
But our store rooms contain enormous numbers of inventions.

However, there are thoughts and concepts that are not possible to put into fact.
If we take the word 'love', for example.
Immediately, everyone has a different concept of the word.
A mother might well have love for her newborn child. A couple might well love each other.
But, if we think about it, there is a vast difference between the love that a mother has for her newborn child and the love a couple might have for each other. We will not go into details but you can work out the difference for yourselves.
Equally, we have the opposite, 'hate'. Once again, it is an abstract concept.
You might well be able to create a physical image of art; a painting, a statue etc., but you would be hard pushed to create a physical representation of love or hate.
You could, using something physical, suggest the concept of love or hate but there is nothing that directly links to the meaning of the words.
We could, for instance, draw a heart, with or without cupid's arrow piercing it and we would know that we are representing love, but if you think about it, we are actually using symbols that have become accepted as representing love and not an actual physical object called love.

We hope you can appreciate the point we are making.
We are suggesting that there is an area in the 4th that deals with and contains the vibrational energy of abstract thought.
This is an important area and we would like, in this chapter, to explore this place and help you to understand how it functions.

Like a number of areas of the 4th it is non-physical, by which we mean that if and when we visit this area there is nothing to see. It is purely an area in which abstract thought exists.
We have already mentioned a couple of similar areas and this is yet another.
The way to enter it, as we have previously described, is by aligning our frequency to that area and we find ourselves there. Of course, there is nothing to see once we arrive. We are in an area of abstract thought.

However, this area is slightly different to the areas we have previously described.
As we enter this one, whether we are aware of it or not, our DNA becomes involved.
The reason is because, with the previous non-physical areas we mentioned, once we had balanced our frequency to the area concerned, it was mostly just a question of delving

into it with our minds, but with this area, deep psychological questions are posed, and to obtain answers, it requires that not only our mind but also our higher self must be involved and thus DNA must start its inevitable process of sifting the wheat from the chaff, so to speak.

So, this is not an easy area to describe nor to interact with despite using words like 'love', 'hate', 'intelligence' and 'thought' in our everyday communications.
We could make a long list of words that we use that describe abstract thoughts and emotions (both of these words are part of what we are talking about), but we will leave you to create your own list if you so desire.
The point we are making is that there are a number of thought creations that are an essential part of our everyday communications that we all accept and understand but that bear no relation to anything concrete or physical.

We repeat, there is an area within the 4th dimension that deals with these abstract words but that are actually very important to our communications and reactions with many aspects of life.
How often do we say, for example, 'I love you', or 'I love doing this or that '?
Equally, we say that we have been 'thinking' about something or have 'mulled over in our minds' something.
We could go on and on giving examples of such words or phrases.
It suffices to take a piece of paper and, on one side of it, write a list of these words and, on the other side of it, try to draw a meaningful depiction of the words to illustrate what we mean.

Yet another example to illustrate the point. If we take the word 'thought', something that we do countless times a day. But, although we might try to create a written description of the word 'thought' we could not draw anything that would immediately depict to someone else that we had depicted the word 'thought'
We do not wish to labor the point but we want you clearly to understand that there are a host of words that have no physical representation. And yet these words exist and have clear meanings to us all. We all know the meaning of the words love or hate, like or dislike, brave or cowardly etc., but they have no physical representation except in a cartoon fashion.
We mentioned that love is often represented as a heart-shaped drawing. If we see a drawing of a heart shape, we accept that it represents the word love, but we think you will agree that it is a poor representation of the magnificence of the emotion of true love, whether it be for a couple truly in love, a mother's love for a child, the emotion someone has for a pet animal or even a consuming love for a hobby.
So, the word love can be applied in many ways to many things, in varying degrees. We chose the word love deliberately because the theme of our planet is love.
Jesus said that he loved us all and urged us to love our neighbors as ourselves, which implies that we should love ourselves. Not in a narcissistic manner but in a deep, platonic, respectful fashion. And yet we really do not have any means of depicting this fundamental aspect of our creation.
Our God is the God of love. Deep down, if we can tap into our God force, we release the emotion of love.

Love for self and for all things. When we truly can tap into this God force called love, we are overwhelmed by this beautiful emotion and yet we have no accurate means of depicting it accept a childish picture of a heart - which does not even depict what a heart really looks like.

We repeat, that the point we are making is that there are a number of concepts, of words that we use every day, but that there is no concrete way of depicting.

This area in the 4th dimension is what we are trying to describe because this is the area that deals with the vital concepts - abstract words.

Before we try to describe this area, let us use one more phrase to illustrate the point.
Let us use the sentence that many of you have said, 'I love my dog or cat.'
Now, try to describe this sentence in pictures rather as many civilizations did.
Already, the personal pronoun 'I' has no accepted picture. But the second word 'love' has to be depicted using the heart shape.
The third word 'my' has no accepted pictorial representation.
It is only the words dog or cat that we could picture by drawing a dog or a cat.
So, from this simple sentence,' I love my dog or cat', we would have the greatest difficulty in representing it pictorially and that is because 'I' and 'my' are abstract terms, despite both of them being deeply concerned with you.
It is only the words love and dog or cat that we could draw.
'I' and 'my' remain abstract.
This is strange, don't you think?
Two of the most important words applicable to you, 'I' and 'my' (as in belonging to me) cannot be conveyed except by using words.
Many other words we could convey with pictures, and dog, cat, bird, house, car and so on we could draw, but two of the most important words we use, 'I' and 'my' or even 'me' if we add a third, cannot be meaningfully described except using words.

Thus, we can appreciate the difficulty people had thousands of years ago, before written languages were invented, describing abstract thoughts using just hieroglyphs.
No doubt they did their best to overcome this problem but it must have been a struggle to invent symbols without the invention of written language.

People often wonder about Latin numerals that did not have zero and did not have negative numbers. These are important to us today and one wonders how Latin speakers, writers or mathematicians coped with describing the concept of zero or, indeed, calculate without having the use of negative numbers.
So, long ago we had abstract thoughts that we could speak but could not, perhaps, describe using just hieroglyphs. The languages must have been incomplete.

Let us trace the whole concept back to see where we are with all this.
In one part of the 4th we have an area that contains the concept of abstract thought.
There is no list of words in this area, just the concept itself.
Then, for those who could tap into this area we had people that desired to depict these abstract thoughts.
But, just using hieroglyphics, many of these abstract thoughts were impossible to create.
It was not until written languages were invented that one could start to express abstract thoughts.

This must have been very frustrating to scribes of long ago who were tasked with writing down the dictates, for example, of a Pharaoh who might have used abstract words in his dictation.

Or did they?

Did words exist for abstract thoughts in those days if there were no signs to depict them, or did Pharaohs have just to use words for which symbols could be used?

We wonder if modern linguists who study ancient symbolic language as we see written in tombs or on clay tablets in various countries and various temples, question the use - or not - of abstract thoughts?

Or do they content themselves with just translating the messages without questioning the missing words? Or yet again, do linguists themselves add the missing abstract thoughts to their translations?

We have spent far longer than we intended giving examples of the difficulties of creating sentences containing abstract concepts, and we have no doubt there will be some people who will do all they can to say that abstract concepts have been accurately depicted in hieroglyphic writings, but our investigations of early methods of communication have revealed that scribes had difficulty in depicting abstract thoughts or messages.

We will just use one more example of a phrase that many a tyrant would have liked to express but had difficulty with.

This is the phrase.

'I am the greatest Pharaoh (or whatever chief of his people he was) that has ever been or ever will be.'

We think that there has been in the past many such people who would have liked to express that thought.

Today, of course, using written language, the phrase is simple but put yourself in the position of scribes in ancient Egypt or any other country that did not have written language.

The sentence we wrote contains a number of words that are abstract thoughts, if you analyse it in terms of what we have previously mentioned, and so one can imagine the difficulties of scribes of those times and they would have been hard pushed to find hieroglyphics that correctly portrayed that - to us nowadays - simple sentence.

However, we have said more than enough to illustrate the difficulty in accurately portraying abstract thoughts. Even today, with all the language we have at our disposition, we might struggle to describe some abstract thoughts succinctly.

Enough said!

Let us, in our minds, link with this abstract thought landscape and see what we can see.

First, we must say that this area does not exist as a physical place.

It is an area of frequency that was created by archangels to contain the concept of abstract thought.

This phrase might seem to be rather meaningless because what we just wrote was, itself, abstract.

Any area that contains physical ideas, concepts or whatever is easy to describe. For instance, if there was a storehouse in the 4th that contained the archetype of every animal or plant to be found on Earth, one would expect to visit such an area and see an example of every animal or of every plant.

So, we would expect to see an enormous zoo for the archetypes of animals or an enormous plant nursery for the archetype of every plant. In other words, we would be surrounded by physical objects.

But in this area, there is nothing except a certain frequency which is, of course, invisible.

This implies a sort of area, a circle for example, that contains the frequency we desire to contact.

But it is not quite like that.

We are going to have difficulty in describing this area.

Before we can enter this area, we have to know that it exists. Then we have to be told the frequency in terms of vibration of that area and, finally, we concentrate our thoughts on that frequency and we suddenly find ourselves there. But there is nothing to see!

It is just a feeling that we are in touch with that frequency.

So, when we visit this area not much happens on the surface.

In fact, what is going on is that our higher self, plus certain aspects of our DNA, receives what we might call a 'download' of information concerning abstract thoughts.

This may seem ridiculous to us modern humans who are constantly being bombarded with abstract words, phrases, thoughts and concepts. So, we are used to dealing with abstract thoughts.

You may have wondered why, when we started this chapter, we spent such a long time and many pages explaining what abstract thoughts, words and messages have evolved into in our everyday lives, but it is our opinion that there was a time when it was not possible, meaningfully, to describe abstract ideas.

It was only when comprehensive written languages were invented that we were able to include abstract ideas into our everyday language despite many of these abstract concepts having great importance.

We do understand that many people will dismiss this concept as nonsense as, today, we use abstract concepts as an integral part of everyday language.

We do not wish to go back and give even more examples but just imagine how difficult it would be to describe in drawings or hieroglyphs the everyday words as we mentioned.; I, me, we, you or life. Even words like God can only be imagined pictorially as an old man with a beard whereas God is not that at all.

Then other words such as kindness, personality etc., would be virtually impossible to describe pictorially.

So, we are suggesting that this area that deals with abstract words, meanings and concepts could only be truly appreciated when written language was invented.

It was all very well to speak certain abstract ideas but if there was no means of recording those ideas, once spoken they would be lost to history.

We will draw this chapter to a close here.

We do realise that it was not a very satisfactory chapter in terms of our explanations but we wish to stress to you that it is one of the most important areas of the 4th because introducing the concept of abstract words, thoughts, ideas and concepts is one of the basis of civilization, and, in all probability, is the basis of the creation of written languages.

If this abstract landscape did not exist and if man had not been able to tap into it and push himself to create words, both spoken and written, to describe abstract concepts, life as we know it today would be not only greatly different but much poorer, not physically in terms of possessions, but intellectually.
As we rise in ascension, in spirituality, so intellect will play an ever greater role and new words will have to be invented to describe concepts that are new to you and that we try to introduce.
How often do we say that words do not exist to describe certain very important concepts?
We will, collectively, have to invent these new words just as words were invented to describe abstract thoughts long ago.

Life is constantly evolving and language must evolve also.
Without inventing new words to describe recently introduced concepts, progress will stagnate.
So we hope that you can appreciate that this area - the area of abstract thoughts, words and concepts - is essential to the progress of humanity as ascension progresses.

CHAPTER 12

THE MEMORY PLANE

You will have noticed that the upper 4th dimension (which we will call the 4th) contains a large number of areas, which we tend to call landscapes when communicating with you. Some of these landscapes appear physical and some of which are 'mental' or non-physical areas.
All of these landscapes, whether they be physical or non-physical, are kept apart by the simple expedient of giving unique frequencies to them.
Thus, no two landscapes can overlap unless intentionally required to do so.
Therefore, you can easily determine that to enter any landscape simply requires linking in one's mind with the appropriate frequency.

It may come as a surprise to some of you to learn that while you are going through your incarnation in the 6th dimension, you always retain links to the 4th.
We have mentioned that you always retain a link to your oversoul group and to one or more guides or teachers who are in 4th.
You also retain links to the areas we described in previous chapters which enable you, for instance in the case of the last chapter, to be able to deal with abstract thoughts.
The degree to which one can link with the abstract landscape depends on a number of things: one's intelligence, one's education, the degree that one's position in society requires one to deal with abstract thoughts and so on. But, we stress, everyone retains links to the 4th.
This link can be strengthened through meditation until one is able to be in two worlds at once, the 6th (the incarnation plane) and the 4th, which is your true home.
When one can do this a whole mass of possibilities opens and history notes a number of people who were able to do this and were thus able to act in an almost miraculous fashion. Jesus is, perhaps, the prime example although there have been many people, largely unknown, who had a similar control over being able to link with the 4th.
All of you, however, retain links to some landscapes in the 4th to assist you with your incarnation.

We wish now to turn our attention to yet another landscape in the 4th that you may use from time to time, although you may not know that it is retained in the 4th.
This area is where memory is stored.

There has been much debate about memory by doctors etc., and brains have been probed to find the area within the brain that stores memories. Of course, doctors fail to find any such area.
Then people turn to mind, despite very few knowing what mind is.
Memory is not stored in any physical part of the human anatomy. This can be demonstrated easily by the fact that, at the demise of the physical body, memory is still retained thus demonstrating that memory is part of the non-physical aspects of a person.

Memory is stored in the akashic record as we have mentioned elsewhere in other works. But the akashic record is, in fact, an amazing, multidimensional area. The akashic record is found in the 5th dimension, but there is also a part that is to be found in the 4th. The reason for this is that memory is important and thus there is a sort of copy of what can be found in the 5th, in the 4th so that people who might have difficulty in connecting to the 5th dimension can still find memories by linking to the 4th.

Whilst incarnate in the 6th dimension, as we have said, you always retain a link to the 4th and so many people find it easier to draw memories from the akashic record in the 4th rather than to try to form a link to the akashic record in the 5th.

Before we delve into memory, might we draw to your attention the importance of memory.

Imagine that memory never existed. We think that you would find life untenable.

Imagine that you just had this moment as your reality - which, in fact, is true.

If memory did not exist, you would have no concept of your name, your address, your age, your situation, any skill that you might have acquired, your job, where you work and so on. You would just have this moment.

Now, the truth of the matter is that you do, in fact, live in this microsecond of space/time. That is all that exists, as we have often explained.

There is no past and no future, just the infinitely small point of time and of space that creates your reality. All the past microseconds of time are stored in the akashic record.

But it is thanks to the fact that you can locate past frames of space/time that you know who you are, where you live, who your family is, where you work or go to school and so on which we mentioned earlier.

As we said, if it were not for being able to contact the akashic record, life would be very bizarre and, frankly, unlivable.

We mentioned the akashic record being in two places, the 4th and the 5th.

The difference between the akashic record of the two places is that the akashic record in the 5th not only contains your personal memory file but the files created by all living entities, and these files can be contacted if one knows how.

So, we, when we want to retrieve books created by other people, go into the akashic record of the author of the books we require and retrieve them from the akashic record in the 5th.

We can also review the lives and actions of anyone that interests us by getting the information from the akashic record in the 5th.

But, the akashic record in the 4th only contains your personal file and you call that your memory.

The file of each person is encoded with a frequency unique to you, or them, so you draw from that file only your own memories.

Can you understand this?

For each person his/her personal file is encoded with a frequency that ensures that when a person tries to remember something, he draws only his own memories from that file.

We think that you will agree that if you try to remember something but that you connected to the memories of anyone else but you, your life would be chaotic!

Now let us start to link all this together.

You actually live in a microsecond of space and time. This moment of space/time is infinitesimal.

But, as soon as any moment of space/time is lived, it is stored in two places. The akashic record in the 5th and, more importantly, your personal file in the 4th.

This is of vital importance to you. We use the word vital advisedly. We mean vital in the sense of being essential to the continuance of life.

As we demonstrated earlier, if it were not for memory being constantly available to you, you would live in an infinitesimally small amount of the here and now and you would have no memory of who you are or anything essential to being able to know anything about you.

Memory is essential to you.

So, we must all be grateful to the archangels who created these personal files in the akashic record and who created the ability we all have to link to a file in order constantly to remind us of who we are and all our personal details in the 4th.

It may seem strange to those incarnate who believe that there is only physical life on Earth, if they could realise that every waking moment they are in touch with a non-physical dimension that constantly sends them memories of who and what they are.

So, in a way, there is not much to talk about concerning this memory landscape but, in fairness, we feel we should attempt to describe it somewhat.

Obviously, if we could stand back and look at this place there would be nothing to see. Although the area contains countless blocks of frequencies (one for each person, animal, plant or mineral) these blocks of frequencies are invisible as are the memories they contain.

But let us try to analyse how the area works. It is, in fact, very complicated.

As we said, and we apologise for repeating ourselves, there is an area for each and every sentient being or object, including for those of us whose incarnations have finished and who are in the spiritual realms.

So, this assumes that, from the moment of leaving the 4th and linking with a baby at the moment of birth, the connection with the memory area incarnates with us. But it is not in any way a physical connection. It is non-physical, by which we mean that one of the auras retains a close link to the personal memory file in the 4th.

Obviously, a newborn baby has no awareness of this link for at least two reasons.

First, the baby has nothing to remember, being newborn, and second, the link between mind and brain is not fully formed.

We could add that the auras are very weak at this time and also the brain is not yet capable of working as it does in a more developed human - or any other creature for that matter.

So, the baby lies in his crib with no idea of who or what he is. Just his basic survival instincts work. The desire for food, sleep, awareness of pain, etc.

It is only when the baby develops somewhat that it is able, via its aura and mind, to link with the memory area in the 4th.

Now, we have mentioned in the past and in this work that a part of us can link to the akashic record, which is a memory area, in the 5th and this can be achieved by linking with the higher self, certain aspects of auras and DNA.

The connection we have to our personal file in the 4th is more direct.

It comes through an aura that is connected to the 4th, into the mind and is transferred to the brain.
Once again, DNA is involved but the process of being able to link to one's personal file in the 4th is more direct than if one were to connect to the akashic record in the 5th.

It is worth mentioning that contact with the personal memory file in the 4th can be interrupted through trauma. It happens, occasionally, if someone has an accident or other trauma, that the link breaks to a certain extent and the person does not know his name, his address, nor any other important details.
Happily, memory usually returns as the trauma reduces, but through certain illnesses the link can be permanently lost and the unfortunate person finds himself, as far as his history is concerned, in the state of a newborn child, i.e., with no idea of who he is or any details of his life.
This is because his mind, being disturbed, is not able to link with his aura which is in touch with his file in the 4th.

We must also mention that certain people with illnesses suddenly link with a part of their file that contains memories of some time ago. Thus the person, usually elderly and retired, thinks that he has to go to work or has the desire to return to where he lived as a child.
Usually, after a while the memory fades and the person returns to normal.
The reason that this can occur is that memories are stored in his file in the 4th in reverse order. By this we mean that each frame of his life is stored one behind the other, starting with the oldest at the front leading backwards to today's memories.
Thus, if the person suffers from a deficient mind or whatever, he can try to link with his memories - as we all do all the time - but instead of linking with the furthest ones, which are the here and now frames, he links with ones nearest the front and thus thinks he is younger than his physical age.
There are illnesses in which the person does this on a permanent basis, loses contact with today and progresses nearer and nearer his childhood.
If he progresses - if we may call it that - to the point that he thinks he is a newborn babe, he can take the final step of linking to before his moment of incarnation, at which point he dies.

If you are young but have old relations; grandparents for example, have you noticed how easy it is for them to remember events that happened when they were young but how difficult it is for them to remember recent events?
They can talk for hours about their youth but if you ask them about events relative to now, they may have no knowledge.
This, once again, is because they can link with memories at the front of their memory file in the 4th but do not have the strength to delve into the depths of their file where recent events are stored.

So, we hope we described enough for you to realise where memory is stored and how memories are retrieved.
We hope, also, that you who are young may understand why elderly people have difficulty with dealing with today's events and you will not mock them for being unable to link with what is going on today.

It is a question of having the psychic strength to locate the back of the memory file.
Of course, the more a person remains active in a mind sense, the longer he can stay in touch with today.

We advise all people that are retired not to sit down and give up on life.
Try to stay mentally active as long as possible and it will help you to be able to reach to the back of your memory file and retrieve today's - and recent events - from your memory file.
We have heard many an elderly person proudly say that he has a good memory and recount tales from his youth as proof of his good memory.
But ask him today's date or who is prime minister or president and he might struggle to respond.
This is what we are talking about.
You might be young now but most of you will grow old so the advice to keep mentally active will be relevant to you one day, so please heed this advice. It will serve you one day.

Having said that, we have given you an overview of your personal file in the 4th and how it applies to you each waking moment.
This, as we hope you can understand, is a very important area in the 4th and we hope that the explanations we have given you will help you to understand where your memories are stored and how you can tap into them.

With that place dealt with we turn to the next.

CHAPTER 13

THE DEATH EXPERIENCE

We turn now to a page of life that is seldom considered.
It deals with death, if we may call it that.

As you know, you cannot die. Your physical body was never alive. It was just animated by your spirit in a highly complex fashion.
Everything that we have discussed in this and in other books was related to the way that all the events that take place in the various dimensions are related to you being able to animate your physical body.
If you could realise in your mind the mass of information we have given you about how life works, it is a staggering number of events that, together, enable you to be who you are.
We have told you much but we have not told you everything because there is much more going on behind the scenes, so to speak, that we have not described. This is because some of it would be too complicated for you to understand but there are matters that we will address eventually when the time is ripe.
All of it is related to keeping you alive and active.

However, we wish to look at a unique area in the 4th that considers death.
What do we mean by this, when we say that you cannot die?
But death can take many forms.
It is possible for a person to no longer wish to continue down the road of life and if this occurs, he has the free will to withdraw from life.

This may seem strange because life is so wonderful.
A number of people in incarnation do not have the strength to carry on so they commit suicide.
The body dies but the spirit goes off to Summerland in the 4th and the person, generally, is astounded by the beauty of life in the 4th dimension and quickly picks up the reins of life once again and carries on in the 4th.

But, once in the 4th, there are people, for a variety of reasons that decide that they do not wish to carry on and want to pull out of life.
Such a person might have been in the spirit realms for long ages and has risen to great heights spiritually but takes a decision that enough is enough and wishes to terminate his journey towards perfection - the Godhead.

Fortunately, the number of people who think like this is very small but there are such people from time to time who wish to terminate their lives, and there exists a place in the 4th that helps them in this choice.
It is not a subject that gives us any joy to talk about and it is the first time that this area has ever been mentioned publicly. You will be the first to know about this area.

We have mentioned that, in the deepest depths of hell, there are people who decide to die and their life spirit is snuffed out, to be replaced by a new recruit coming from the 7th to replace him.
However, we are not talking about that type of event.
We are talking about noble spirits who feel that they have done enough and decide to die.

As we said, all people have free will and some decide that they do not wish to continue down the long path that leads to perfection.
This, of course, is their free will choice.
In heaven, no one is forced to do anything.
It may seem crazy to decide not to continue down the path of perfection as each step taken leads one to ever more beautiful areas and ever greater sensations of bliss.

But some people decide not to go on.

There are angelic beings - human archangels - that come to talk to these people, not to try to dissuade them, but to discuss the motives of why such a decision was taken.

We recognise that people who have been in the spirit realms for long ages and who have made great progress are wise enough to make up their own minds, and who are we to try to change it for them?
However, to us who are full of the desire to continue to help you, who are reading this book, and all life as you go through your incarnations, it seems strange to want to stop and cease to be.
We look forward to reaching ever greater heights of spirituality and it would not occur to us to want the journey to stop.
But some do take this decision and, in this chapter, we will consider the place set aside for such people, what it looks like and how the process of removing life works.

As you can imagine, this place or landscape has its own unique frequency, so anyone wishing to enter it to die would need to know the frequency and have to take the necessary steps to match their frequency to that of the death landscape.
We must say that not everyone in the spirit world knows about this place because, for obvious reasons, it is not a topic widely discussed.
It is not that somebody has taken the decision to hide this place. It is just that life in the 4th dimension is so wonderful that almost no one considers wanting it all to end.

We think that most of you, if you were in Summerland or even part of the higher areas that we have described, would agree that to wish to escape from it would verge on folly.
But, as we said, there are, from time to time, those who take the decision to pull out of life.

This area is physical as opposed to those that we have described that can only be felt emotionally.
What does it look like?
If you were to try to imagine this landscape you might well imagine a bleak, barren, sad place - a reflection of the attitude of someone who wishes to terminate his life in deep depression.

In fact, it is quite the opposite.

We will say at this point that none of us that are involved in giving you the information that we have done over the years, and will continue to do so endlessly, have ever visited this area.
We do not waste our time in learning to link to a landscape that we have no intention of ever visiting. We wish to go on to the glorious end.
The information we give you comes to us via the human archangels who work there supervising the death process.

This landscape is, apparently, extremely beautiful.
It is, in effect, a large and magnificent marble palace, with beautiful gardens surrounding it.
Why should this be?
The answer is simple.
Those who choose to terminate their existence do so because they feel that they have done enough, served enough and do not wish to do more.
But these people are wonderfully, blissfully happy because, generally speaking, they have lived for many years in the heavenly spheres and have advanced enormously. If you could see such a person you would see him glowing with starlight. Such would be his level of spirituality.

We break off here to remind you that when we say 'he', we are just using linguistic convention. We include ladies in our descriptions. We will also say that, generally, these people have progressed so far spiritually that they have passed any sense of identity.
But we must call them something so we will follow convention and call them 'he'.

So, these people, being so holy, have created this marble palace with their minds.
From the exterior, it resembles somewhat the sort of palaces that were created in the 16th or 17th centuries for French or Italian kings. A huge, multi-room palace, decorated both from the exterior and interior with carved decorations depicting all sorts of things: flowers, animals, saints and so on.
The rooms are large, often following the golden ratio tradition.

Everything is made of marble of all sorts of colours.
We must say that it is all created by imagination although, to those who go there, it appears real.
We can only say that if you were to imagine the most beautiful palace on Earth and multiply that image by ten, you would have some idea of what it looks like.

The grounds are laid out with 'parterres' similar to those created in palaces long ago.
Beautifully laid out flower beds, sculptured trees, fountains, paths - all immaculate.
It is, apparently, dazzling.
Of course, the landscape looks after itself. It needs no maintenance.

When it is known that a person wishes to terminate his life, a number of human archangels appear to organize and control the event. It takes a lot of love and skill to terminate the existence of someone.

So, there is no question of sadness. The person who wishes to terminate his life is full of joy knowing that he has done his best over many years to serve God.
The archangels who will conduct operations are, themselves, full of love, joy, understanding and sympathy.
The whole event happens in an atmosphere of love and joy. There is no question of sadness.

The person whose life is to end has been fully briefed as to what is to happen.
The person concerned is led into a beautiful room, once again all made of marble, with pillars, statues and wonderful carvings.
He is asked to lay on a marble bed, if we can thus describe it, and the archangels stand around.

The process consists, in essence, of removing the soul from its attachment to the person.
If you have followed our previous teachings you may remember two things.
First, archangels, when they created the person, took a piece of life spirit (which also is the whole of God) and attached it to an embryo 'something' and then gave that 'something' a logos which told it what it was going to be - in this case a human.
Now, this is where it gets a bit complicated because a person, long before he gets a physical body, if he chooses to have an incarnation, not only has the spirit of God associated with him but has a certain amount of DNA.
Over time he developed his auras, his higher self and a number of other things that we have never talked about, although we will one day when we hope you will all be able to understand.

We could say that the spirit of God is the most important, and this would be true. But many other things are equally important and need to be separated from the person before he can cease to exist.
We must also say that the God spirit is encased in a sort of protective egg shell which is there in association with the God spirit to protect that God spirit.
We will also say that, although the egg shell, which is normally called the soul, can be removed from the God spirit, that God spirit must never be harmed because it is not only that person's God particle but it is also the totality of God. This is difficult to understand and we have explained it at great length in other works.
Each and every object alive contains a minute portion of God but that portion is also the totality of God.
So, the person's God's spirit must be removed with the greatest care.
The DNA, the logos (which is attached to DNA) must also be removed with care.

How is this done?
Even for someone discarnate - in the heavenly spheres - none of the pieces that need to be disassociated with the person are actually part of that person. They are all contained in boxes - if we can say that - that are attached to auras.

Even for the person discarnate, he can never see the various parts that need to be removed. They are all of tremendously high frequency and thus invisible to most people.

That is why very advanced human archangels are required to assist the person who wishes to die because, thanks to their very advanced state, they can see most of these boxes that contain the various parts that need to be removed.

Using processes that it would be futile to try to explain, these boxes are removed from the auras of the person.
However, they are not disposed of.
If any object were to disappear or be damaged, all life would instantly disappear.
This is because all is one and every part of the organisms that go to make up a person are, in fact, all that exists.
Although each person thinks that he has personal 'bits and pieces', in fact it is all an illusion. There is only one, and that one is God, so although these bits and pieces appear to belong to a unique person, it is the only set of bits and pieces (that are illusionary when associated to any one object) and are rather like a hologram in which an image, if looked at closely, consists of a myriad of tiny versions of the same image.
Obviously, life is not quite like that, being much more complex, but you get the idea.

So, as these pieces are removed, they are placed in the care of true archangels that are there to accept, protect and care for all these bits and pieces. Please excuse us for using the crude term 'bits and pieces' but we do not wish to fill pages describing each time the many parts that need to be removed.

Equally, the Spirit of God - the God particle - is removed and placed in the care of the true archangels who melt away and do whatever they do with all these objects.
Nothing dies in this sense. All the bits and pieces can be recycled into or in association with another human.

Meanwhile, the person who wishes to die is lying on this marble bed. He feels nothing.
All the action is taking place in his auras which are somewhat remote from his spiritual - but, to him, physical - body.
Gradually, as the bits and pieces are removed from him, he ceases to be conscious. He passes into a sort of deep slumber.
Finally, or should we say gradually, as the bits and pieces are removed from his auras, the connection between his auras and the person ceases to be effective and the person starts to become less visible.
When the last part is taken from the last aura, the body fades from view and effectively ceases to be.

So, the spiritual archangels fade away back to where they came from, bearing their precious cargo of these life elements.
Quite what they do with them and where they store them, we don't know but we do know that they are reused in the creation of another person.

Now, what about the person who died?
Once all the bits and pieces that went into the creation of the person are removed, the person disappears.
He disappears because he never was!

He was only an illusion created by all these life elements coming together to create the impression that he existed.
The life was in the various bits and pieces - and there are quite a lot of bits and pieces that come together to create this holographic image that we call a person.

But the whole thing was an illusion.
Do you find this staggering?
If you do not perhaps you have not understood the implication of what we have stated.
We will explain again.

You are in incarnation as you read this.
This implies that you have a physical body and a number of auras, each one containing a spiritual version of you.
You can think, talk, walk, have intelligence and a multitude of elements that make up your life, giving you an independent identity which will last eternally, first in the spirit realms, then during your incarnation if you choose to have one and then for the rest of eternity back home again in the 4th dimension.

You can be a noble spirit or a crass, egotistical hypocrite. The choice is yours but you will have a distinct personality, unique to you.
You can create all sorts of things, become an expert in all sorts of disciplines. You can go on in the spirit world to become a great saint if you wish.

But it is all an illusion.
In fact, you are part of the oneness that we call God, and if your connection to all the bits and pieces that are connected to God are removed, you disappear because who you are, all that you have achieved, is an illusion. It never was. It was only the bits and pieces that are connected to God that created the illusion that you existed.
What we wrote above is not quite true. It is true that you only exist as an illusion but what you did with your life remains as a testament to the fact that you lived.
We cannot all change the world like the great saints or sinners, but every act you take has a ripple effect on all life rather like dropping pebbles into a still pond of water. The ripples spread out endlessly.

So that is the reason that you exist. To create life-changing effects both on yourself and on everyone.
The slightest thing you do spreads out endlessly throughout the ethers. What you do never stops and, eventually, touches and affects every living organism throughout the world.
This is because we are all one. Billions of people and billions of animals is all an illusion. There is only one pretending to be everything.

That is why everything you say or do has a knock-on effect on every living object in the world; humans, animals, plants and minerals.
This is why we encourage you to be a good person.
This is why we encourage you to stop eating animals.
This is why we ask you never to harm anything but to help all life when appropriate.

All is one pretending to be a multitude.
The death experience we described earlier demonstrates that we don't really exist because, as the God particles are removed from a person, that person vanishes because he was just an illusion.
It is only the acts we perform, the words we say that remain as a testament of who we were.

So, we will end this bizarre chapter here and move onto the next subject.

CHAPTER 14

THE RUBBISH TIP / WASTE MANAGEMENT

Let us now turn our attention to yet another somewhat unconventional aspect of life that is connected to life in the 4th.

You may remember us mentioning at the beginning of this book that we apologized to you for not fully describing all the areas or landscapes that are contained in the various auras or dimensions but, upon consideration, decided to concentrate mainly on the 4th. We have, in other books, mentioned many events connected to other dimensions and have suggested that the way we present these books to you, although they can be read as solo, standalone volumes, actually are linked as if they were one huge compendium.

We have given you, in other books and this one, sufficient information concerning how life is connected to you, so we decided we would deal with some of the many fascinating areas within the 4th that you should know about to assist you to progress towards perfection as we move more and more into ascension.

We also mentioned that this information is not only intended for you but for future generations because much of what we are telling you has never been revealed to the greater public before and we can say that even in the secret, mystery schools, some of what we reveal to you has never before been allowed to be talked about.

We, who give you this information, have been tasked by those above us to reveal as much as we think you will be capable of understanding.

The reason is this.

We are moving into a monumentally important period of Earth's history. It is called ascension.

Ascension is much more important than merely using the word 'ascension' would imply. It is a gradual move of the human race towards perfection.

This turn of the wheel of life will not take us all the way to perfection but it will be a giant step into the light. A step greater than any other step in the past took.

In order to move closer to the starlight of God, implies that one has knowledge.

One cannot become an expert on any subject unless one has knowledge of that subject and to become an expert on spiritual life implies knowledge of the spiritual areas of life. This is why we are giving you as much information as we can on the non-physical or spiritual planes.

Some of you may find these books, or the chapters within them, unacceptable.

You are free to dismiss them, although we assure you that every word we have given you in all the information; books, videos, essays and statements, are true as far as we can possibly verify.

We have no desire to mislead you and we never will.

But, just as beauty is in the eye of the beholder, acceptance of what we tell you is in your hands, so to speak, and we can only present information and leave it up to you to understand or not, accept or not. We will not try to convince you either way.

What we give you is true - every word - as far as we know. What you accept as true is your concern.

Already, this book, volume eight in the series, contains a mixture of information, some of it previously revealed by us and others and some which has never been revealed before. The last chapter, entitled 'the death experience', was new, never before revealed to the public.

We go on to another topic.
This topic will deal with rubbish!
What on earth can we mean by this extraordinary phrase?
We certainly have rubbish on earth and we have explained how the negative forces from the lower 4th, the demonic forces, are there to dispose of any and all physical entities that have outlived their usefulness and how these negative forces dispose of the physical remains by breaking them down and reducing whatever object it was to its constituent atoms which can be recycled to produce other similar, or different, objects.
Even this is much more complicated than it seems and we would like to devote part of this chapter to the processes that must take place in the physical realms to reduce objects to their constituent atoms and how these atoms may be reused to create more life.
So, let us return to what we mentioned several books ago about how physical life is created.
What we are going to choose as the topic of our discussion will be humans, but we ask you to accept that what we say concerning humans will equally apply to all life; animal, vegetable or mineral.
The only difference being that, obviously, a rock lasts a lot longer than a tomato, but the process remains the same.

Now, the stumbling block in what we wish to say is this.
We mentioned to you, and we are going back to talking about humans here, is that floating about in the air of planet Earth are a number of atoms, each and every one destined for a particular human and, further, each and every one of these atoms are destined for a particular part of that human.
By which we mean that there are a certain number of atoms (oxygen, hydrogen, helium or whatever) that have a frequency attached to them that corresponds to the frequency of any particular human.
These atoms remain in suspension awaiting the call sent out by a human for a certain number of atoms, once again of oxygen, hydrogen, helium or whatever, that this human requires.
We will repeat this as it is an amazing miracle and is worth fully comprehending.

At the moment of birth of a human, not only is a baby born with a physical body but, at the same time, released into the atmosphere is a number of different atoms that this baby will require as he grows to manhood and to last him until he draws his last breath and his physical body dies.
Assuming that what we have said above is true - and it is - can you fully appreciate the staggering skill of whoever or whatever organizes this for every living thing and throughout all time?
Can you imagine how, from the moment of conception of a baby in the womb of its mother, some entity calculates exactly the number of atoms of the different elements contained in the periodic table the person will require and places those elements (atoms,

if you will) in all the food, drink and air that this person will require throughout his lifetime and organizes the person's life so that he uses up these atoms or elements throughout his life - no more, no less.

Each and every one of these atoms, elements, molecules (call them what you will) are encoded with the exact frequency of that person and will be used by that person and no other.

It does not seem possible and we forgive anyone who rejects this information as nonsense because we, too, find it almost incredibly hard to believe.

However, people much wiser than us inform us that it is so, so we accept it as truth.

But, if we think about this, it does imply that life is much more complex than we have yet described, and we have written many thousands of words over the years to you explaining many complexities about life.

We said that there are elements floating around - some in the air and some in food and drink - that have a person's exclusive frequency attached to them and so are reserved exclusively for that person but it is yet more complicated than that.

A person has many parts to him; skin, bone, flesh, liver, heart, spleen, lungs etc. Would you believe that the elements we mentioned above not only are encoded with a person's unique frequency and thus are reserved exclusively for that person, but even more amazingly, each molecule, atom or whatever is sub-coded with a frequency that reserves it for a certain part of that human?

So, we have, for example, an atom of oxygen that has the code of a certain human and waits to be ingested in some way by that human.

However, it is also encoded with the sub-frequency of a certain part of that human; skin, blood, bone, flesh or one of the organs. It is the same for other atoms of oxygen reserved for other uses of the body.

This implies that each part of the human has his personal frequency, but also the frequency of any particular part of him.

Therefore, a human has a frequency unique to him but also, attached to that frequency, a sub-frequency corresponding to every part of his body.

There are atoms that vibrate to the same frequency of that human but, further, also contain a sub-frequency corresponding to a particular part of the person's body and that atom will link with that part of the body and no other.

So, you have to understand that for a human, you, for example, there are a large number of atoms - or whatever you wish to call them - that are in nature somewhere, that have your frequency and the sub-frequencies of various parts of your body.

Just to take oxygen. You may need oxygen to help you breathe, so there are sufficient oxygen atoms to satisfy your requirements concerning breathing.

Now, you may journey around somewhat, so oxygen atoms are placed in the atmosphere to help you breathe no matter where you may find yourself in the world.

Then, if there are other parts of your body that require oxygen, there is more, each atom encoded to assist whatever part of your body requires oxygen.

Each oxygen atom is encoded to assist one part of your body and will only ever be used for that purpose.

The same applies for each element that your body requires.

When you ingest food, obviously there are not only the items that you require contained in that food.

Due to the fact that some elements contain your frequencies and some that don't, your body extracts only the elements that correspond to your frequency and distributes them to the various organs of your body.

Those elements that do not concern you are eliminated as waste and return into the earth or rivers and lakes, eventually to be picked up by the plants or animals and will, eventually, find their way to the people who have the frequencies relevant to what is contained in the diverse food.

This waste food eliminated by your digestive tract we could consider to be rubbish!

It is disposed of, in towns and cities, by channeling it into waste disposal plants where the elements are broken down into their constituent parts (atoms, etc) and thus they are recycled, and the elements returned either to the soil or to the atmosphere and these elements will be used to grow more plants, either to feed humans or animals, and the process of the body extracting only those elements that a body requires continues, the unwanted elements being once again eliminated as waste - rubbish. And so the process continues as each element still contains the frequency of a particular human and also contains the sub-frequency corresponding to a particular part of that human.

Waste eliminated by people that do not live in towns or cities is disposed of by other means - waste disposal tanks or people just 'doing their business' wherever they can, but the process of this waste being recycled remains the same.

The circle of ingestion, elimination and recycling goes on endlessly thus ensuring that there are sufficient atoms necessary to the needs of all life, as all life, eventually, is drawn, by the law of mutual attraction, to those atoms necessary for the well-being of that person or creature.

This is an incredible process.

No doubt some of you are wondering why it should be necessary for any atom to be encoded with a frequency unique to any one person?

Why should it be so complicated?

The answer is that, although all is one and the concept of individuality is an illusion, God decided, in his wisdom, that all life should start out as a multitude of individuals so that each individual could have experience and those experiences should be fed back to God, which is done via the akashic record.

So, it was decided that, to keep every person separate from any other person, the elements that create his body should be unique to him.

If any atom was created suitable for all people, gradually this concept of individuality would become confused and people would lose their sense of individuality.

Atoms contain auras and auras can memorize the thoughts and emotions of people.

So if any atom, say of oxygen, was suitable for all people, the memories associated with that atom of oxygen, when a person dies and his body is disposed of, (the atoms being used to create more food ingested by other people) the individual, eventually, would find himself somewhat confused.

His mind would have a sense of who he is as an individual but his body would contain atoms containing the thoughts and emotions of others that had used that atom of oxygen before.

Can you understand this?

It is not easy to explain but for you to retain your sense of individuality, it is essential that every atom that you ingest contains only your frequency and no other frequency.
We will repeat this one more time in an attempt to clarify the point we are making.
Atoms contain auras and auras can memorize the thoughts and emotions of a person who uses that atom. When the person releases that atom, if it did not have a unique frequency, someone else would eventually use that atom to assist him.
Each person has a unique sense of identity. But, if a person used an atom that had already been used by someone else, that atom would have associated with it the thoughts of a previous user of that atom.
As atoms can last a long time, any one atom, if it did not have a unique identity and could be used by anyone, would gradually have associated with it the thoughts and memories of a number of people.
These thoughts and memories would clash with the sense of identity of the person using that atom.
Multiply that by the countless atoms that constitute a person and you will see that any person would not only contain his sense of identity but the identities of countless people. The result would be chaotic.

But we have not answered the question as to why each atom not only has your frequency associated with it but a sub-frequency that informs the atom as to which part of your body it must act.
The answer is that each part of your body has a separate sub-frequency that enables it to develop or decline independently from any other part.
In that manner a person may have, for instance, a defective heart while the rest of his body is perfectly healthy. So each part, each organ of a person, although collectively creates a person, develops or declines independently from other parts.
So, each part, each organ requires more or less atoms in its drive to remain healthy and thus needs more or less atoms to achieve this goal.
That is why each organ contains a sub-code and why each atom contains the sub-code relevant to any organ or any part of the body.
The body tries to draw from the food ingested the atoms in sufficient quantities to assist any ailing part of the body.

While we are mentioning organs, may we touch on the problems of transplants?
People that have had transplants note at least two things.
1. The body tries to reject the transplanted organ. The reason is obvious. The transplanted organ contains a frequency inimical to the person who is given the organ and thus the body tries to reject it.
2. Sometimes a person who receives a transplant notices a change of personality. The reason is that the atoms that constitute an organ have, in their auras, the personality of the donor and this can clash with the personality of the receiver of the organ.

Now, when we started this chapter, we mentioned the word 'rubbish'!
We apologise for using this rather uncouth word but there is in the 4th an area that deals with unwanted matter.
We wish to link what we have so far said in this chapter about atoms etc., to the area that disposes of unwanted matter.

If you have followed what we said in this chapter about atoms you may have questioned what doctors say about the body regenerating itself almost as if atoms wear out and need to be replaced.
Doctors proudly state that the body you now have is not the same body that you were born with because, with regularity, you cast off worn-out atoms and they are replaced by new atoms that are full of energy.
They may not refer to atoms in quite this fashion but they have noticed that atoms of the body are replaced quite regularly.
This is true!

Atoms that combine to create your body help keep your body healthy by containing a certain amount of life force and they give up this life force as they attempt to keep you alive and healthy.
The rate that atoms are replaced depends on the functions that any atom fulfills.
Atoms that make skin, for example, need to be replaced at a much greater rate than atoms that create internal organs.
But, sooner or later, all atoms give up their power and need to be replaced with fully charged atoms.
One can liken the event to the batteries that keep an object, a clock for example, working. Sooner or later their charge diminishes and the clock starts to run slow. So the batteries need to be replaced for the hands of the clock to correctly display the time.

Even physical atoms have a non-physical aspect to them and when an atom has used its energy and needs to be replaced it goes off to this area to be disposed of.
Of course, another atom is immediately drawn into the body to replace the worn-out atom.
In the meantime, the atom no longer of service to the body goes off to the area in the 4th and is disposed of.

We would like to say that it is recycled but this would not be quite true.
In physicality, atoms tend to last a long time but that is because atoms that are taken from the air, for example, have not been given any task to do and so are like batteries waiting on the shelf of a shop or store.
Once they are put to work, they wear out and need to be replaced.
This is why everything needs to be maintained.
In the case of sentient life; plants, animals and humans, food is necessary to get the replacement atoms.
Even buildings and other structures need constantly to be maintained as the atoms wear out.
The exception is a few items like stones and water that seem never to be replaced. It is understandable in the case of stones because they just lie about and do not serve life in the sense we are describing. Water is a puzzle because it is used all the time by all life but

the atoms that constitute a molecule of water never seem to lose their power. We do not know why but there must be a reason and we hope to discover why one day.

Naturally, if and when we find the answer, we will inform you.

But, eventually, worn out atoms go off to this rubbish tip (disposal / waste management site) in the 4th where they are disposed of.

We will attempt to describe this area and how it works.

Basically, as you may have realised from previous chapters, the areas in the 4th where any event is taking place break down into one of two types.

Either the area is physical in a spiritual sense or it is invisible.

The fact that an area is or is not visible to us in no way affects its efficacy. It is just that some events require a physical plane or landscape while other events are non-physical or mental in nature. Thought being a typical example of a non-physical area.

In the case of atoms, the area is physical but, eventually, the atoms will move to become invisible so we could say that this rubbish area is a bit of both.

We repeat, once more, that we called this area a rubbish tip or disposal /waste management site because it corresponds in many ways to the rubbish or landfill areas that you have on the earth plane, so to make it understandable to you we use that phrase.

We will also add that us, in the light realms of the 4th, being full of happiness and joy, like to keep our descriptions amusing when we can and this area gives us the opportunity to lighten the tone of our description.

So, if we visit this area, what do we see and what do we feel?

The first thing we notice are a number of advanced people dealing with diverse matters. These people have volunteered to work in this area and have been trained to deal with the various atoms as they arrive, sorting them out according to type.

By which we mean that there are groups that deal with disposing of oxygen, others dealing with hydrogen, others helium and so on.

The reason is that each type of atom has specific properties and this requires specific treatment to dispose of them.

You have a similar system on Earth where various items are sorted at their arrival at the rubbish site and dealt with according to type.

Certain plastics get one treatment, certain liquids receive another treatment and so on.

We should perhaps say that on Earth, attempts are being made to recycle certain materials. This is good but we will point out that the objects made from recycled materials tend to be less dynamic than those previously made.

This is because the power remaining in the atoms is less than when the atoms were put to use in the first place and thus any object made from recycled atoms is less vibrant, if we may use that word.

Eventually, the atoms reach a point where they are so empty that they are sent off to us for disposal.

However, we heartily endorse the recycling of atoms on the earth plane and it actually makes our job easier as there is less energy that needs to be removed by us from an atom as we prepare them to disappear.

To return to our rubbish tip!

There is a constant stream of used atoms pouring into the rubbish tip area and there are a number of people who reception them and sort them according to atom type, as we mentioned earlier.

We will also say at this point that there are more atoms than your periodic table suggests but they are all known to the people who work in the rubbish tip area and they are all sorted.

So, you have to imagine this area and all these people receiving worn out atoms which are sent down different conveyor belts to be treated by others.

Obviously, the reality is much different from this but we use this simple analogy in order to give you an image of what goes on.

Perhaps we should describe how and why a worn-out atom returns to the 4th. The answer is simple. All is one and all is a function of consciousness.

Physical life - the incarnation you are experiencing at the moment - is a sort of illusion. However, it is made to appear real and to achieve this God's archangels created a 'life' in the 6th dimension.

The basis of this life is atoms. But atoms come from the 4th. They appear in your reality as physical objects in order to create the illusion of solidity but atoms are spiritual creations given a frequency that enables them to seem real to you and to create all that exists in your reality.

By the law of mutual attraction, virtually all things in so-called physicality (the earth plane as far as you are concerned) retain a strong link to the place of their true creation - the spiritual realms - and thus return home when they have outlived their usefulness, their incarnation we might almost say, in physicality.

Of course, as you look at the night sky and see the myriad of stars, you must understand that these stars and their associated planets and moons also have atoms that come to the end of their usefulness and thus return to this rubbish tip area in the 4th.

We hope you can therefore appreciate that there are a considerable number of atoms of all types returning to the 4th and being terminated in the rubbish tip.

That is why it is necessary to sort the atoms according to type and that they are further sorted according to the amount of spiritual power remaining in them.

If we can continue with the analogy we used earlier by likening the rubbish tip area in the 4th to rubbish dumps on Earth, anything useful is retained and separated from the atoms.

In this case it is the spiritual energy left in an atom that is withdrawn from the atom, handed over to archangels, who devote their existence to this task, and that spiritual energy is purified and can be reused to create more atoms to replace those taken out of life.

What remains is an empty husk, so to speak.

We apologise for continually using words or terms from the earth plane but, as we have often said, words do not exist in modern parlance to describe some spiritual functions so we have to use analogies in order to convey our meaning to you.

Sanskrit contains many more words that refer to spiritual things or acts but we think that it would be rather confusing if we continually embellished our discussions of spiritual events by adding a sprinkling of Sanskrit words that very few would understand.

So, we have to use words, terms or phrases from, in this case, the English language in an attempt to clarify our meaning.

So, to repeat, used and tired atoms are drawn, by the law of mutual attraction, to the spirit world and are attracted by the same law to the rubbish tip area.

They are sorted according to what types of atoms they are into various directions and are funneled off to areas where skilled operators remove the spiritual aspect from each atom.

The spiritual aspects are handed over to archangels who recycle them to create more atoms.

The husk must then be got rid of.

Now, at this point we refer back to the previous chapter where we mention that, in the case of a human who wanted to die, as his spiritual aspects were removed, he disappeared because he never actually existed. It was the spiritual aspects that gave the illusion of existence.

It is the same with the husk of the atoms.

As the spiritual elements are carefully withdrawn so the husk gradually disappears until it fades from existence.

This happens because it never was.

It was the spirit that gave the appearance of life. Once the spirit is withdrawn, the atom ceases to be.

All is one!

That which happened to a human must happen to an atom, as all is one.

So, the rubbish tip area contains a vast number of used atoms in the process of being recycled.

The spiritual aspect is withdrawn and passed to archangels but, as this process occurs, the husk gradually disappears because it was only an illusion created by archangels who, under the guidance of what we call God (but which as we have said is consciousness), and so when the spiritual aspect of an atom is withdrawn the husk ceases to be.

This is a very clean and clever manner of dealing with atoms and of recuperating unused spiritual energy.

You may have noticed that we did not refer to dark matter and dark energy - antimatter. As you can imagine, even though 'dark' atoms - if we may thus refer to them - do not seem to be connected to life as 'light' atoms are, in fact, they are an essential part of life and are of equal importance as light atoms.

Life must be kept in balance and so all atoms, whatever colour we ascribe to them, play an equal role and so wear out equally.

But it has been noted that if they came into contact, they would cancel each other out in a very short space of time. This energy, being cancelled suddenly, would reveal itself by an enormous explosion. Both sets of atoms, black and white if we can thus refer to them, contain the same amount of God force, but organised in a sort of positive or negative fashion.

It has often been noticed that to cancel power in a rapid fashion often causes an effect, in this case a rather violent one.

It is just the natural effect of a positive and a negative force - negative in a plus and minus sense, not a holy or diabolic sense - being cancelled that results in a sort of third effect, an explosion.

However, the process of dark atoms being eliminated is exactly the same as the process that light atoms go through.

The difference is that the process takes place in a parallel aspect of the 4th, next to the original rubbish tip, and the God force is removed in exactly the same fashion in which case the empty husks of the dark atoms just disappear as before.

The God spirit removed from the dark atom is cleansed as is the God spirit of the white or light atoms, at which point they both become safe and can be mixed to create more atoms.

Light or dark atoms contain the same God spirit.

The change of colour comes about by manipulation of the spirit by archangels at the moment of construction.

Each atom is given a sort of logos that tells it if it is going to be a light or a dark atom. At that point, they must be kept apart until the logos is removed by archangels and then they may safely be mixed.

We have done our best to describe this rubbish tip area to you and we hope that you have understood even if some of you cannot accept it.

So, once again, we will end this chapter here and move on to yet another topic to be found in the 4th.

CHAPTER 15

THE GOD FORCE

You may have noticed how there was a connection between Chapter 13 and Chapter 14 in that, as the spirit force was withdrawn, so the physical part disappeared, as the physical part was an illusion created by the spirit part.

Thus, we had two parts to life.

1. The spirit part, and
2. The physical part, even though that physical part may have been in the 4th or the 6th dimension.

As all is one, it matters not where life is to be found. It is all one life.

This leads us onto the next chapter - this one - which will deal with an area in the 4th that maintains the link between the spirit and the physical.

We repeat, when we talk about physical, we might be referring to life as you know it in the 6th dimension or life as we know it in the 4th. It is the same life, the main difference being one of frequency.

Life continues endlessly.

You may have the impression that it is in distinct phases and the way it is viewed at the moment of physical birth and physical death, assuming one chooses to have an Earthly incarnation, we suppose that we could say that it is. However, if one can step back to see the broader picture, one realizes that life is just one long spiritual experience and, if viewed in that fashion, it goes on endlessly as a composite whole.

It started endless ages in the past and will go on for endless ages into the future.

We intend to devote this chapter to the part of the 4th that helps organize the spiritual aspect but, before we do that, may we take a moment to ask you to consider the length of your life?

We do not refer to the length of your incarnation but to the length of your existence from the moment that you were selected to become a human by archangelic forces, and for how long you will exist until you merge with the Godhead.

Could one trace on a piece of paper the vast number of one plus almost endless zero's as in million, billion, trillion and on and on years that you will exist?

Once something has been created by God, normally, it cannot die.

The exceptions we noted in Chapters 13 and 14.

Excluding these exceptions, human life endures virtually eternally, and during that vast length of time it is expected that one would grow intellectually and spiritually.

If you consider someone like Jesus, he is considered by many to be the most advanced human ever to walk the Earth. We must say that Jesus does not see himself in that light. He thinks of himself as a humble pilgrim walking the path to perfection but with a long journey still ahead of him.

Nevertheless, compared to most of us, we will say that he is a very advanced soul.

But can you imagine, if you apply yourself to the spiritual path, where you will be in several trillion years' time.

Certainly, we would have difficulty in describing such a person and yet that is the destiny that awaits us all.

But out of all that long existence you will have one incarnation in the 6th dimension. This is the one that you are going through at the moment.

Before that and after that moment - and out of all eternity it is only a moment - you will soldier on in various parts of the 4th.

Now, this is where we wish we could talk about something without our meaning being misconstrued.

We wished that we could mention the 'R' word - reincarnation.

We use that word with the greatest trepidation because, as soon as we do, people will seize on it and declare that reincarnation is a fact despite our saying many times that you only come to the earth plane once.

We have tried and tried to drum this into people but it will only be when your incarnation ends that you will find the truth that reincarnation is a falsehood.

There are even people who claim to have had near death experiences that claim multiple incarnations.

We cannot convince such people but we assure you that once your Earthly incarnation terminated, that is the end of that chapter of your life.

However, life goes on endlessly and you will progress from level to level as far as your continued life in the 4th is concerned and we wished we could liken it to a form of reincarnation - from level to level - either higher or lower levels. But long and bitter experience has taught us to avoid the 'R' word.

However, we do have the right to talk about the incarnation you are all going through at the moment.

This is what this chapter will deal with, or rather the place in the 4th that helps link the endless spiritual ages to the one short 'physical' incarnation.

So, can we describe this area?

Unfortunately, it is one of the non-physical places so in linking to it there is nothing to see.

But, if we open our minds we can, to a certain extent, link with what is going on in this area or landscape.

We wish that there was a more definite way to describe these many areas that we attempt to portray in this book but a number of them, being non-physical, cannot really be described using the languages with which most of you are familiar.

As we mentioned, Sanskrit has a lot more descriptive words but even in Sanskrit not every area has a descriptive word and, as we said, not everyone has a mastery of Sanskrit. Therefore, we ask that you accept that these areas exist and we leave you to accept our descriptions or not.

So, there is in the 4th, an area that has been created that helps link the endless spiritual aspects of individual life to those who choose to have an incarnation, which includes you of course.

We might well ask why such a place needs to exist and what purpose it serves?

The answer, as is often the case, is both simple and complicated.

The simple answer is that you are in two parts, as we have mentioned above.

You always retain a link to your spiritual aspect and this does not happen by magic.
It needs a mechanism for you to have a physical incarnation but, at the same time, have the spiritual or non-physical aspect operating behind the scenes.

We do not know of any simple means of describing this double effect but we could liken it to you driving a car.
You are concentrating on safely driving your car along a road but, behind the scenes, so to speak, are a mass of parts all combining to make the car work.
Without all, or most of these parts working correctly, the car would go nowhere. But, assuming that all the parts work, your car gets you from the point of departure to your destination.
But it requires two aspects.
1. That the car works, and
2. That you drive the car correctly.

We do appreciate that this may be a poor analogy of the area we wish to describe to you but if it enables you to appreciate that, in the case of a car, you need two aspects working together to get you safely along to your destination, it will have served its purpose.
Life is similar except the motivating force is invisible and you have to guide yourself through life.
We could, of course, liken the area we will describe to the factory that constructed your car, but we do not wish to push the analogies too far.
Suffice to say, for the purposes of this chapter, that there are actually three parts to it.
1. The one God force that all share.
2. You, in your incarnation, mainly under the influence of your personality, and
3. This area which provides the link from 1 to 2 and back again.

We have, in other works, done our best to describe the very complex mechanisms that take the one God force and link it to you and we have also described as well as we can how, from this one spiritual force we call God, all life in any dimension and throughout all time was constructed.
If you are not familiar with all this, please refer to our work which, we understand, are available for free if you link to the internet sites set up by those on Earth that work with us and to whom we are grateful for their loving service both to God and to our organization.
So, let us try to explain as best we can how this area creates a permanent link to you and to all life between the one God force and the individual lives that all live whilst they are having an incarnation in the 6th dimension.

There is, in this particular area of the 4th, a mechanism that creates conditions, permanently, that enable those incarnate to have a link to the God force. We must say that, although each and every life-force benefits from this link, not all people are aware that it is in place even though it operates within them all the time.
In fact, in this area in the 4th there are a number of angels and archangels who control the mechanism.
When we mention angels, we refer to human angels and archangels who have kindly volunteered to devote vast periods of their existence to ensuring that the mechanism

works flawlessly. If ever there is a problem, they immediately step in and repair that problem.

So, to put it in simple terms, the God force is funneled into this area.
You may protest and say that we have stated that the God force works in other areas.
What you have to understand is that the God force can be compared to a holographic picture in which there is one picture seen when one looks at the hologram. However, if one examines the picture closely, it can be seen that the main picture is actually composed of a myriad of small pictures, duplicates of the first large picture.
Obviously, God is not quite as simple as that but if you can understand how a hologram is constructed it will help you understand how God operates.
God exists as a constructive force - a single entity, if we may thus describe God - but God is able, via his archangelic aids to be in many places at once.
In this and in all cases, it is not a part of God that is available. It is always the totality of God that can be in many places at once. If this were not the case, there would be no life.
It is the fact that everything physical and non-physical contains the totality of God that makes the life in all dimensions, all auras.
It might be worth picking up a small pebble and looking at it closely because when you gaze at it you are looking at the face of God!
However, we digress.

In this area in the 4th is placed the God force.
This force is invisible but the angels and archangels are so advanced, so holy that they are able to feel that presence and to guide it to you who are incarnate on Earth.
Many of the world's population have no idea that they only exist as physical beings thanks to this God force pouring into them at each moment, each frame of life and it is that, that creates life.

So, what these angelic beings do is to take the God force and direct at each and every object on Earth whether it be animal, vegetable, mineral or human.

It is directed into each atom because it is these atoms that come together to create everything according to the law of mutual attraction.
You, for example, exist as a human being, thanks to an immensely complex system of various parts - some of which we have described in other books - coming together to create your body, your mind, your personality, your higher self, your ID, and your DNA, both physical and non-physical just to name a few parts of you.
But, behind the scenes is the God force that is being directed into you from the 4th, from the area we are talking about.
This goes on for all life in incarnation, no matter what it is.
It happens to you from the moment of your birth, when the God force is sent to you and continues until the moment of your demise when, by the law of mutual attraction, your spirit returns to the 4th.
This is an impressive feat accomplished by this group of angels and archangels who are able to ensure that this influx of God power flows into all life on a permanent basis.
This has been going on ever since the first life forms were sent to Earth to have an incarnation and will continue until life is no longer needed on Earth, which will be a long, long time in the future.

We have to say that these angelic beings are not visible to us, being so advanced compared to any of us who comprise the Great White Brotherhood, because they vibrate to a frequency outside and above our level of sight and comprehension.
We know that they exist and what they do thanks to other archangelic beings who contact us and inform us of their presence within this area of the 4th.
We do not know how many of them there are nor do we know whether they become tired after a while, leave and other angelic beings replace them.
We only know that there are always sufficient to ensure that the process of directing the God spirit to all life incarnate works all the time.
We repeat that if there was not this place in the 4th that receives the God force and directs it to you, there would be no life incarnate.

There is not much more that we can tell you about this vitally important area so we will recapitulate.
There exists in the 4th an area where there are a number of angelic and archangel humans.
They receive the God force, which is sent to them by other even higher angelic beings, and as they receive it, they send it to all life incarnate on Earth.
As we have told you, everything is alive from the smallest grain of sand to the mightiest creatures and humans.
It is this God force that creates life incarnate for all things.
Their place in the chain of life cannot be underestimated.
It is thanks to these angels that physicality exists in the 6th dimension that you call incarnation.

To what degree these angels are aware that you exist we do not know but you should send your thanks and gratitude to them because, without these angels sending you the God spirit, you would not be alive and reading this book.
This stupendous event has occurred ever since the first life forms incarnated long ago and will continue until incarnation is considered no longer to be necessary.

There is much that we do not know about them.
We do not know how they deal with the fact that incarnation is actually an illusion.
But we do know that they treat incarnation as a living fact and thus pour God's force into you and into everything all the time.

As this action by the angels charged with sending you this life force is so important, we could write volumes about it but for the purposes of this book it suffices to give you an overview.
Detailed descriptions must wait for another day.
It suffices that you are aware that there is an area in the 4th that receives the God force and sends that force to all objects and entities incarnate.
This is achieved thanks to the tireless efforts of angels and archangels who reception that force and direct it to all things incarnate including you who are reading this book.
So, we will end this short chapter here and turn to yet another new subject.

CHAPTER 16

THE LIFE PLAN

We could write a compendium about the different areas within the 4th that contains elements that would, or should, be of interest to you as many of these areas affect you in your incarnation either directly or indirectly.

However, there must be a limit to what we describe.
We understand that there are a number of readers of our books that want as much information as possible and for our books to be as comprehensive as possible.
It is true that, in the past, we have presented books in a rather limited way because we were afraid that those with short attention spans would not read large volumes.
This could be considered to be playing to the lowest common denominator.
We apologize to those who really are keen to learn as much as possible about life and so, from now on, we will present larger and more complete books, presenting as much on any subject as we feel applicable.
This will, of course, create more work for our Earthly scribe and thus slow down somewhat the production of books but if they are more complete and present more information, it will be worth it.
Certainly, from our perspective, we wish to give you all as much information as possible so we will create, from now on, more complete and informative volumes. We rely on our Earthly scribe having the energy to write large volumes of text.
So, we ask you all to be patient from now on as we undertake the task of creating larger books.

We turn to the next item of interest, the next plane or landscape in the 4th that concerns you.
It is this.
There exists in the 4th dimension an area that deals with the production of life plans.
You may have heard that you incarnate with a life plan.
These life plans are not suggested in a haphazard fashion nor are there an unlimited number of them.
It would be inappropriate for there to be an unlimited number of life plans and would create chaos on Earth, so there are a large but limited number of life plans available for selection by a person desiring to have an Earthly incarnation.

According to the personality and interests of the candidate preparing himself for incarnation, a selection of life plans would be presented to the individual and he selects, after much discussion with his guides and teachers, which life plan would best suit him.
Then his life plan is tucked away in his higher self and remains there guiding the person incarnate as he starts his incarnation.
It pushes him, if we may thus describe it, along the path he chose before incarnation and will continue to do so until the end of his incarnation.
So, we have given you a brief overview of a life plan and how it functions.
But let us now return to the beginning and explain in detail as much as we can about life plans.

We hope that you can appreciate that life plans are essential to helping a person through his incarnation.

We could liken it to the rudder of a ship which guides the ship across an ocean from one port to another, the port of departure to the port of destination.

Without a rudder, a guiding system, the boat would just bob about on the ocean at the mercy of wind and tide.

It is the rudder that guides the ship safely across an ocean.

Of course, there is not just the rudder. There is the captain who decides where the ship should go and a helmsman who turns the rudder so that the ship follows the captain's directives.

So, the analogy is not totally correct but we want you to understand that a life plan is essential to guiding you through your incarnation.

Let us return to a moment in the 4th that a young person - almost, one could say, a soul - is placed in the care of an oversoul.

We have already described the function of an oversoul but for those who do not know what an oversoul is, let us say that it is a grouping of like-minded individuals forming a collective and travelling through time together.

It has been likened to a platoon or company in a military group or a house in a school.

It is a group of people, some of whom have been in the spirit world for a long time and some of whom are recent arrivals.

But an oversoul is very important. It acts as a base, a home, a safe haven that a person can return to when he feels he needs to be comforted and reassured. It is his home in the 4th. However, there is nothing physical to see.

It is purely people of like minds sharing their life, their love for each other because they think alike and have similar hopes, aims and ambitions.

An oversoul will remain with a person no matter where he resides; in the 4th, in incarnation or even should he wish to explore life, or lack of it, elsewhere.

If only people incarnate would realize that they have an oversoul and belong to it, life would be much more peaceful.

We mentioned life plans and oversouls as if they are two separate structures and, to a certain extent they are. But, if we can use a few Earth examples, it might help to explain a connection.

Let us take the case of a hospital. Someone decides that he or she wishes to create a hospital and so that person gathers around him a group of like-minded people (from his oversoul group) and they plan how they intend to create this proposed hospital (a life plan, in a way).

This hospital gradually takes form and, hopefully, provides a noble service in caring for the sick.

We could use other examples; businesses for instance, the creation of political parties, etc.

It is often a case of people from the same or similar soul groups creating a project and planning it out, which can be likened to a person's life plan.

As with most analogies, it is not perfect but we hope it helps you understand what soul groups and life plans are.

While we are on this topic, may we ask you to note that in physical life there are a large number of possible business, charitable or social organizations that can be set up but, nevertheless, the number of options is not unlimited.

It may be possible, for instance, to create a commerce of some sort and each commerce will be unique but they will all follow a similar concept, taking a product or an idea and selling it to the public in exchange for something, usually money.

So, although there are a multitude of commerce's, they all stem from one idea, how to make a profit from selling something to someone. This could be likened to a life plan.

The concept of hospitals, care centers, old people's homes, etc., come together as another form of life plan.

We could go on and discuss politics, armed forces and so on but the concept is the single, similar idea to do something.

So, we hope that you can see that from the huge number of collective creations of businesses, care services, newspapers, factories, banks, etc., there are actually a limited number of plans that are behind the plethora of ideas.

In the case of you, the public that follow our teachings, there is a fair chance that you belong to the same soul group as us. We know that most of you are gentle, kind and spiritual people seeking, in your own fashions, the same objectives as us which is to gain knowledge in a bid to rise in the ascension process.

A soul group does not have to be limited to just a few souls. A soul group can contain millions of people, and as we all rise in spirituality together, so we can all join, reduce our individual egos and start to think as one noble entity.

Equally, we must say that there are other soul groups who think in a diametrically opposite fashion to our soul group and, once again, these might consist of huge numbers of people.

Amongst such a soul group, would be those quite at home with the concept of harming life: robbers, hunters, murderers, terrorists, etc.

These people, too, have the right to think and act as they have chosen but we must say that such people, generally, lead unhappy lives and will pay for the path they have chosen when their incarnation ends and they have to go to hell.

We all have free will. Some choose to do good and some choose the opposite.

The point we wish to make is, in each case, as the student human is shown around heaven, so he naturally feels drawn to a certain type of lifestyle.

Although, as soon as he arrives from the 7th to the 4th and he is placed in an oversoul, if it is noticed that his developing personality is not compatible with the oversoul that he is currently in, he can move to an oversoul in which he will feel more at ease.

Then, assuming that he wishes to have an incarnation, he will have a selection of life plans from which to choose, and with much discussion with his guides and teachers, he will select a life plan which will attempt to guide him through his incarnation.

This implies that each group, the members of one oversoul, if they desire to incarnate will be shown a selection of life plans, but each bouquet of these life plans will be connected to the type of personality an individual has and what he hopes to achieve from his incarnation.

Therefore, each group has a wide but limited number of options to choose from.

In the case of good people, the sort that might belong to our soul group, the life plans might cause the person to be born into terrible hardship, live a life of poverty in order to test him to the limit.

There is an example of this in the Bible where a person was asked by God to sacrifice his son as an offering to God.

We must say that in real life such a suggestion would never be made to anyone, neither by God nor by his angels. It is just a story to demonstrate what we are trying to explain.

At the last minute, Abraham (the man in question) was told to spare his son and he had passed the test of his faith in God.

We do not expect any good person to be faced with such a choice but it is common for a good person to be born into a poor family and to have to struggle all, or most, of his life in an attempt to make ends meet.

This is the nature of life, generally, for good people.

They choose a life where they are tested.

They could give in and turn to crime and we suppose that some do.

However, the difference between good and the opposite sorts of people is that a good person knows deep down that if he does a wrong act (stealing, for example) in order to feed his family, he knows that it is not correct.

Someone from the opposite end of the spectrum would steal without a second thought and might even feel proud of himself for getting away with the act.

While we are talking about good and not good people, may we say that we have a word missing in the English language. If we describe a person as a good person, within reason we all know the sort of person we are describing.

However, in the opposite case we have a number of people to whom we have difficulty in ascribing an appellation.

We do not wish to describe a person, the opposite of what we consider to be a good person, as bad, nor evil, nor misguided.

A person who chooses to act in an antisocial fashion is part of us all as we are all one. So, we do not wish to condemn the person as being bad, nor evil, nor misguided, as he has chosen a path through life that is legitimate, even if his actions are seen as antisocial.

Evil people there are. Fortunately, they are few. But there are a large number of people that choose to act in an antisocial manner. We don't really have a word for such people.

Also, we must say that not all such people are poor, working class people. Some are, but many of them, being close to the animal instinct as opposed to good people who are closer to the spirit world, find it easy to progress through life.

Many of them are just ordinary people, who turn their hands and their minds to petty crime but there are a considerable number of highly educated, highly positioned in society who have this antisocial aspect prominent in their makeup.

They would be successful businessmen, politicians, bankers, lawyers and even some royalty of various countries, who have chosen to follow this rather negative path and who do not hesitate to push any advantage that they think will advance them either in terms of influence, power or finance.

If we may paraphrase an expression somewhat, the aim of such people is to 'rob the poor to feed the rich'.

However, although we appear to be criticizing such people, and we must say that we regret that they have taken this path, nevertheless, they are our brothers and sisters. More, they are us. We are all one. They are us and we are them.

They and us are two faces of the same coin so to speak.

Let us take this expression and push it somewhat.

Imagine that it was a gold coin. It may have two faces, heads and tails, but they are all stamped into the same gold coin.

If we imagine that gold coin to be God, both faces are the face of God.

We apologise for that rather simple analogy but we want to express that whatever path anyone takes through life; they are still connected to all of us and to God.

However, we also wish to make the point that people, their oversouls to which they belong and their life plans, from which they choose if they are to have an incarnation, are all connected.

The personality of a person attracts him, by the law of mutual attraction, to the oversoul to which he naturally feels drawn and then he is presented with a number of life plans and one is chosen which will remain with him and will help guide him through his incarnation.

Naturally, once his incarnation finished, he returns to his home in the 4th and to a greater connection to his oversoul, and this life plan, which remains in place to a certain extent, becomes more flexible and he has greater freedom to reach beyond the confines of incarnation and beyond the limits that his life plan placed on him.

We will repeat, just to make it perfectly clear, the process that occurs as a young soul is selected to be a human and how he progresses from that early stage into and through an incarnation.

In the 8th dimension there are a large number of points of life that could be considered to be singularities. There are a vast but finite number of these singularities, one for each and every grain of sand, drop of water, plant, animal and potential human. But none of them have yet been chosen to become something. They are just points of life.

As usual, let us consider just humans.

At the far end of the life spectrum there is a stream of humans who have reached perfection and who merge with the Godhead and thus disappear from life as we know it. This would leave a void and if it was allowed to continue as a one-way stream of humans disappearing into the Godhead, eventually, there would be no humans left neither in incarnation nor in the heavenly spheres.

Nature abhors a vacuum and so, as people merge with God, they must be replaced. Therefore, archangelic beings decide what needs to be replaced. This could be almost any life form but, as we are just considering humans, let us suppose that a certain number of humans need to be created to replace those that are in the process of merging with God. It may seem strange, but there must always be an exact number of different life species in creation. This is an immense number but that number is required, no more, no less. Therefore, for each human that reaches the end of his long journey to perfection and blends with the God force, he must be replaced by a new human being selected to replace him.

The archangels reach into the mass of singularities in the 8th and select, at random, the number of potential humans they require and put a stamp, a logos, on them that tells each singularity that, from now on, it is going to be a human.
This is how you were chosen to be a human.

We have often talked about this and we do so again to make new students aware of where you came from. We have also said, and we repeat, it was purely by chance that you were selected to become a human. You could have been selected to become anything: animal, vegetable or mineral. Indeed, you might not have been selected at all and could still just be a singularity in the 8th.
But, having been selected to become a human, you are destined to live a life of extraordinary wonder, beauty and happiness. Do not imagine that this incarnation you are currently going through is all there is to life. You live in a magnificent palace and all you have seen so far in incarnation is the coal store. When your incarnation finishes and you return home to the 4th you will have the right to explore the rest of the palace.
You are, indeed, the chosen one, as you will learn once you return home.

Therefore, once selected and once given a stamp - a logos, as it is called - that tells you that you are destined to become a human, you move from the 8th dimension to the 7th. Why should this be?
Amongst other rather complicated reasons that we have explained elsewhere, you start to develop a personality.
Without personality, you would just be a sort of zombie. It is personality that makes you what and who you are.
So, in the 7th, you start to develop the first glimmerings of personality and a recognisable form of human starts to appear.
You are permanently developing your personality until you have matured to the point that you can move on.
Also, towards the end of your sojourn in the 7th you will attract the attention of a person who will become your personal guide. You will also attract the attention of a number of angels who will start to care for you. An oversoul will be selected for you.
Eventually, you transition to the 4th and merge with your oversoul group. So, at this point in the 4th, you will have a definite personality, a guide, you will belong to an oversoul group and you will also have angels nurturing you.

As you should know by now, time has little or no relevance outside of physicality, but we will use time as we attempt to describe life progressing through the heavenly spheres.
So, for many years, a young person will be shown around the different areas of the 4th, including, amongst many more, the landscapes that we have described in this and other books.
Obviously, there are many more landscapes shown to the student human than we have so far had the opportunity to explain to you.
We would like, as this book progresses, to explain more of these areas but it takes time for us to explain to our scribe the nature of these landscapes so we must progress slowly.
The point we wish to make is that a huge number of landscapes are shown to the student and note taken of which interest him and which do not.

All this information influences his personality in the same manner that information influences you.

This takes time, so the student may stay in heaven for a long time, measured in Earth years, before he is ready to take a decision as to the next stage of his progress.

We must say at this point that the student human realizes that he is immortal and, no matter what he chooses to do, he will live forever.

It is also made clear to him that life either in the 4th or the 6th, if he decides to have an Earthly incarnation, is really a series of lessons and the aim is to progress to perfection.

Some student humans accept this information eagerly and start to devote their lives to following the path to perfection. In this case, he chooses a sort of life plan in which his purpose is exclusively to learn all he can about the spiritual path, and very advanced humans and even human angels take charge of this person, educate and guide him along the path that they, themselves, are on.

There is no need for such people to have an Earthly incarnation so they remain in and progress through the various levels of the 4th.

We wish we could compare how such a person, as he leaves one level and progresses to the next, as being reincarnated from one level to the next, but as we have previously said, long and bitter experience has taught us not to say such a thing as so many people will immediately seize on the 'R' word (reincarnation) and say that it is proof of reincarnation from heaven to Earth. It isn't, as we have so often said. In this case it is like moving upwards in class in a school. Moving from one year to the next, the lessons becoming more advanced as the person advances.

There are quite large numbers of such people who would not profit from an Earthly incarnation but, equally, there are others who show little interest in the spiritual path and it is this group that are shown that they could, perhaps, benefit from visiting Earth and experiencing life in so-called physicality.

No one forces anyone from this group to come to Earth but the opportunity is offered to them.

What happens if a person shows an interest in, perhaps, having an Earthly incarnation is that, first, they meet with members of their soul group that have had an incarnation and these people explain what it was like to go through an incarnation on Earth.

Some people who had an incarnation had a relatively easy time on Earth while others suffered terribly.

The student will meet with many such people and will listen carefully to the stories recounted by those who once had an incarnation.

He will listen to those who had an easy ride through their incarnation and he will listen to those who had a really tough time.

He will also be taken to some of the levels of hell and learn what errors these people made that caused them, by the law of mutual attraction, to be in hell.

Equally, he will visit some of the higher spheres and talk to the people that had an incarnation but who devoted their incarnation to helping all life.

In other words, he will be shown every facet of life on Earth, how life, when it was in the darkest swing of the pendulum was terrible indeed and how, now that the pendulum is swinging into the light areas, is beginning to be more pleasant.

We wish you to understand that, among the many young humans considering their future, there are many different personality types.

We have mentioned those that chose a holy path and thus did not need to consider an incarnation.

The life plan would be to follow the path to God and thus their life plan is decided and they just have to follow it.

At the other extreme, believe it or not, there are a few people who are naturally drawn to what we might call a psychopathic trend.

All students are shown all aspects of life in physicality from the deepest evil to the highest good.

Those good students, when they visit the planes of physicality that deal with the lowest that man can sink to, feel disgusted and rapidly turn from any such thoughts.

But the psychopaths amongst the students would be delighted to find that such areas exist and feel very much drawn to those areas.

We must say, at this point, that heaven contains most of the aspects of life but the bad is kept strictly apart from the good. It is only on Earth that all aspects of life are combined, which is one of the purposes of life on Earth.

It gives the opportunity for those who are undecided about which way to go to experience all the facets of life in order for them to decide which path to accept.

We return for a moment to the 4th.

We mentioned that there were a number of students who automatically chose to follow the path of perfection and thus did not need an Earthly incarnation.

We wish to say that there are also a few who decide to be so evil that their guides refuse to allow them to have an incarnation.

When we say that their guides refuse to allow them an incarnation, it is not quite true. No one in the 4th has the right to impose his will on another but if a guide or teacher is confronted with someone who is really evil, he suggests that, perhaps, an incarnation would not be the best place for him to express his evilness. He would suggest that one of the areas of hell would best serve his desire for evil and hopes that the student follows his advice.

A guide would take the student to a place in hell where, by the law of mutual attraction, the student feels drawn and arrangements would be made for the student to be placed there.

In a way, that would be the student's place of incarnation.

However, if the student insists on having an Earthly incarnation, arrangements are taken, a life plan is selected by all, and the student is born on Earth.

The annals of history are full of the crimes subjected on countless people and animals by such people.

It is true that, once their incarnation terminated, they have to go to hell to repent - which they were made aware of before choosing to incarnate - but still they could not resist incarnating in order to satisfy their psychopathic desires to control and harm life.

Some are drawn to physical harm - torturing people - but many, particularly in modern times where in so-called civilized countries physical torture is no longer acceptable, these people turn their psychopathic minds to torturing people mentally or emotionally.

Such people often rise to positions of power and pass laws which plunge the public into financial hardship or destroy their lives in other fashions. Torture can take many forms.

We won't go into details. We are sure that just by looking around you, you can see the vast number of people who are facing terrible hardship because of the actions of this relatively few number of psychopathic people who get pleasure from their actions.
At the same time, we must remember that there are a large number of people who chose to incarnate in order to experience this hardship.
So, the psychopaths perform an important role in life by providing the conditions that enable vast numbers of less powerful people to suffer.
This may seem crazy if we think of it in a shallow fashion but if we can realise that there are people who deliberately choose to incarnate in order to experience what suffering feels like, we can realise that we need the psychopaths to create the conditions which permit others to suffer.
It all comes down to the life plans people choose.

If you are struggling to comprehend what we said above, let us create an analogy. An analogy that we have used before.
Imagine that someone has the desire to become a great, world beating athlete.
Even when he was at school, he would have this desire and would take steps to try to be better than his schoolmates at the chosen sport.
Then, once he leaves school, he would join a sports club and a coach would notice the person's talent, take him under his, the coach's wing, so to speak, and help the student to progress.
This would include long training sessions where the young athlete would have to spend hours pounding around a running track, equally, hours in a gymnasium doing weight training and so on just so that the public, who sit at home eating harmful food, drinking harmful beverages can applaud the athlete every time he wins.
Let us assume that this athlete becomes the best in his field and becomes world champion.
This fame lasts a few years until another young athlete rises through the athletic ranks and becomes better than the person we are considering.
This is inevitable.
Techniques improve. Food improves and, dare we say, drugs may play a part.
In any case, the first athlete we were considering becomes a 'has been' and someone else becomes world champion at the chosen sport.
The first person is forgotten by the public who turn their attention to the latest star.
So, what was the point of all the suffering the first athlete went through? It ended in failure.
However, from a spiritual point of view the forgotten athlete made a great sacrifice, made a great service to mankind.
It is better to have been a 'has been' rather than a 'never was' which is the case of all his once fans who sat at home and applauded him as he won his sport trophies.
But even those who sat at home and watched him on TV served a purpose.
Without the public encouraging and applauding his efforts, the sport would serve no purpose.
Athletes need the public just as the public need the athletes.

Now, all this is connected to one's life plan.

Let us return to the area in the 4th that contains a list of all possible life plans.
Before we do that, let us just remind you that as a young human is shown around heaven and is introduced to every possible aspect of life, his guides, teachers and whatever group of angels are supervising his education, take careful note of the subjects to which the student feels drawn, those that he rejects and all this helps form his personality.
So, by the time a person is ready to take charge of his life plan, everyone connected to this young human, who is, we remind you, still in the 4th dimension, has a clear idea of his likes and dislikes.
Eventually, he is taken into this area in the 4th that deals with life plans and he is shown a large selection of possible life plans from which, together with his helpers, the student human will make a choice.

This place, it is true, contains a huge list of possible life plans but it is not a list in any way that you could imagine.
First, we must say that it is part of the akashic record. Although we have said that the akashic record only contains information relevant to life forms, every time a person chose a way through life, going back over many thousands of years, the result of each and every life lived by anyone was stored in the akashic record and certain wise people decided to select many of these life experiences and group them together so that, as life progressed and became more complicated, a sort of list could be consulted to help humans as they progressed through life.
We think that you can easily imagine that when life first started, first as aquatic elements, then as stone creatures, as we have explained in other works, there was no need for life plans as life was so basic, so primitive.
It was not until a really recognisable form of human with family and hierarchical structures started to be created that the concept of any sort of direction to a life began to form.
It was from these early forms of personality structures, all fed into the akashic record, that the concept of life plans were created.
Over vast lengths of time, as life developed and as personalities grew more complex, all of which was stored in the akashic record, angelic beings had the notion of creating a separate area just for life plans.
This has grown over time and now is a recognisable area within the 4th that can be visited and, from the many life plans available for perusal, a young human can select, with help, the life plan most applicable for him.

How can we describe the process of selecting a life plan?
The young human, his guides and helpers attune their vibrational frequency to that area.
There is nothing to see but, stored in the memory of this area, are all possible life plans.
There are advanced angels in that area that are able to link with the personality of the young human and, by consulting the guides and helpers that accompany the student into the life plan area, are able to project into the mind of all concerned a list of all possible life plans that might appeal to the student and his guides and helpers.
This projection is not easy to describe. It is done by placing into the mind of all concerned the concept of the life plans suitable for consideration by all concerned.

So, the young human, his guides and angelic helpers find that they have this large list of possible life plans in their minds and they all combine and discuss which one would be most suitable.

One would think, logically, that student humans would choose to be born into wealthy or royal families.
However, in the akashic records section of the 4th it is possible to take a potential life plan and project where its progression would take it.
In many cases it can be seen that to be born into a rich or royal family would lead the person astray and would not result in the path that the person would like to follow.
It has been said that all power corrupts and absolute power corrupts absolutely.
Naturally, if a psychopathic student is shown such a life plan, he would accept it immediately, but others would reject such a life plan.
After much cogitation, a life plan is selected and it is placed, as a sort of concept, in the higher self of the student.

Now, as we have said, not all people incarnate by any means. We have mentioned those that stay in heaven and study spirituality. We have mentioned true psychopaths that prefer to reside in hell so that they can give vent to their worst desires.
Then there are a large group of what we might call ordinary people who prefer to stay in the 4th because they do not feel drawn to a physical incarnation.
However, there are people who feel attracted to incarnation.

This is your case as it was with us. One of the few requirements in belonging to the Great White Brotherhood is to have had an Earthly incarnation at some time.
Many of our members had an incarnation at a time in Earth's history when life for ordinary people was hard indeed. Such times would be difficult for modern people to imagine and, no doubt, many of them were glad that incarnations in those days were short and so they were released from the brutality of those days quite quickly.
But we are talking about life plans, not the delights or otherwise of incarnations as such.

All people, whether they choose to have an incarnation or not, are given a life plan.
We must always try to remember that all life is one, and in the case of humans, if one person is given a life plan, all must be given a life plan.
It is generally thought that only those undergoing an incarnation on Earth have or need a life plan and those in the spirit world, for some reason, do not have or need a life plan. This is not true.
All people, including those who choose to spend time in hell in order to be able to exploit their tendencies for cruelty and those who follow the holy path, have distinct life plans.
We hope that you can visualise that someone who chooses to go to hell would choose a life plan that would place him in a position where he was able to exploit his tendencies for cruelty and hatred whereas those who follow the holy path would select a life plan that would attract him to noble experiences.
Ordinary people that choose not to have an incarnation would select a life plan not dissimilar to those who do choose an incarnation.
Finally, we consider those humans who do choose to have an incarnation.
Let us try to describe how this works.

As the young human is being shown around heaven, as we said, he may meet with those members of his oversoul group who, at one stage, had an incarnation and have now returned to the 4th.
Discussions would take place with those whose incarnations were long ago as well as those whose incarnations were more recent.
He would meet people that came to Earth as men, women, homosexual or with no gender desire, handicapped and every sort of skin colour in order to understand what life on Earth is like.
Before incarnating, the young human would have very little concept of gender, race, skin colour or what limitations being handicapped gives.
Therefore, it is important that he meets with a variety of people in order to learn from their life experiences - the result of their life plan - because the life plan, in conjunction with personality, pushes the person in a certain direction. The law of mutual attraction ensures that he meets certain people and has certain experiences.
One might imagine that there would be a vast number of life plans that one could select but, as we said earlier, the choice is, in reality, not that large.

The first choice is to consider gender; male, female or homosexual. Most people decide to become either male or female. The number of homosexual people is relatively small despite evil people pushing young incarnates to experiment with gender change.
Next would come skin colour. According to the skin colour options, most would either be born into Eastern or Western countries. Obviously, there are an increasing number of people of immigrant parents, dark skinned, born into European countries but the actual number is still relatively small.
Then there is class. We could say that there are basically three types of people; the poor, sometimes referred to as working class, then white collar, more qualified people, then those who are relatively rich.
After that we must consider education. Some are poorly educated, some receive a better education and a small group who receive higher, university education.

From what we have described above, one can see that the choice of life plans is not unlimited. Far from it.
Depending on the personality of the individual, he would be attracted to a certain lifestyle and thus he would select a certain life plan.
As we mentioned, logic would dictate that a person would choose to be born in a rich family and have an easy ride through life but wealth is no guarantee of pleasure, nor of happiness.
Many rich people are deeply unhappy and have disastrous incarnations.
In any case, when a life plan is being considered, it is possible, to a certain extent, to follow into the future the result of selecting a certain life plan.
This is because life is more complicated than just choosing a life plan.
A life plan, in conjunction with personality which, when gender, race, colour and so on are all added together will create a certain path through life. If one follows that life into the future, it can be seen that this would or would not create the life that the person desires.
So, as all these factors are considered by the person wishing to incarnate, in conjunction with discussions with all his different helpers, a life plan will be decided.

This would include his gender (male, female or other), country of birth, skin colour, type of family, etc. Eventually, one or more families are selected for that person to incarnate into.

As one lady in one of those families becomes pregnant so the young candidate prepares to incarnate into that family.

And so a child is born.

The aims of the incarnation can be many and varied.

It might be to have a selfish, unkind, egotistical life or it might be to have a noble, helpful passage through life, assisting all life as best as possible.

Most just decide to incarnate in order to experience life in physicality. These people are not unkind nor are they noble spirits. They are just ordinary people.

Therefore, we hope that you can see that a life plan is not a stand-alone thing.

It is closely connected to personality, and to a certain extent, is influenced by what soul group one belongs to.

At all times, as the person is going through his incarnation, he is being overshadowed by at least one guide who remains with him at all times and ensures that the person does not stray too far from his life plan which, as we said earlier, is contained in his higher self.

You may remember us telling you that higher self and akashic record are closely connected and are, effectively, the same thing.

Therefore, the life plan, selected from the akashic record, stays with the person throughout his incarnation, and the life plan, plus his personality, plus various other parts, ensures that the incarnation follows the path set out for it before incarnation was chosen.

We will end this chapter here. We have deliberately explained life plans in as great a detail as we can and we hope that you have understood most if not all of it.

CHAPTER 17

THE ABRIDGED AKASHIC RECORD

We have done our best to show you, who are going through your incarnation, the link between a number of aspects: the life plan, higher self, akashic records, personality and so on.

We suspect that many of you, as you move from day to day, from problem to problem, had no idea of the many aspects contained in the 4th that are, in fact, there to assist you if only you could link to them.

Of course, to make the connection with these areas requires that you know that they exist and that the connection from those areas, those forces, are connected to you via your various auras.

There is not one second of your incarnation that you are disconnected from your oversoul. Not one second that your guide is not with you and not one second that your life plan is not available to guide you through your incarnation.

All of the aspects that we have mentioned in this book, and many more, were provided for you to assist you in what you and your guides and helpers knew would be a trying time.

You chose to incarnate in order to be tested. You deliberately chose to incarnate in order to try your strength in a world that would try to drag you down.

It is a sort of tug-of-war with negative forces pulling on one end of the rope and you, on your own, pulling on the other end.

Of course, you on your own cannot overcome the mass of negative forces trying to make life as difficult as they can for you. That is why all the forces from the 4th that we have mentioned - and more - were provided to you, were incarnated with you in your auras. Together, you, plus all the forces from the 4th, if and when you learn how to link with them will overcome the negative forces. They are no match for the power of God which is contained in the forces that are available to you and are waiting patiently in your auras for you to harvest them and use them in your path through life.

All this was explained to you before you incarnated and they are still available to you. As we have explained in other works, when you incarnate, you are largely connected to physicality and all the advice given to you is put into your higher self which is also connected to the akashic record.

Now, many people scratch their heads and wonder why they are on Earth having an incarnation. They can see no point in it and wish that they had never been born.

Even when they are told that God's forces are available to assist them, they see no difference in their lives.

They seem to spend their entire lives in a state of battling with problem after problem and it never seems to improve.

There might be moments of relative calm but that calm seems to be the calm before the storm, and soon afterwards, another series of problems turn up, as you knew they would.

We are sure that you who are reading these words know exactly what we are talking about and we who give you these words know from first-hand experience what we are talking about as we all had incarnations at one time or another.

As we have mentioned elsewhere, life today compared to life long ago is fairly civilized. Some of our group who went through an incarnation long ago, recount tales of their incarnations that were horrible beyond imagination.
Long ago, there was no limit to the brutality inflicted on people but, thankfully, as the pendulum of life swings into positive so life is slowly improving.
However, things are not yet perfect and most people in incarnation could do with all the help they can get. Fortunately, that help is available to them and is contained in their file in the akashic record.
If and when that help can be located, it can be retrieved from the akashic record, passed through auras into the higher self and then moved through the imagination plane into the mind and finally the brain, at which point you (the ID) can analyse that information and incorporate into your personality and either take action to link it to you or not. The choice is yours.

At the beginning of this book, we said that we would teach you how to link with these forces and how to incorporate them into your lives in order to make you the positive force you should be. The actual technique is so simple that it will only take a few lines to explain but we will reserve this information until the end of this book.
The aims and objectives of this volume is to explain to you the how and the why of these forces, why and where they exist and we want to continue to explain the actual reasons as to why they exist.
There are many texts going back over thousands of years that mention how to connect with these forces and there have been noble souls such as Jesus and Buddha that explained the technique for drawing these forces into your life. Unfortunately, many of these texts explained their objectives in such a manner as to confuse people rather than help. This is often because, over the years, the actual teachings of the sages have been distorted through mistranslations or by deliberately distorting the original teachings to keep people from discovering the simple truth about linking to the spiritual forces.

We will explain the technique for drawing the forces from the 4th and incorporating them into your lives but our aim is to do much more than this. We wish you all to have an in-depth knowledge of what is going on so that you can become experts on the how and the why of the way life, both physical and spiritual, works.
So far, we have given you 7 books. This one is the 8th.
We have also answered many of your questions on a variety of topics and will continue to do so.
We do not wish to appear to make ourselves seem more important than we are but we can honestly say that the information that we have given you, if collected together, is more than has ever been revealed to the public before.
We will also say that we will not stop until we have explained to you - the public - all that we know about life.
It is our aim that, eventually, what we tell you will be considered to be the greatest compendium of spiritual and physical life and will be considered to be the go-to information to explain life in simple and truthful words.

There are countless tomes published that claim to explain aspects of life. Some are close to the truth and some are just works of fiction.

No one incarnate, unless he has access to knowledgeable people in the spirit realms, can gain access to true information.

It is not possible for anyone in incarnation to understand the complexities of creation.

We are fortunate in that, not only do we have access to knowledgeable humans who are part of our group, but as a decision was taken by high angels that the public should be made aware of as much truth as it is possible to explain, very wise angelic beings kindly answer any questions that we may ask and so we can present information to you that no other group can.

We do not wish this to sound arrogant. We accept this heavy load of explaining complex truths to you and have put in place a chain of people in the desire to transmit all these facts about life to you.

Others, incarnate and discarnate are being trained in telepathy and the various psychic skills to bridge the gap between our world and yours, to ensure that no matter what happens the flow of information will continue in an unbroken chain until our goal is achieved.

So, we present this priceless information to you and leave you to accept or reject the information.

Having said all that, let us find another area in the 4th to describe to you.

We wish to describe an area, a landscape, that permits someone to link with his personal file, not in the akashic records that we have already talked about, but a file in the imagination plane that enables information from the akashic record and the higher self to be accepted and transmitted onwards without distortion.

Once again, this is not going to be easy to explain and it is an area that we have studiously avoided mentioning so far because we wanted to keep the chain of information from one aspect to another simple and logical.

In other works, we said that information was transmitted from the higher self into the imagination plane, into the mind and, finally, into the brain.

This is true for a lot of information.

However, everything concerning your life plan, your personality and so on is so important for you, that a special area is set up in the 4th that links directly to your imagination plane and allows you, if you are willing to open your mind somewhat, access to your life plan and its associated components.

You may ask why this should be and how it really functions?

That will be the subject of this chapter.

As you know, life in incarnation is complicated. You are expected at almost every moment of the day to make decisions over problems presented to you.

It matters not at all where you live, what sex you are, your age, your status - rich or poor.

All the time life sends you problems and you are expected to find an answer to each and every question.

We have already told you that the answers to any question, any problem are already provided in your higher self and, if and when you have a problem, it suffices to reach into your higher self and bring forth the solution.

Let us try to explain how this works.

It does not seem logical that life is sending you problems, but that the answer is already available. But it is so.

The way this works is as follows. We will explain but you will find that it takes a stretch of imagination to accept it.

The truth of the matter is that, as time does not really exist, the past, the present and the future are all just one moment. It is all part of the singularity that life is.

So, believe it or not, a million years in the past or a million years into the future are happening now. The million years in the past is all part of the now moment as is a million years in the future. They are all part of the now moment.

We have mentioned frames of time rather like a cine film photographing a scene in a film.

This is so, and each frame is stored in the akashic record.

However, the time has come to explain another facet of life that, so far, we have not mentioned.

As far as we know, very few have discussed this topic, so please be prepared to have your understanding concerning how life works to be jolted somewhat as we present a new paradigm.

When we explained about the frames of life, we mentioned not only was each frame stored in the akashic record but we also said that between each frame, life was destroyed. So, between any two frames of existence, there was a void and life started again.

What we did not tell you was that each time life started again, each new frame was, in fact, a totally new beginning of life.

Not a continuation from the previous frame, as it seems to be, but a brand-new creation of everything. It is the fact that the new frame seems to be so similar to the last one and the one before that, that gives the impression of continuity, rather like the frames in a cine camera filming a scene from a movie.

But, in fact, each frame is a totally new life creation. Life stops between any two frames; the previous frame is recorded for posterity and then life is recreated from scratch all over again.

What this means is that all we have explained to you in the books that we have given you, explaining life before the so-called big bang, through the creation of life by God and his archangels in a kindergarten and from the moment of the so-called big bang to the present, is all created in a microsecond of time as you know it.

This is possible because time does not exist. There is only sequence of events - one thing following after another.

Now, we don't know if you have managed to understand this extraordinary sequence of events, so we will explain again and then we will link it to the subject of this chapter which is about you being able to control your incarnation.

We need you to be able to understand this part before we move on to explain the next part.

So, let us start again.

Life is a series of snapshots created and recorded. Billions of times a second, life is created and destroyed, created and destroyed.

You, as you read this, have the impression that you are going through your incarnation as one smooth act. But, in fact, life resembles a cine film, single frame after single frame being joined together to create a roll of cine film.

Life is like that but there is one fundamental difference. In real life, the one you are living, between any two frames, life is completely destroyed and the whole of creation from the very beginning up till now is recreated in each frame.

Although you have the impression that your life follows on as one smooth passage through existence, in fact you are being destroyed, re-chosen from the 8th, moving to the 7th, then to the 4th, choosing an incarnation on Earth and being here reading this book. This may seem impossible, but it is so.

A total, fresh, new creation is constructed from zero, through what history considers to be billions of years up to now, in a flash - a very small space of actual time as measured on Earth.

We will not give the exact moment in Earth time that these events occur as this information could be used by evil people to create weapons.

Suffice to say that the length of each snapshot is very short indeed before it ceases, is stored in the memory of the akashic record and life finishes and restarts.

The implications of this are many and important.

First, we mentioned that when humans were required, archangels reached into the bank of singularities in the 8th and selected, at random, the number of required singularities and gave those singularities a logos that told them that they were going to be human.

But we just said that, each microsecond, life was annihilated and recreated from scratch. This would imply that archangels would reach into the bank of singularities and select, at random, any point of life and give it a human logos. If this is the case, and it is being done billions of times a second, how is it that the archangels do not put a logos on you that sometimes is human, sometimes vegetable, sometimes animal and sometimes mineral?

How is it that you are not selected to be a grain of sand or a raindrop?

The answer is that humans are constantly needed to replace those joining with God so there are always humans being chosen.

It is true that singularities are selected at random, but each time life is created, that human logos links with you because you were chosen to be who you are.

So, the logos is created as a human and destroyed billions of times a second but you, and all other humans, are a force that continues endlessly.

This is very difficult to explain and very difficult to understand, so if we may, we will expand on this concept.

But before we do that, we need to state something else that has seldom been mentioned. As life is created and destroyed countless times a second, the life that is created is virtually a copy of the previous life.

There is only one life picture and it is created and destroyed, created and destroyed but each creation is a carbon copy of the previous creation.

One way of imagining this is to visualise a printing press, printing endless postcards for instance. Each postcard would be an exact copy of all the previous ones.

This printing press, to continue with the analogy, has been printing these postcards since the beginning of when God first had the idea of creating life countless eons ago and will continue printing these postcards for countless eons of time into the future.
Each postcard represents a frame of space-time so the printing press would be capable of printing these postcards billions of times a second.
What would the picture on the postcard look like?
It would be blank. There would be nothing printed on the postcards because there is nothing in creation.
Before you chuck this book away thinking that it is created by lunatics, bear with us and give us a chance to explain.

We repeat, life is created and destroyed then recreated but each creation is a blank sheet. There is no creation, yet there obviously is!
So, we need to explain this conundrum because you exist and are surrounded by creation of all sorts.
You exist, your family exists, your friends, your abode exists. There are shops, cars, airplanes, countless people, countless countries and a mass of fauna and flora, etc.
So, if nothing exists, where does all this come from?

Although life is created and destroyed billions of times a second, there are some things that cannot be destroyed because these things are what create the whole system.
They are outside of all this and organize the creation and destruction process.
We call this force God. For those who have difficulty with the word God, it is sometimes called 'the all that is'.
Whatever term you wish to use for this creative force, please believe us when we say that this force exists.
Now, this force creates, in conjunction with a group of archangels, this group of blank life frames being created and destroyed billions of times a second.

Now, this is where we come to you.
God and his archangels decided to create conscious beings of all sorts; animal, vegetable, mineral and human, in order not only to clothe this blank postcard but to create experiences so that God could have an interesting life and learn from the experiences of the created life.
So, he created from himself all that exists as points of consciousness. That is all that exists. God pretending to be all that exists whether it be animal, vegetable, mineral or human.
He created only one life force but endowed each point of life with the logos to be either animal, vegetable, mineral or human by giving each and every point of life, each singularity - not only a logos that informs each singularity what it is going to be - but also endows each singularity with consciousness. That gives it the impression that it is what it was selected to be, but also endowed it with personality which gives each singularity the sense that is it is a unique 'something'.
In the case of humans, it is the personality that gives you a sense of who you are.
Personality creates the ID, the person who looks back at you in the mirror.
Further, it creates a place in your makeup that is termed the imagination plane.

Now, the imagination plane serves many purposes, some of which we have explained in various books.

But we wish to return to the subject of this chapter.

We hope that you have read and understood what we previously said to you concerning the fact that nothing exists, because we have reached the point where we need to construct into that blank postcard (frame of life, which is all that exists) the world you live in.

We will just repeat before we explain more that each frame, each postcard if you will, is not only blank but it is the same bank picture repeated endlessly. There is only one.

But there is one for all life.

Therefore, you live in a world where, billions of times a second, blank frames of life are being created exclusively for you.

The person next to you has his blank frames created exclusively for him and on and on around the world and throughout time.

It is the same picture created over and over again exclusively for you - the same blank, timeless, space-less moment, endlessly repeated since the beginning of creation and going on until the end of creation - that flashes into your consciousness.

This means, strange as it seems, that you have always existed and always will because you live actually in a single frame of existence which only lasts a microsecond.

But you have consciousness and personality and it is these two things, augmented by DNA and a number of other aspects that enable you to imagine the life you lead from your creation in the 8th dimension eons ago in Earth time until you finally merge with the Godhead.

It has been noted that, perhaps, in our last statements we did not make abundantly clear what we stated, so with your permission we will reiterate in different terms what we said.

Our intention was to explain that there are, in considering this aspect of creation, basically two parts to it.

The first is the part that was constructed by archangels long ago in order to create the concept of life progressing for all things.

Each and every living object, and most things are alive whether they be animal, vegetable, mineral or human, has attached to it a sort of singularity that we described as postcards.

The point that needs to be made is that there is not just one for all living things. It is the opposite.

Every living thing has, if we may use this postcard analogy, its own printing press churning out these blank pictures (please excuse the contradiction in terms).

So, every animal, every vegetable, every mineral and every human ever since life was created on Earth has its own unique printing press, if we may thus describe it, churning out billions of blank postcards per second. These postcards are, of course, the individual frames of space-time.

We will repeat in order to make this abundantly clear.

Everything has connected to it a mechanism that is creating countless frames of space-time, billions a second but the point to retain is that it is being done for all things individually.

You have this mechanism that creates billions of frames of space-time (that we referred to as postcards) exclusively for you.

Each and every person also has a unique mechanism churning out frames of space-time, totally unique to him or her. Every animal, every plant, every grain of sand or drop of water also has the same thing going on.

If you could calculate the number of lifeforms - animal, vegetable, mineral or human that exist - there would be a mechanism for creating a unique series of frames of space-time for each and every one of these objects as if each object, no matter what it is, has a code attached to it that links it to its printing press and it is churning out blank postcards exclusively for that object.

This has been going on since the dawn of creation and will continue endlessly into the future.

We repeat also that life is created, totally destroyed and recreated billions of times a second and further, the new creation does not start where the old one left off. It starts from the very first moment when God had the idea of creating life and follows the progression through until this moment.

All this, which would appear to have taken countless trillions of years, can happen in a flash because time as you know it does not exist - it is part of the illusion of 3D incarnation. If time does not exist, a microsecond or a million years are the same.

But we repeat. Each and every object, no matter what it is, if it has the life force attached to it, it has this mechanism that creates frames of space-time exclusively for that person or life form.

It is not one system for all things. All things have their own system exclusive to them.

That was the first part of the story.

We wish to say that although these moments of space-time, these blank postcards as we called them, are created by archangelic forces and thus, in a way, are connected to the God force, they can and are being destroyed billions of times a second before the totality of life is recreated.

So, they are not entirely representative of God which cannot be destroyed.

However, we move on to part two.

This involves talking about living objects which include animals, vegetables, minerals and humans.

As we have already stated, God (in his infinite wisdom) decided to create all these objects and put the totality of his life force in association with each and every object.

Anything created by God cannot be destroyed and so, despite life being destroyed and recreated billions of times a second, any life force created by God remains intact as it is created from the God force and therefore cannot be destroyed.

It is outside of and remote from the creation/destruction cycles.

What do we mean by 'anything created by God'?

This would start with every atom. There is the totality of the God force at the heart of every atom.

Atoms combine to create all that exists and that includes what is called dark energy as well as the atoms with which you are familiar.

So, everything that you see around you is created by atoms. Atoms are alive as they contain the God force, so everything you see is alive.

They cannot be destroyed because the God force cannot be harmed.

Let us return to you, if we may, and the fact that there is a mechanism that is constructing your individual moments of space-time as we said and as we likened to blank postcards. These blank postcards which, we remind you once again, contain all the myriad of events that have occurred since creation first happened up till this moment, need to be clothed, if we may use that word, by information that is not available to the creation of the actual postcards, the fleeting microseconds of space-time.

The picture is created by you.

You have the unique ability to paint a picture in each blank postcard because God gave you all of his power and you are in fact God. God in the form of you.

Other people, animals, plants and minerals also contain the God force exclusively and individually in them.

We need you to understand this vital point.

You exist because you are God. God made you in his image. Not a part of God but the totality of God.

All that constitutes you is because you are all that constitutes God.

God is such a marvelous entity that he can transform himself into you even though you may not realise this and even though many religions try to deny this fact and term it blasphemy. It is not blasphemy. It is a fact that you are God in the form of you.

We will go on and repeat what we have said before.

Not only is God capable of transforming himself into you but he is capable of transforming himself into every man, woman and child that has ever lived, is living or will live. Also, he is capable of transforming himself into every animal, every plant, every mineral, every drop of water and everything that exists.

This is a wonderful thing to contemplate and should be carefully considered.

When you look at yourself in a mirror, you are looking at God who has transformed himself into you because he wanted to give you eternal life.

He also did this with every object that surrounds you. Everything is God who has transformed himself into all that surrounds you no matter what it might be.

If you can realise this, we ask you to consider the implications. Everything surrounding you, no matter what it is, is God transformed into that object.

Further, as it is God, whatever you are considering, not only is it God but as you also are God, you are it, whatever it is and it is you.

So, if you harm something, not only are you harming God but you are harming yourself. Think about this. Jesus mentioned that we all were God and he also mentioned that to harm something is to harm oneself.

We also wish you to understand that each and every moment of space-time, each blank postcard has a picture painted onto it by you, but each blank postcard is exclusively yours. No other person, animal, vegetable or mineral has the same blank postcards as you. They all have their own blank postcards exclusive to them and they all fill each blank postcard with their own images created by them, no matter what they are: animal, vegetable, mineral or human.

Each and every object has its own series of blank postcards and each and every object creates its own images with which to paint or clothe each postcard and the thing that paints the images, animal, vegetable, mineral or human, is God. God being exclusively that 'thing' no matter what it is.

Therefore, if we can go back to considering you, you are all that exists. You live alone as God, creating endless images on postcards or microseconds of space-time that are created exclusively for you and nothing else exists outside of what you create through your imagination.

You may remember that this chapter is to describe a place in the 4th that deals with you linking that place to your imagination plane in order to be able to clothe or paint images onto the countless blank postcards created exclusively for you.
So far, in this chapter, we seem to have explained many things – well, two really - the blank postcards which are created and destroyed billions of times a second and you who is God and are thus capable of creating images with which to clothe each blank postcard or each moment of space-time depending on how you wish to imagine these moments.
But we have not really talked about the subject of this chapter which is the place in the 4th that brings these two aspects together.
We felt that we needed to do this, to present this information, because, although we have mentioned it before, we wanted to make sure that you understood the creation of life and so we have done our best to clarify these two points:
1. The blank postcards or microseconds of space-time that are created exclusively for you, and
2. The fact that you are the eternal God and you are God taking your form (human) and having your experiences.
So, we will consider just you because this chapter is about you and how you create the life you are having.

The basis of the existence of God is something we call consciousness.
This word, consciousness, despite being an ordinary, everyday sort of word, is difficult to describe. It has different meanings depending on how it is used and is actually, in the way we mean it, the creative force that enables you to be God having an existence that you call 'your life'.
Now, if someone hits you on the head, it is said that you lose consciousness. What does that mean?
We do not wish to get involved with medical terminology but to lose consciousness implies that, for a certain time, you are not aware of life carrying on as normal.
This may last for a few seconds or for quite a long time but the point is that while you are unconscious you are not aware of life evolving around you.
There is a blank, so to say.
So, we could say that to be conscious is to be aware that life exists and you are part of it and create or observe life as it unfolds.
If you can accept that simple statement it means that consciousness equates to awareness.
To be aware implies that life is going on, and in many various ways, involves you.
To be conscious implies that you are aware of life and either are part of creating events or are the victim of events created by others. When we say victim, we do not necessarily mean something unpleasant, although it often is in incarnation. We mean that you are affected by events created by someone or something else.

So, let us return to the heart of the subject.

You must be aware that, in fact, you live alone as God in a blank world in which nothing exists except the fact that 'you are'.

You are all that exists and you exist as a point of consciousness and that point of consciousness is God.

However, God has given you imagination and it is thanks to that imagination that you are able to create all that you see and all that you experience.

But you do it on your own as, in reality, nothing else and no one else exists except this point of consciousness that you think is you and is, in fact, God.

Obviously, the reality is more complicated than that and we have explained how, despite you being the only life form that exists in your reality, you can react and interrelate with other life forms in their realities.

But for the purposes of this chapter we do not wish to get lost in a maze of complexities about life.

We repeat, you are a point of consciousness and you are the only thing that exists in your world.

But you have imagination and it is thanks to that imagination that you are able to clothe your blank postcards, your microseconds of space-time, to create what you call your reality.

As you should know, each postcard, each microsecond of space-time, is stored in your personal file in the akashic record and can be perused in order to create memory and also, the last few postcards can be observed in order for you to create a continuity of what you decide to create in order to give a smooth progression to your life which is being created for you with the help of your life plan.

At long last, let us turn to the place in the 4th that concerns the subject of this chapter. Because, in your file in the akashic record, there is every aspect of all of your life which, we remind you, goes back to the moment that God first put his spark of life into you in the nursery planet that we spoke about in a previous book and which is also contained in the information stored in every postcard, every microsecond of space-time since you were first created. To constantly re-examine all this information each time you wish to remember something or every time you wished to link the last few frames or postcards to your 'now' moment in order to create a smooth transition from one microsecond to the next, would create impossible complications.

So, in the 4th has been created a special file from your existence that contains only a relatively few frames or postcards. Further, this place only contains relatively recent events thus bypassing all the events covering, effectively, trillions of years so that you can directly link to recent events, recent memories.

This information, stored in your file in the 4th, is linked to your imagination plane and thus, if you wish to remember something or wish to link with day-to-day events occurring in your life, it suffices to link with this abridged version of the akashic record contained in this area and just the events concerned with your immediate past are instantly fed into your imagination, passed to your mind and to your brain and you have at your disposal just the memories that are significant to you as you pass from 'now' moment to 'now' moment - which, in fact, is always the same 'now' moment.

So, we hope that you can understand what is going on.

You exist as a point of consciousness that is called God or 'the all that is' and that Jesus referred to as 'I am'.

You are all that actually exists in your reality but can be linked to other people, animals, minerals, etc., as required in order for you to create your reality.

Next, the world you live in, and all other life form's worlds, are created and destroyed in microseconds and each new creation, or postcards as we called them, are actually blank.

But from the akashic record, it instantly contains all of your creation from the moment of your creation long ago up till now.

However, in order to make life easier to live, there is a file in the 4th that contains a shortened version of your personal file, only containing the events and memories that concern your recent past (possibly from the moment when you as a baby could first remember things) and that file is linked to your imagination plane and allows you to relate to life in a simpler fashion.

Although this file in the 4th containing only recent events applicable to you is reserved exclusively to you, you should understand that each and every person has the same thing available for him as he has his own version of the 4th dimension and his own file containing his recent past events.

This is also applicable to animals, vegetables and minerals. They all have the same dimensions that you have and thus, in their 4th dimension, they have the same memory file that is exclusively applicable to them, individually.

We wish to say that this memory file in the 4th is separate from the true memory file in the true akashic records relevant to you. Your true experiences are stored forever in every frame, in every postcard of the akashic record but the latest bit is copied and placed in your file in the 4th.

This implies that it is separate from the true akashic record and is constantly being updated from microsecond to microsecond but it will not endure eternally as your memories in the true akashic record will. It is a sort of temporary file.

That really is all that we need to say about this file in the 4th.

So, we will repeat, there is, in the 4th, a place that contains the latest part of your experiences and memories. It is a shortened part of the akashic record and is put there so that you can locate a simplified version of your personal akashic record file. It may be considered to be a sort of temporary file in computer terms. As you are the only person that exists in your reality it concerns only you.

But, of course, all other things exist in their reality and thus have the same temporary file in their reality, totally separate from yours.

Information from this file is passed directly to your imagination plane and from there it is passed to your mind and brain and you create your next frame of space-time, your next postcard as a smooth transition from the last, the last coming from your file in the akashic record and the latest one, the 'now' frame, being created by you in conjunction with your life plan.

We do appreciate that this was a very difficult chapter to comprehend and we don't expect all to follow it.

But we have told you about this memory file, how it works and why it is necessary.

The information concerning how the 'now' moment can link to the past, present and future we will reserve for another day.

So, we will end this chapter here and turn to yet another topic of moment and pith.

CHAPTER 18

THE SPIRIT LINK

We think that you will so far agree that in this book, which is the 8th in this series, we have given you quite a lot of information, some of it we have talked about before and some of it is new, not only to you but to all people.

We intend to go on as far as we can in describing areas in the 4th that relate to you, many of which, if you incorporate into your lives in incarnation, will help to smooth your path.

We wish at this point to turn our attention to an area which will also be new.

There is an area in the 4th that relates to the difficulties of connecting to the spirit world because it has always been the intention of God's archangels that life in incarnation and life in the 4th should, effectively, be connected as if they were one life.

It is unfortunate that people choosing an incarnation seem to be cut off from the 4th although, as we mentioned in the previous chapters, you are always connected to your oversoul group, your personal guide and to your life plan but your life plan, although decided upon while you were in the 4th before incarnating, you carry with you through your incarnation.

So, quite apart from all the aspects we mentioned in all the previous chapters, we think you would agree that it would be beneficial if you could have a permanent connection to your oversoul and also a direct relation with the guides that, at the moment, are obliged to help you behind the scenes, so to speak.

There are a number of reasons why, when you incarnate, you feel cut off from the 4th dimension.

We have already stated in this book and in others that your life plan is tucked away in your higher self, as are the memories of the time that you spent in the spirit world before incarnating.

Many people imagine that the reason for this is because, and we quote to a certain extent, 'life is a school and to be told the results of the examinations would negate the object of the school lessons'.

This is, of course, not correct.

Although life in incarnation is an education, there is no examination at the end of it.

There is no group of people preparing questions for you to answer and, above all, there is no concept of pass or fail as there would be in a traditional school environment.

Despite what we said in the last chapter about creation being destroyed and recreated billions of times a second, which was true, the aim of life is to progress spiritually and smoothly from the starting point, at which you were barely conscious, to its conclusion, which is to reveal the fact that you are God himself.

Speaking of the statement that we revealed to you that you were God, we have no doubt that some of you accepted that statement as a working hypothesis and some of you rejected it for a variety of reasons.

Whether you could accept or you rejected our declaration that you are God, may we ask how many of you truly feel that you are God?

There might be a few that suffer from delusional problems that might state that they are God but, apart from those few who might have mental problems, how many of you can honestly say that they feel that they are God?

We suspect that the answer is zero!

Even we in the spirit world, including our friends and colleagues that have been in spirit for a long time, recognise that they are a long way from revealing, by their actions, that they are God.

Indeed, the closer one approaches the throne of God, it seems the more that one appreciates the distance yet to travel.

And yet, the path to God is not one of movement.

It is simply the degree that one can remove one's ego.

In other words, the barrier that separates us from the God that we really are is the very sense of personal identity that God instilled in us at the very beginning of our creation.

So, this seems to be a very strange conundrum as is so often the case with life. We have two forces apparently opposing each other - or rather it is the same one force in this case, God - acting in opposing fashions.

On the one hand we have the wonderful, perfect love power that is God, and on the other, we have the same God force that creates life (whatever life can be considered to be) as a somewhat primitive force sent out to struggle its way back to its creator. And all this, apparently, is so that God can benefit from the experiences of his creations.

As we have said before, it all seems a bit pointless and countless people throughout the world and over the millennia would agree.

But, is it pointless?

If God is as wonderful as he seems, then surely, he would not make such a complicated thing as life just in order to gain pleasure from watching us all struggle through life.

So, perhaps we are missing something. Perhaps there is some element of life that we have overlooked or that, for some reason we are not aware of.

We would not imagine God to be a psychopath, despite the manner he is portrayed in the Old Testament of the Bible and in various other religious texts, nor as he is preached from the pulpits of certain churches, nor yet as imagined by some followers of these religions.

We might well imagine that some followers of these religions might, themselves, be psychopaths and we might imagine that the writers of these texts and a certain number of preachers might have been or are psychopaths, but it seems to us from our individual and collective experience that God is the very essence of love.

We use the word love in the diametrically opposed sense to the meaning of the word psychopath.

Indeed, we give a far deeper meaning to the word love than can possibly be expressed using words.

We take its meaning on until we connect it with the sense of total unity. All things coming together to create oneness.

We do appreciate that what we said does not seem to imply love very much, but we want you to reach out with your mind and try to imagine what it would be like if you could incorporate each and every element of life; animal, vegetable, mineral or human into your own life, until there was not one iota of difference in your mind or in your heart between the smallest atom of sand and you, yourself.

If you could really feel the life, the vitality, the beauty of everything in the depths of your heart, of your very soul, that is the meaning we give to the word love.

A far cry indeed from the tyrannical person that God is often portrayed to be.

Now, we said that the object of this chapter is to describe to you the area in the 4th that relates to the difficulties in connecting your life in incarnation to life in the spirit world.

Please notice that we did not say that this area deals with creating that link.

So, just what is the purpose of this area and what does it actually deal with?

This, surprisingly, is going to be somewhat difficult to describe, so explanation of its various functions might be rather long-winded, if you are familiar with that rather old-fashioned term.

Let us start at the beginning and take whatever time required in order fully to describe this place and how it relates to you in incarnation.

Further, let us explain what is needed in order to be able to have a permanent link to the spirit world for those who desire to have such a link.

We must also consider what would be the advantages, if any, of creating (opening) such a link and also discuss any possible disadvantages of having this link installed.

We must go back, for a few lines, to talk about your life in the spirit world before you chose to incarnate. From that we could consider if any of that information would be beneficial for you to know.

Please bear in mind that this area in the 4th that is the subject of this chapter has been created with the intention of providing a link between the spirit world and the world of incarnation.

If you have studied our previous teachings in this book and others, you will be aware that there is a plethora of diverse areas in the spirit world and we are not at all sure that complete knowledge of all of them would be necessary while you are in incarnation.

We will also mention that there are huge numbers of people in the spirit world - those who have not incarnated and those who have returned after an incarnation - that have very little knowledge of the huge number of areas in the spirit world that could be learnt about.

Indeed, if you have read our books, watched the videos and read the lessons that we made available to you, you probably have more knowledge than the average person in the spirit world.

Most people stay in their own small world and do not bother with the wider issues we make available to you.

Life in spirit, due to the happiness, beauty and peace, tends to act as distractions, especially as time does not exist. There is no night-time in Summerland, which is where most people live, and so life continues as one joyous day. Unless someone specifically requests to be educated about any subject, they live a peaceful, untroubled life, never being hungry, thirsty, fatigued or ill and there is no incentive to look further, mentally, then the moment of joy that they are in.

So, we can understand that they do not disturb their peaceful lives by investigating the things we explain to you.

We tell you that in order to make you aware that, for huge numbers of people, they have no idea of the things we talk about and also to make you aware that to be able to link with such people or to link with areas of ignorance would bring you no benefit.
So, the question is what is the purpose of this area in the 4th?

As we started to tell you, before getting sidetracked somewhat, quite a lot happened to you from the moment you were created as a point of life - a singularity - in the kindergarten or nursery planet before being transferred to the 8th dimension of our planet, then being selected to become a human, moving to the 7th, then to the 4th, at which point you joined your oversoul and your life in a meaningful sense really started.
So, to you in incarnation, would any of all that information be beneficial to you in incarnation? Only you can answer that question and we will not try to answer in your place.
However, from the moment that you joined your oversoul and were assigned a personal guide, once you joined the 4th, things get more interesting.
As we have told you - and if you are a bit lost, we refer you to previous chapters of this book and other works - you are shown around many of the areas of the 4th.
You took the decision to have an Earthly incarnation so, once again, we leave you to consider whether or not such information, if you were aware of it in your incarnation, would be beneficial to you during your incarnation or not.
After all, if you have studied the information we give you, you already know more or less what you would know if this area in the 4th helped you to obtain it.
So, have you found this information helpful in living in incarnation? Only you can answer this question.

We suppose that the answer depends on the type of person you are. You who read our books are not typical of the general population of Earth. You, who study the information we give you are what we call awake as opposed to the general population who tend to be asleep. We refer to those who go to work, come home, watch TV and drink either coffee, tea or a few beers.
We do not criticize these people but we could not say that they are awake in the sense we refer to. We refer to people like yourselves, who have curiosity and take the trouble to ingest the mass of very difficult to understand information we give you.
We consider that to be awake.
So, if you had been born with this information already placed in your mind, would it help you to battle through your incarnation or not?
As we said, only you can answer that question and we would not presume to answer the question for you.

As you know, the mass of knowledge available to you to investigate and study before incarnating is virtually endless.
Once again, it depends on what sort of person you are as to the amount of knowledge you seek before incarnating.
Some seek very little and some seek vast amounts of information.
It is the same in incarnation. Some seek very little knowledge and some seek a vast amount.

We will also point out that information does not necessarily have any connection to spirituality, either in the spirit world or in incarnation.

Even among those who avidly seek knowledge, not all of it is connected to spirituality by any means.

So, if you were to have knowledge from the 4th placed in an active part of your memory, what would you wish to know?

Would it satisfy you to learn about the spiritual aspects, the sort of things we talk to you about or would you wish to learn advanced knowledge about any subject that interests you and to which you might feel drawn as a career path?

Would it satisfy you just to know what your life plan is?

Would it help if you could speak to your guide(s)?

Does your guide have any advanced knowledge that he would be willing to share with you?

If you wish to know, we who are in the spirit world are in daily correspondence with our Earthly scribe who writes these books, etc., that we give you.

Although our connection is close and we can communicate telepathically with him as easily as you might communicate with a friend using a telephone, we almost never advise him as to what path he should take through life and he has learnt never to ask us.

Therefore, in your case, being able to talk with your guide would advance you little.

You are here to live and learn through the decisions you take each day and your guide will not interfere with your decisions.

You may consider your life plan as a sort of school and your oversoul as your house within that school. Your guide acts as a sort of house master, not a teacher. The guide's role is to keep a watchful eye on you to prevent you straying from the path the life plan has mapped for you.

The teacher is life itself. It is from the problems presented to you and the decisions you take to resolve those problems that are your teacher.

So, out of all that, your life plan, your oversoul, your guide, what amongst all that would help you sail through life?

Indeed, if you knew all of your life plan in advance and you knew what problems, what tests, what trials and tribulations life held in store for you as you progress through your incarnation, how many of you would have the strength to carry on and see your life to its end?

It would take a person of exceptional courage and fortitude that would have the moral strength to know of the trials awaiting him and not be concerned by them.

It is only when we look back at the tests we had and that are now behind us that they become bearable.

Knowledge of the future, especially in incarnation, can be a scary thing.

If we can quote from the life of Jesus as reported in the Bible.

Apparently, he was aware of the fate that awaited him and all the suffering that was coming towards him. Even Jesus was frightened of this but had the strength of character to face his fate without trying to escape from it. It is claimed that he mentioned that, if it was God's will, he would drain the bitter cup to the last drop.

Now, we are not saying that this is literally what happened to Jesus but we are suggesting that an advanced soul can be made aware of his future and even advanced souls can dread the future.

So, to repeat, to have knowledge of what the future holds in incarnation is not always a good idea.

To return to this plane in the 4th that deals with associating the spiritual or non-physical aspects of life to a person incarnate, what does it deal with and what purpose does it serve?
The fact of the matter is that we seem to have three stages in our real lives.
1. Life in the spirit realms from the moment of conception to the moment, in your case and ours, a decision was taken to have an incarnation.
2. The actual incarnation.
3. The endless life in the spirit world after our incarnation.

If we think about this, we have, roughly, three stages in our incarnation.
1. The, hopefully, carefree life before school starts.
2. The years we spend at school.
3. The rest of our adult life.
So, life in incarnation follows approximately life in the real world.

But, as we said at the beginning of this chapter, it was hoped that life would continue as one smooth path from the moment of our creation by God's archangels in the kindergarten planet long ago, until the moment we blend back to the point we came from, which is God.
But, as you should know if you have followed all of our various teachings, a decision was taken, for those deciding to have an incarnation, to remove the spiritual or non-physical aspects from our awareness in order for incarnation to be a school-like experience to enable us to create aspects of our personality by interacting with people of good, bad or indifferent personalities and to allow our life plan to unfold without too much interference from the spirit aspect.
As we also said, the real information is tucked away in our higher self but access to the higher self is reserved for those who take the trouble to realise that it exists and who also take the trouble to gain access to it.

So, at the moment, we have this sort of barrier put up between us in incarnation who are totally involved with daily life and the higher self. Access to the higher self can only be obtained through meditation, etc.
Even then, this access is not automatic or unlimited.
Access to a higher self and the information it contains is a hard-won battle and we have explained earlier why it is not a good idea to have full, unlimited access to information coming from the non-physical planes.

You must realise at this point two things.
1. It is not actually the higher self that contains the information. It is contained in the akashic records. This information can be passed to the higher self but it has, first, to pass from the akashic record to this plane we are trying to explain to you and then it passes from this plane into the higher self and from there it can be transferred into your mind.

2. Access to all the information about you, your life in the non-physical planes and what
   your life plan has in store for you could be a very frightening thing. So, don't be in too
   much of a hurry to look into your future.

We still haven't answered the purpose of this plane that can act as a link, actually, about
your life as stored in the akashic record and that which could be passed into your
cognizance via the higher self.
When the whole of creation was manufactured by God's archangels under the directions
of God, the archangels projected their thoughts long into the future and created, in
principle, everything that would be needed to make life work from the dawns of time up
until all life was more or less perfect.
So, this area was created as a potential for the future when man, once he chose an
incarnation, would have the strength of character to know about the difficulties he might
have to face but would be able to accept these difficulties without them disturbing him.

We think it's fair to say that, at the moment, if you who are reading this book knew that
some difficulty was coming your way, you would have at least two reactions.
1. You would feel scared, and
2. You would take whatever steps you could to eliminate the problem.

How many of you, if you knew that a serious problem was coming towards you and that
your life plan had decreed that it was something that you needed to go through in order to
temper your soul, could face that difficulty calmly and not let it worry you?
Very few of you - or us - we would suggest, could just let some horrible experience
approach that we knew we had to go through without affecting us somewhat.
Even Jesus, in the analogy that we mentioned earlier, was worried about his fate.
This, of course, implies that Jesus had a connection to his file in the akashic record, via
the plane that we are talking about and had access to his higher self.

There is an important point that we don't know if you have picked up on. Your file in the
akashic record contains information about your future.
This is a very important aspect of life that is often talked about but which no one
understands.
The question asked is, does the future exist?
Scientists and philosophers have often debated this subject. Some believe that it does and
some believe that it does not.
Those who believe that the future exists try to create arguments to explain their points of
view but, to be honest, are not very convincing and those who think that the future does
not exist, until it arrives, argue that as time is a linear progression, it has to stop with the
'now' moment and, as the future has not happened, it is not relevant, if you see what we
mean.
The fact of the matter is that it is true that there is only the now moment but those now
moments can stretch back far into the past and also a certain way into the future.
The future is seldom set in stone.
Let's just take a simple, childish example. Imagine that you take a child's balloon and you
fill it full of a lighter than air gas.
Logically, if you release it you know that it is going to rise into the air. That is its logical
future but let us suppose that for some reason the balloon explodes. This could be for a

number of reasons; the fact that someone pricked the balloon with a pin, the fact that it was over inflated, the fact that the balloon had a manufacturing default and was weak in one point.

Whatever the reason, the balloon goes 'pop' and fails to rise into the air.

We apologise for using such a simple example but we did it for a reason.

We did not want argumentative people to try to find an alternative reason for any example we might use.

In the case of a child's balloon, we have only two states. When it is filled with a lighter than air gas, assuming it is released, it can only have one of two outcomes. Either it rises or it goes pop - excluding the fact that it might have been poorly knotted, and even in that case the balloon does not rise into the air.

So, to eliminate all arguments let us state that the balloon has one of two possible outcomes. Either it rises or it doesn't.

The question is what was the outcome of the balloon - what was its future?

If we hold the uninflated balloon in our hand and we have at our disposition a flask of lighter than air gas, who can predict what will happen?

If we inflate the balloon, will it rise or will something prevent it from rising?

This is where the story gets very complicated for a number of reasons and so we ask you, if you are interested in the future, to pay close attention.

The akashic record contains the records of all living things for all eternity and this includes, to a certain extent, the future of all living things.

But it does not contain the record of any inanimate object. So, we could not find a record of a balloon in the akashic record.

It is true that atoms are alive and it could be argued that if atoms are alive, any object could be stored by linking to its atoms.

But atoms are not directly stored in the akashic record.

They have to be linked to something animate - alive one might say - before that living object is stored in the akashic record.

It is not so much that atoms are stored but the history of the logos that the atoms constructed that is stored in the akashic record.

Therefore, to return to our balloon, we will not find the history of the balloon in the akashic record.

However, we could, if we knew how, link to anyone involved with that balloon from its manufacture, transport, sale and to the person who inflated the balloon, assuming that we could locate any particular balloon.

We do realise that this story is starting to sound ridiculous, but having started with the mention of a balloon, let us continue.

The point we wish to make is that the life history of each and every person who was ever involved with our balloon is stored in the akashic record.

So, let us get to the point where the latest person is going to try to inflate our, or rather, his balloon.

This moment is stored in the akashic record and one would expect the story to end there as the future has not happened and so we do not know if the balloon rose into the air or if it fell to the ground.

However, all living things are immortal and so, in the case of the person who is thinking of inflating his balloon, he is immortal.

Further, if someone lives forever, he must be alive now although we call that now moment the future.

Think about this. If you are immortal - and you are - you are not only alive at this moment but must and will be alive in the future. If you will be alive in the future you must be somewhere, doing something and observing life as it passes into the future.

We are tempted to use the word 'history' to describe your future but as history always implies events in which you were involved in your past, the word history would give a wrong impression.

We are not sure that a word exists that implies events happening to you in your future so we will just do our best to describe future events.

We repeat, if you are immortal and conscious in the future, logic dictates that you would have a 'history' in the future.

So, if we could locate that person as he inflated his balloon in the 'now' moment, we should be able to follow his history into the future and see if the balloon rose into the air or did not.

Now, seeing if a balloon rose or not may not be of great consequence, even if it was your balloon, but if you could see that something was going to happen that would bring a negative outcome to your attempt to inflate and release the balloon into the air, could you take steps to alter the outcome?

This is where we start to tread on difficult ground.

Not only do you have a life plan but your life plan can interact with other people and sometimes your life plan might intend you to help someone and, by altering your life plan, might have catastrophic knock-on effects for other people.

We are going to create in our imaginations another scenario, one that we hope will never happen.

Let us suppose that you are planning to go to the seaside but you look into the future and see that the weather is going to be unpleasant so you decide to stay at home.

Now, let us suppose that you were meant to go to the seaside in order to save someone who would drown. The fact that the person drowned would not only be a terrible shock for the family of the deceased person but let us suppose that, as a result, the children would be placed in care.

This would dramatically alter the personalities of the children and might cause unhappiness to their children and for generations to come.

Now, it could be argued that if the original person had looked far enough into the future, he would have seen that he was being sent to the seaside to save someone, but if that person only looked at his immediate future and tried to make his life more pleasant, the unfortunate consequences of his somewhat selfish act would, in that imaginary case, be catastrophic.

Therefore, looking into our future must be done with great care and, generally, action should not be taken out of self-interest but only in the case of helping others.

You will find, as you develop your sensitivities, that your guides will look into your future and mentally suggest certain courses of actions.

These may be to save you from getting into sticky situations or in order to place you in a position to help someone.

But the guides will never look into their futures in an attempt to ease their lives and neither should you.

You should only ever act to avoid catastrophes in other people's lives.

Once again, we have got somewhat sidetracked in our description of this area in the 4th that, effectively, tries to link your akashic record file to your higher self.

We do this deliberately as it is a non-physical area and thus there is nothing to see and there is nothing to relate to.

It is an area that exists, and for those who know how, it can help the person to relate his incarnation to his non-physical existence. Thus, there is nothing to see and not much to feel.

However, the effects of linking to this area can be dramatic at the moment as mankind, or very few of them, has not yet developed how, safely, to connect to the spirit world, especially the akashic record.

The effects on human life as it stands at the moment could be catastrophic indeed.

That is why we concentrated in this chapter more on the dangers of connecting to the area we are mentioning and suggest that you do not attempt to interfere with your life plan.

It suffices, if you are wise, to leave well alone and let your life plan, your higher self and your guide(s) take care of your incarnation.

It will be for future generations to link with this area.

So, we will end this chapter here and turn, yet again, to another area in the 4th.

CHAPTER 19

THE HAPPINESS PLANE

In this chapter we will explore yet another area in the 4th that you may be interested to hear about.

Many of the areas that we have previously described were related to mysterious and somewhat frightening non-physical planes.

But this time we are going to describe the area that deals with happiness.

Now, you may think that happiness is a natural state that depends on good events that occur from time to time in your life and to a certain extent it is.

But have you noticed that some people appear, naturally, to be happy and buoyant by nature and some people appear nearly always to be miserable and unhappy? It is only major good events arising in their lives that cause a smile to appear on their faces.

Others there are that seem nearly always to be of good humor and they nearly always have a smile on their faces and it is a pleasure to be around such people.

Well, you may have difficulty in accepting this but there is an area in the 4th that is charged with happiness and if one can link to that area one can imbibe that vibration and thus naturally be a happy and positive person.

Once again, we must say that this is a non-physical area so when one links with it, there is nothing to see. However, as we often say, this place exists.

You may be questioning how this area can possibly influence anyone to be happy?

The short answer is that we all have auras and these auras reach out into a variety of dimensions, either physical or non-physical.

So, assuming that this area exists and it is possible for someone to link with it via that person's auras, it suffices that the emotion of happiness can be transmitted to the auras of the person concerned and then that energy is transferred into the psyche of the individual and that person feels happy.

That happiness is not dependent on any good event occurring in the life of the individual. It is a natural state that the person feels most of the time as that energy, that frequency is being transmitted to the individual all the time.

We think that you can appreciate from our previous talks that when one is influenced by a vibration coming into the psyche from whatever source, that person responds to that vibration, that frequency. Some people are more susceptible to frequencies affecting them than others.

For instance, there are people who can meet a stranger for the first time and can instantly form an opinion about that person. They can sense if the person is a nice, kind, and generous person or whether the person is the opposite of those emotions.

Nevertheless, if someone is under the influence of the ray of happiness, that person, generally, is liked as his emotions of gaiety are infectious and can influence nearly everyone that he comes into contact with.

We will just mention that there are people that are jealous of anyone happy and instantly feel alienated towards such a person.

One would think that all normal people would desire to be happy, but there are quite a large number who get some sort of relief from feeling unhappy and by trying to spread unhappiness throughout their sphere of influence.

As you may have guessed, if there is an area in the 4th that transmits a vibration of happiness, in order to keep life in balance there is an equal and opposite area that transmits unhappiness and it is up to us to decide which area we wish to link with.
Although this chapter will deal with the happiness plane, perhaps we will also talk about the unhappiness plane which is just next to the happiness plane and thus deal with both topics in this one chapter.
Although it gives us pleasure to talk about happiness it gives us no pleasure to talk about a plane that transmits vibrations that creates emotions of miserableness.
But that area also exists and so we must mention it

But to return to the plane of happiness.
This area is constantly broadcasting this frequency like a radio, TV or telephone system does, but in a similar way to a radio, TV or telephone broadcast station, the fact that these frequencies are being transmitted does not automatically infer that people pick up these frequencies.
In the case of radio, TV or telephone, of course, some piece of apparatus is required before the signal can be decoded but in the case of psychic frequencies being transmitted from, in this case the 4th dimension, it has to be picked up by an aura.
Further, the psyche of the individual that we are considering has to be attuned to that frequency before the happiness plane can influence that person.
So, although the aura may pick up the signal being transmitted from the 4th out into the cosmos it is only when the relevant area of personality can attune itself to that frequency that it can truly influence any individual.
Until the individual is able to attune himself to the frequency of happiness, he cannot incorporate that frequency into his personality.
We will just mention at this point that the same applies to the emotion of unhappiness.
The area is broadcasting the concept of unhappiness out into the cosmos which can be picked up by an aura of anyone. From there it can be transferred to the personality of any individual, but the person concerned has to attune his frequency - within his personality - before that person can feel unhappy.
The process in both cases is virtually identical. It is the opposite in its effect (happy or unhappy) but the process of accepting the emotion into the personality is the same.

Perhaps at this point we can consider how a frequency or plane is able to broadcast its vibration into the auras of people. Let us realise that there are, in fact, quite a large number of areas in the 4th that deal with a variety of topics and each one is kept apart from any other topic by having a unique frequency.
You will find, if you examine the logistics of how life can influence people - or indeed, plants and animals - that vibrations (frequencies) play a fundamental role.
In other words, virtually every aspect of personality consists of planes in one or other of the dimensions broadcasting its sphere of influence by encoding each and every emotion with a frequency unique to that emotion.

If you have studied the other information we have given you concerning how life is constructed, you will have noticed that the vast majority of aspects of life involve frequencies, each one separate and unique from any other frequency.
We cannot calculate exactly how many aspects of life there are that are encoded by unique frequencies but the number is enormous.
As we said, virtually everything that we see or can feel emotionally contains frequencies and each frequency is a unique frequency.
Just to mention humans, each human vibrates to a unique frequency, and this since humanity was first created. It is because of that, that the akashic record exists.
It is the same for each animal, plant and each and every mineral.
We could go on and say that each planet and all the aspects of gravity and every other aspect of life has a unique frequency. Thus, you can see that it is quite impossible for us to estimate the number of different frequencies there are throughout the multiverse, but it is fair to say that is thanks to all these frequencies that life as we know it exists.

So, this plane that we are discussing is broadcasting its frequency out to the cosmos and, effectively, is picked up by everyone's auras and from there it can be transferred to a part of the personality of any human - or any other life form for that matter - but plants, minerals and animals do not all have the ability to respond to their personalities to the same degree that humans can.
Therefore, we tend to limit our investigations to humans but we will also say that there are many pet animals such as dogs that can respond to the happiness plane and can be extremely happy, providing they are loved and cared for correctly by their owners.

Now, the thing is that although everyone receives the happiness vibration, not everyone incorporates it into their personality.
We have mentioned in other works that to accept a vibration requires that what we call a 'pigeonhole' be created in the mind before any aspect of life can be accepted. It is the same with this. The happiness plane is being received all the time by the person's aura but if a person does not desire to accept this frequency it remains in the aura and does not get transferred to the personality.
We will just mention here that mind and personality are closely linked and, from this perspective, can be considered to be the same thing.
Therefore, it is up to the individual to open the door, so to speak, and for all his personality to be flooded with happiness - or the opposite, unhappiness - because that emotion is also pouring from its plane in the 4th into the aura of each and every human and from there can be transferred to the personality of the individual, providing, of course, that the person has created a pigeonhole in which to place the unhappy emotion.
We mentioned that personality and mind were closely related, and if it were reasonable, we would call that area mind-personality, as they are more or less one.
However, we need, always, to be careful and as we have previously described mind and personality as if they were two separate areas we had better continue thus or some people might be confused.
Life is complicated and confusing enough without us adding fuel to the fires of confusion!
But for those able to accept that mind and personality are more or less the same thing, we suggest that you do. Not that it makes a lot of difference in reality.

The main point to bear in mind is that there is an area in the 4th that broadcasts happiness and unhappiness as a concept into the auric planes, is picked up by a person's aura, and from there can be accepted into a person's makeup, thus rendering him naturally happy or unhappy.

We would like to try to describe how the emotion of happiness is created and contained as a power in an area of the 4th but we are not sure that we can.
Certainly, if one visits the plane of happiness, which one can do by the now familiar act of creating in one's mind the same vibration or frequency as that area, and having linked to that area one feels very happy, but as to the actual mechanism that tells that particular frequency that it is connected to the emotion of happiness (or unhappiness in its adjacent plane), that is a mystery.

What we are not sure of is if the frequency in the 4th concerned with happiness transfers to the personality that feeling or whether the frequency, once accepted by an individual, triggers a response of happiness that is contained in personality!
Can you see the difference?
Let us explain again and then we will tell you our point of view.

In the 4th is a plane that contains a frequency that is constantly being broadcast out to all life.
It is picked up by the auras of living objects.
From there, it remains in the aura until a person, or any other living thing, creates in his mind-personality a pigeonhole in which to accept that frequency.
Then, from that point on the person is naturally happy or unhappy depending on which vibration he accepts into his mind-personality.
That is one way of looking at the question.
Another way is to consider that the emotion of happiness, if we ignore unhappiness and just concentrate on happiness, is actually contained in the mind-personality and this frequency from the 4th triggers the response of happiness which is contained in the 4th.
In our opinion we are reasonably sure that it is the latter.
The emotion of happiness is part of personality as are a myriad of other emotions and it requires that the frequency from the happiness plane in the 4th unlocks the happiness emotion already contained in personality.
This, to us, seems a more logical answer to the question although, if pushed, we would have to admit that we have no real proof either way.
And in a sense, it matters not which way around the system works. It is the fact that one can link to that vibration in the 4th and, as a result, one feels naturally happy. It is that what is important, although we will also admit that curiosity pushes us to try to find the truth about any subject we investigate. We do not like unanswered questions.

Of course, if we accept that happiness is contained as an aspect of personality, it begs another question. Where in personality is happiness formed?
We could also ask what purpose it serves?
If we think about happiness, we could raise a number of questions.
Something tells us that happiness is connected to the God force as, surely, to be filled with the power of God would make one happy.

However, if one can link to happiness's opposing force, unhappiness, then can that be part of the God force also?

God, in our galaxy, was selected to promote love and for those who have experienced true, unconditional love, happiness comes automatically as a handmaiden of love.

So, we appear to be going around in circles somewhat.

Is, for example, unhappiness connected to the negative forces?

We observe that people who are naturally unhappy tend to be rather negative in their outlook on life, but there is a great distance between feeling negative and being involved with evil.

From what we know about evil people, they generally fall into the class that we would call psychopaths and, once again, from what we know about psychopaths, they are seeking happiness from their negative, selfish behavior whereas truly happy people tend to be only too willing to help others if and when they can.

Indeed, that is the fundamental difference between psychopaths and good people. A psychopath considers exclusively his own needs, wants and desires and feels happy when one of his plans works.

Good people get happiness if and when they can help others and the more people - or any other life form - a good person can help the happier and more contended he feels.

So, we have this strange conundrum once again.

On one hand we have those who are naturally happy doing what they can to help all life, and on the other hand we have psychopaths who gain happiness when one of their plans comes to fruition despite, or because of, the unhappiness they cause to others.

There is an old adage that says, 'To be happy, it is necessary that the others are unhappy.' That would seem to be the leitmotif of a true psychopath.

But the point we wish to make is that both groups are seeking happiness.

So, we need to step back, outside of cogitating about happiness versus unhappiness, good people versus evil. We need to look at the problem from a different angle.

As you may know, it is said that a problem cannot be solved from the level of the problem. To solve a problem, we need to rise above the problem and look down upon it from a higher direction, so to speak.

Where can we turn to find people higher than us that, hopefully, have more wisdom than us?

The obvious answer is to ask the wonderful, knowledgeable human angels who so often answer our questions when our knowledge fails us.

Perhaps we can say something about communicating with angels before we share their wisdom with you.

The first thing we would say is that, normally, communication between us and angels does not occur. They are so far ahead of us in their personal vibrations that they are invisible to us and also, for the same reason, we cannot speak to them.

Second, they have their own work to do and many deal with matters of helping all life far outside of anything that we could conceive of.

Next, to contact us, which they kindly do from time to time, they have to lower their frequency somewhat until they resonate to the same frequency as senior members of our group.

We can put questions to these senior members and they can ask the human angels. Then, of course, their answers are transferred to us and we can tell you. But what we tell you often starts from information coming from human angels.

Lastly, we have been informed that these angels are supremely happy and some of that happiness is transferred from the auras of the human angels into the auras of the senior members of our group.

We are informed by the senior members that, although they are naturally happy, their level of happiness receives a tremendous boost, thus indicating that happiness is variable according to the degree of holiness of the individual.

So, we seem to add another layer to the subject of happiness ... holiness. As we have mentioned before, when we mention holiness, we are not referring to mealy mouthed priests or other representatives of various religions. Holiness, to us, is represented best by the words and actions of someone like Jesus. We leave you to study the life of Jesus and decide for yourself what holiness means.

But let us now explain what the human angels told us about happiness, how it works and so on.

We will not quote verbatim what we were told. We will explain in our own words.

The subject of happiness or its opposite is rather more complicated than was previously mentioned.

All that was explained in this chapter as regards the areas in the 4th that contain the concept of happiness or its opposite is true, as are the statements concerning those concepts being picked up by the auras.

Where what we told you and what the human angels said varies, is that, apparently, DNA is involved. This we were not aware of but, knowing how DNA is involved with most aspects of the psyche, it doesn't surprise us.

So, from the auras, the happiness (or unhappiness) emotions are picked up by DNA and that DNA - not all of life's DNA but a certain aspect of it - judges (if we may use that term) to what degree the emotions of happiness, just to consider happiness, should be incorporated into the personality of the person concerned and from there, once the decision is made by DNA, the required degree of happiness is allowed into the personality of the individual.

It is thanks to DNA that people can have different degrees of happiness in their personality.

The happiness plane in the 4th broadcasts the emotion at full strength and it enters the auras at full strength.

From there, the DNA takes the happiness emotion, filters it according to the makeup of the person and then this adjusted quantity is passed, via the chakras, into the heart area of the individual and he feels a permanent degree of happiness in balance with the rest of his makeup, particularly his personality.

In the case of the person who is attracted to unhappiness, the process is the same except the chakra that receives this emotion is not the heart chakra but one of the lower ones.

We hope that you have understood this explanation and we would like to extend our sincere thanks to the angels who provided this explanation.

We could say more about the happiness plane, but we consider that we have given you sufficient information for you to know why some people seem happy most of the time and why some people seem unhappy.
All that remains is for us to tell you how to open yourself to the vibrational frequency of the happiness plane and start to receive that emotion.

One of the easiest and surest ways of doing it is through meditation and that will, over time, automatically link your auras with that plane amongst others.
However, for those who do not wish to meditate we suggest the following course of action.
When you wake up in the morning, give thanks to God for another day and thank God for the fact that his angels and your guide(s) are looking after you.
Start your day and go through it feeling as positive as you can, welcome all the good events that arrive throughout the day and thank God for them.
At the same time, welcome the problems of the day knowing that they are just tests of faith sent by God and that the solution is already on its way in the degree that you put your faith in God.
Never give way to misery or unhappiness, no matter how great the problem seems to be.
Always try to stay positive and happy, laugh in the face of adversity and you will find you will be helped through the problem by your guides and God's angels.
If you continue like this all day, when you go to bed, thank God for all his help and then put it all behind you and sleep soundly.
When you wake up in the morning, repeat the process and continue each day like that, always staying happy and positive no matter what happens, and gradually you will incorporate the happiness plane into your personality.
At the same time your faith in God will increase and you will attract more and more angelic help.
If you follow what we have described you will feel happy all the time. You will deal with problems better and God and his angels will become part of your personality thus making you a stronger, more positive person.

We will end this chapter here and move on to the next plane for discussion.

CHAPTER 20

THE BRILLIANCE PLANE

You may be under the impression that we are running out of areas in the 4th to describe to you and that we would be starting to scrape the bottom of the barrel in our attempt to find more topics to talk to you about.

This is not so.

There are virtually countless areas, or landscapes as we sometimes call them, in the 4th.

Not all are related to incarnation and not all areas would it be wise to describe to you. Some would be outside of your current level of comprehension and some, if you investigated them, would put you in danger as they would open the door to investigating dangerous aspects of life.

The problem is that there are not just the humans, plants, animals or minerals that you are aware of. Nor yet just the demonic forces that we have described. Nor, once again, the fairy world that we have mentioned. Nor, finally, the horrible entities in the 1st and 2nd dimensions which, once again, we have mentioned.

These beings, some of them are dangerous and some of them are friendly.

Some, there are, that are neutral but the areas they live in would have a disturbing effect should you visit such areas.

Indeed, it is not unknown that people who have severe drink or drug problems, open the door into one of these areas and have terrifying visions.

Some people mock those experiencing Delirium Tremens (DT's) and talk of seeing pink elephants but we can assure you that these areas are real and the creatures (etheric) that live in them would cause the bravest person to blanch.

It is not funny for those who experience the visions brought on by DT's.

We should have sympathy for those who, through excessive drink or drug consumption, see these monsters. We should do all that we can to help such people rather than mocking them.

But even all that we just described is not the end of the various life forms contained throughout the dimensions.

Life is endless and there is always the need to keep things in balance. So, for every nice entity to be found in the astral realms there must be an equal and opposite number of negative beings.

Further, the archangelic forces that serve God and have been doing so for billions of years created, in etheric or astral form, a large number of entities, some of which we would call positive and an equal number that we would call negative.

We will also remind you that humans were never intended to incarnate to Earth originally, and thus the area in the 6th dimension that you call your universe was never intended to be created originally nor were a number of aspects of the 4th, and indeed the 5th, and that all had to be created once the decision was taken that man should have what you call an incarnation.

The point that we are making is that there are landscapes and monsters that inhabit those landscapes that man was never intended to interact with.

It is only since incarnation was created that the likelihood of entering dangerous landscapes and thus interacting with dangerous entities came about.
So, we cannot blame God's archangels. The danger comes from the fact that human's development towards incarnation overlaps the domains in which the negative - from our perspective - areas or beings live.

We hope that you have understood this short explanation about some of the dangers of describing the negative landscapes and the negative creatures that inhabit them.
Everything is vibration and if we described these areas it would peak the curiosity of some people and, by the law of mutual attraction, would draw people to those areas.
This would benefit you nothing and could destroy your minds.
Curiosity is a positive attribute when correctly used, but morbid curiosity about negative - to our eyes - areas and creatures should be strictly controlled.
We repeat, to come into contact with some of these areas would destroy you so we hope that you will heed our warnings.

You may wonder why, if we do not want you to visit certain areas, we mentioned them.
The answer is twofold.
1. We promised to tell you as much about the non-physical planes as we could and so we feel obliged to mention them.
2. Any good parent would explain to his children the dangers of negative frequentation and, as we possibly have more knowledge about these areas than you, we warn you to stay away from them.

Having explained that there are a number of areas or landscapes in the various astral and etheric planes that it would be better not to investigate, let us turn our attention to an area that it is safe to mention in the 4th and it is this.
One of the many areas we could talk about is the area, landscape or frequency, that deals with brilliance.
We have spoken about brilliance, or genius, before and we have described it as having the ability to jump from known facts on a subject to a conclusion on the subject without taking the logical steps that most people would have to take to progress from the question under discussion, considering all the known facts and puzzling, step by step, the points that would lead to a conclusion.
Further, anyone blessed by being brilliant usually comes to the correct conclusion as opposed to the average person who, after considered examination of all the facts, frequently comes to the wrong conclusion.

There is an area in the 4th that contains the concept of brilliance or genius.
We all know what the word genius means but few of us understand what brilliance refers to.
Although it equates to genius, we like the word brilliance as it describes light.
God is light, pure starlight and so this area which is described as the brilliance plane, if one visits it, shines with star light.
So, this gives us a clue that anyone blessed by brilliance is able to contact this area and link to the power of God which takes the form of star light.

God is attributed with being the source of all knowledge, all wisdom, and if one can visit that area and incorporate at least some of that power into his psyche, he can act in a manner that is described as genius or brilliance.

We will go on to say that it is not in the gift of anyone to incorporate all of God's power into his psyche or personality.

To do so would destroy the person, even the most brilliant of them. The power of God is infinite and is beyond anything that could be imagined by anyone.

Although to incorporate a small, carefully measured dose of God's power in someone results in genius, let us try to imagine the total power of God by talking about atomic fusion.

It has been noted, regrettably, that atoms contain power and to split an atom can release that power.

Let us further question how many atoms there are in existence?

Everything is made of atoms combining in some way.

Every mineral, plant, animal, human, planet and, indeed, dimension is created from atoms combining in some way to create all that exists.

Each and every one of this unbelievable number of atoms contains the total power of God. If it was possible to detonate, together, all of these atoms, could you even begin to conceive of the enormity of the explosion?

That is the amount of power that would be incorporated into the psyche of anyone who could link with the totality of God's power.

So, we hope that you can realise the danger of anyone linking to the totality of God's power ... rather too much of a good thing.

However, it is possible to link to a small portion of that power and then we say that the person is brilliant, a genius.

The person himself might not recognise himself as a genius because it is stated that genius is 10% inspiration and 90% perspiration.

This may or may not be true but it is fair to say that most geniuses have to put quite a lot of effort into obtaining conclusions, but we must recognise that a genius can obtain a result where the average person would just flounder. So, even a small amount of God's power goes a long way.

Now, as we did with the last chapter, we need to define where God's power is contained. Either, it seems to us, that is contained in this brilliant area in the 4th or it is contained in the personality of the individual. As was mentioned in the last chapter, probably DNA is also involved.

So, let us ignore what we said in the last chapter about the happiness plane and commence our investigations from the beginning and see where they lead us.

After all, to base any new investigations on the results of the last might be a dangerous procedure and could lead us to wrong conclusions.

This has happened many times in the past to huge numbers of so-called experts, and we must not fall into the trap of following in their footsteps. Let us start with what we know.

We know that everything is vibration (frequency) combining in some fashion to form all that exists, whether it be physical or non-physical (astral).

Further, we know that the only things that exist are atoms. These atoms might combine to create all that exists in the 6th dimension physicality - which is the reality in which you live - or they might exist in other dimensions forming all that exists in any dimension. We know that people struggle with this concept. They can accept that they live in a physical universe, but because other dimensions are invisible to most people, many think that they do not exist and are a figment of the imagination of misguided individuals one step removed from the lunatic asylum.

However, for those who have learnt to visit some of these dimensions and, even more, to those who live in other dimensions such as the 4th where we live, it is obvious that dimensions are as solid and as real as your dimension is to you. It is only a question of difference of frequency. The atoms that combine to create life in other dimensions are as real as the atoms that constitute your world. It is just that they vibrate to a different frequency that makes them invisible.

But for those who can accept that life is indeed universal, it comes as no surprise that other dimensions than yours exist and also that, for life to exist in other dimensions, it requires a solidity and that solidity is created by 'astral atoms' combining to create all that exists in other dimensions.

Therefore, this brilliance plane must be constructed by atoms combining to form this area.

We also know that each and every atom contains the totality of what we refer to as God, also known as prime creator or the all that is.

So, whatever dimensions atoms are contained in, each atom contains the one creative force. Not a variation of that force according to which dimension they are found in but the one, unique creative force that is everywhere in existence.

Next, we know that this creative force can be manipulated by what is referred to as consciousness.

It is thanks to consciousness that we have animals, vegetables, minerals and human life forms on Earth plus, of course, all the so-called fairy realms and other spirit forces, some of which we have spoken about at the beginning of this chapter.

The God force is quite simply the creator of life and it is consciousness that enables the God force contained in atoms to combine to create everything. That combination plan is called a logos.

The point to bear in mind is that everything, everywhere, is the one God force contained in atoms that come together under the direction of the logos, and then consciousness creates the unique frequency of everything, keeping all things apart.

This seems rather complicated until one has created a pigeon hole in the mind in which to store this information. Once one has the ability to store this information in the mind, it all becomes simple and obvious.

The point that we are coming to is that all the areas in the 4th that we have so far described, plus countless more, are created from atoms combining according to the logos given to that area and as each atom is alive, once they come together to form something, that something is alive and has consciousness and, more, it has a unique frequency. All is one, so what you are, each and every area or landscape in the 4th is also.

Therefore, we hope that you can see that the brilliance or genius area in the 4th is alive and is conscious.

It may not look like you but is every bit as alive as you are and, as all is one, there must be a link between the brilliance area and you.

We could go on to say that, as all is one and that one is God, everything is you and you are everything.

Although this is true, we must also say that it is true that everything is kept apart by individual consciousness and individual frequency.

That is why there appears to be a difference between you and the brilliance plane, just to consider these two things.

Before we continue to try to unravel where brilliance (genius) is contained, let us break off and state a couple of things.

Logos, consciousness and your personal frequency, combine to create what is called 'ego'.

Ego is quite simply the fact that you feel different from any other person or object no matter what it is. We could also describe ego as selfishness, as selfishness is a feeling of self as opposed to anything else.

The extreme example of ego or selfishness is a psychopath.

A psychopath is someone who considers that only his thoughts, hopes, ambitions and desires count and he has absolutely no consideration for the same feelings that others have.

They will go to any lengths they feel necessary to remove any person or anything else that stands in their way to achieving their goals.

We will also say that the object of your existence, your creation, is to remove, ultimately, any trace of ego and at that point your journey ends.

For those who think that they are close to perfection and thus close to the end of their journey, let us say that we congratulate you for the strides already made but you will find that you have a virtually endless journey still to take.

The more one removes ego promoted faults, the more one discovers endless depths of ego still remaining.

The destiny of all of us is to finish in the arms of God but there is a long way to go for all of us.

We spend a huge amount of time in the spirit world, gradually removing egoistic thoughts, then go on through the angelic stage and, finally, spend eons of time as archangels before removing the last fault and then we can take the final step of merging into the Godhead.

The journey is virtually endless, but every step taken brings us joy.

At the beginning, those who are psychopaths are constantly seeking happiness through power, money, and all the other things that one sees that psychopaths accumulate, but nothing brings them lasting happiness because they are looking in the wrong direction.

Happiness comes in the degree that we can help others, not ourselves.

But let us return to what we were examining.

We mentioned that there was a link between the brilliance plane and you.

We also mentioned that the brilliance plane has a unique vibration but you also have a unique vibration.

So, it is a case of 'never the twain shall meet'.

However, all is not lost.

Assuming what we said about the brilliance plane is true, it is obvious that some people are able to link to that plane by accident or design.

Before we go on to investigate the brilliance plane and how it can link to humanity, may we mention yet another way that, from time to time, genius can be transferred to a person, and may we say that in very exceptional cases, animals.
We wish to mention Nirmanakaya.
We have mentioned these special angelic entities before, but we will do so again to complete the picture.
The word Nirmanakaya is Sanskrit which indicates that their presence has been known about for several thousands of years.
A Nirmanakaya is a non-human creation, an angel would be the nearest description to anything that you could understand.
Each and every land mass, which should really be considered to be a country if it was not for egotistical humans desiring to carve areas out that they can control in order to impose their will and thus impose their power over the population, is under the control of a Nirmanakaya.
Nirmanakaya normally have no interest in humanity and only a passing interest in the fauna of the country he oversees.
It is actually somewhat difficult to know what the function of a Nirmanakaya is as they take no interest in the actions of humanity on the land masses under their surveillance, and even in countries where huge and negative deforestation is taking place, it does not seem to concern them. At least, they do not seem to take any action to negate man's effects on the countries under their jurisdiction.
Perhaps they take long-term views and realise that, in the case of countries where deforestation is taking place, either man will realise his error and will replant the forests or their country can cope with the effects of man's actions.
After all, before man came on the scene, much of the world was covered in forests of one kind or another.
Man has, over the centuries, deforested much of Europe for example in order to create space for planting arable crops, to build houses and to burn for fuel. It seems not to have caused much long-term harm to the land as such, although it has caused much harm to the animal population of those places.

But, nevertheless, Nirmanakaya exist and, we repeat, each and every land mass or island is under the control of a Nirmanakaya.
Where they come into our story is that although Nirmanakaya are not normally interested in man, they do, from time to time, take a young human under their wing and somehow install the concept of genius or brilliance in them.
Thus it is that we have, throughout history, a few geniuses, some of whom became well-known, some of whom seem to have remained in the shadows and some who date so far back in the history of Earth that their works have become lost in the mists of time.

Now, we do not know why Nirmanakaya select people from time to time and put the genius thread with them, nor do we know if somehow they link the person to the brilliance plane we are discussing.

We should, perhaps, admit that we could find this information by delving into the file in the akashic record of any person who was thus treated by a Nirmanakaya, but we must be honest and tell you that as that file would not contain information about a Nirmanakaya, the Nirmanakaya in question not being human and thus not mentioned in a person's file, makes it almost impossible to trace the thread of genius back to its origin. So, we don't spend the energy thus battling.

But we do know that some people, very few, are selected by Nirmanakaya and become geniuses.

However, the number is so few that we can ignore it except to say that Nirmanakaya are a subject worth investigating, and it would be instructive to find out how and why they select people and how they install the 'gene' - if we may use that word - of genius in them.

We do not know very much about Nirmanakaya, but we do know that they select some people and help them become geniuses from time to time.

Logic would suggest that there must be a reason for this but we do not know why it is done nor how it is done.

Let us return to the genius or brilliance plane (as we prefer to call it) in the 4th and try to tell you what we know about it.

Like all the many and diverse planes or landscapes in the 4th, it is created from vibrations or frequency.

As we have mentioned before, to enter it requires that one incorporates into one's personality that frequency. Unless and until that is done, it is not possible to link with that frequency. The exception being, of course, if one can link by accident to that frequency.

As we did with the last chapter, which was about the happiness - or unhappiness - plane(s), let us say that it is a bit more complicated than just having the desire to link with the brilliance plane or many people would do so as most of us would like to be brilliant.

However, if we study history and consider the lives of brilliant people, these people were not necessarily happy people and we consider that to be happy and contented far outweighs the desire to be brilliant.

Indeed, our investigations of brilliant people have shown that many brilliant people have led deeply unhappy lives and for a number of reasons.

Before we go much further with this subject, let us look at a few of the reasons why brilliant people are not always happy people.

The first reason, we would suggest, is jealousy. Brilliance or genius is a rare gift and in a logical and fair world, others who are not brilliant would admire, plaudit and promote such people to places of leadership and do all they can to assist such people to push life forward.

However, very often the opposite obtains.

There are many people who may be fairly intelligent but lack the spark of genius.

However, they may have ego highly developed.

Having spent long years studying a subject and having become highly qualified in their chosen subject, they do not take kindly to others bypassing their achievements without doing very much study at all.

If we may generalize, to become qualified in any subject does not necessarily require much intelligence, it simply requires a good memory.

To pass an examination simply requires to have memorized similar questions to those being asked in the examination and trotting out the answer.

The problem - sometimes, not always - is that the person who passes the examination because he has a good memory and thus is considered to be qualified as an expert on a particular subject, might develop an inflated ego.
But as you can imagine, if someone else comes along who has not studied the subject under question but, because he is brilliant (a genius), he might well propose new, innovative methods of presenting information far in advance of the first person who contents himself in repeating collective wisdom that has been proposed for ages.
When that happens, ego kicks in and the first person feels his position as an accepted authority on a subject threatened.
So, he does all that he can, in conjunction with his colleagues, to discredit the genius.
This has happened over and over again and thus leads to deep unhappiness in the genius who might well find his ability stifled by those far below him in quality but far above him in power.
We fully expect that things will alter for the better in due course as we move further into ascension.

There is another type of person who has genius tendencies but that one could not describe as having common sense.
Genius on its own is not sufficient. Unless it is linked to common sense and/or a profound sense of what we call 'feet on the ground', genius serves little purpose.
We find this displayed in certain types of autistic people that are referred to as 'autistic savants'.
These people were once referred to as idiots. Such a description, highly offensive, we would not apply today.
Autism is a very interesting and complicated aspect of life and, perhaps, we will write an essay on the subject.
We criticise no one and we certainly would not criticise or mock anyone who has what is referred to as autism.
But, there are a small number of people who only have a tenuous grasp on everyday life - that is referred to as common sense - but have a genius level of a particular subject.
This could be almost anything: mathematics, art, music, almost any subject.
This talent, to be able to complete the most difficult tasks in the subject that their genius attaches itself to, never ceases to amaze the average person who has no idea of what is going on.
Set an autistic savant the task of creating something in his selected subject and he or she will produce answers far beyond what any normal person could conceive of.
The ability in this one subject is truly amazing, but it is often the case that they are incapable of dealing with normal life and have to be cared for.

We mentioned these people because there is often a link with other geniuses who seem not to be normal in the sense that the average person considers normal.
They are sometimes referred to as eccentric.
One gets the impression that life has made a trade-off with geniuses. They have traded brilliance for common sense to a greater or lesser degree.

This is interesting and is worth investigating.

If it is true that genius or brilliance, which is our preferred term, can vary in its degree of attribution to a person and it is true that someone who has total brilliance on a subject has almost no grasp of everyday life, it would seem that a genius has to give up a portion of common sense in order to obtain a portion of genius.

It is as if genius and common sense are opposed.

The more genius one has the less common sense the person has.

This is, of course, a generality and there are, no doubt, numbers of people who have a degree of brilliance but also have enough common sense to be able to cope with life.

We stress, at this point, that when we mention brilliance or genius, we are not in any way referring to those who have cunning highly developed and thus have developed the skill of exploiting others in a very clever manner to benefit themselves.

Cunning, in our terminology, is an evil concept whereas brilliance or genius never knowingly harms anyone.

But to return to what we were saying about the trade-off between brilliance and common sense.

Please understand that we are generalizing here and we do not wish that the people reading this chapter who try to find fault with what we say, fly into an indignant rage and point out that there are cases of someone brilliant who is also perfectly capable of coping with life. Of course there is, but it has been noted that the more brilliant a number of people are, ranging from eccentric to autistic savant, the more they seem remote from what is considered normal, everyday sort of people who manage to cope with their incarnation through common sense.

It has been noted that, quite often, the more a person is brilliant, the less common sense that person may have.

We repeat. We are not saying that all people display this tendency nor are we suggesting that all those who struggle coping with incarnation display brilliance.

We are generalizing but we are also mentioning fact.

So please accept what we are saying as a point for discussion, even if you disagree with our, and many psychiatrists, conclusions.

If it is true that there might be a trade-off between brilliance and common sense, we should try to consider why this should be.

However, let us return to the area in the 4th that contains the brilliance plane.

To do so, as with all the planes or landscapes, simply requires attuning oneself to the appropriate plane. In this case, as it is a somewhat physical area, it shines with a brilliant white light which is the power of God, greatly reduced compared with the true, unbridled power of God but, nevertheless, gives us an indication that what we are observing is linked to the power of God.

This is, perhaps, not surprising, as to be connected to God will surely mean having total knowledge. It is hardly conceivable that God would not know everything that there is to know about every subject imaginable. That is one of the natures we attribute to God ... total knowledge.

As God manifests himself as pure starlight, total knowledge would be the most powerful, brightest and purest light: starlight.

As we have already mentioned, total light would destroy us through its total power and so this area contains a reduced version of God's power.

Nevertheless, when linking to this area, the light is magnificent.

We would like you to note that light is a frequency and starlight, which is pure white light, contains all the frequencies that combine to produce light in equal quantities so there is no shade of red or blue in starlight. It is pure white of a dazzling power.

In the heavenly spheres we do not have atmosphere to alter the colour of pure white, nor do we have any colours coming from atoms in space that alters the whiteness that you see from a star in the night sky.

You may not know this, but space is not empty. It is full of atoms, the sort of atoms that you know about and also atoms of dark energy.

This is because the galaxy is just as alive as you are and, just as your body is composed of countless atoms, so the galaxy has a living body and that is composed of atoms.

As the galaxy is alive, it has consciousness and thus has emotions.

As each atom has auras, these atoms can emit colours according to the emotion that the galaxy is feeling.

These colours can alter the perceived colour being emitted by stars. You may not notice much difference when you gaze into the night sky but, in fact, you never see true white star light. It is always coloured by the emotions of the galaxy as the star light shines down on you.

However, in the brilliance or genius area, we see true white star light, which is the light of God.

So, it is totally pure white light.

Although, as we said, the light is reduced in power so as to not harm anyone linking with it, it retains its purity and is quite remarkable to see.

However, we who take the trouble to link with that plane might be disappointed to realise that we are not transformed instantly into geniuses. We remain with the level of intelligence that we had before linking to that plane.

So, we realise that this area, this brilliance or genius plane, does not directly transform anyone who links with it into a genius. How disappointing!

But we do know that this area exists and we do know that it is connected to brilliance or genius, and we further know that genius becomes so through a connection to that area.

After all, if people were not affected by that plane there would be no point in it existing. God does not make useless things.

If this area exists, and if it emits pure white light and that light is the fount of all knowledge, this area must be connected to transferring brilliance or genius to certain people.

But not to us, apparently! Obviously, there is more going on here than meets the eye.

So, we must investigate further.

It is clear that the brilliance plane does not directly create genius in the person but is somehow connected to genius. We must turn to the actual people who become geniuses to see how it works.

We must, as is so often the case, look to personality, and possibly, DNA to find the connection.

To cut a long story short, with the help of our angel colleagues, we think we have the answer.

It turns out that, before incarnation, at the moment that the life plan is decided upon, certain people decide to incorporate brilliance into their personality in order to explore this talent.

But, it is done at a price.

Apparently, it is not possible to be a genius and have total command of common sense. The reason is as follows.

When a person's life plan is decided upon, a large number of decisions are taken. We have mentioned most of them before but, for the sake of clarity, we will repeat some of them.

The decisions taken include the sex of the person, his country of birth, his family and, as a result of the above-mentioned decisions, he is born into a rich or poor family and that influences his education and career path. So, for most people who are born into an average family, only so much intelligence is required, and in order to survive on the earth plane, a certain degree of what is called common sense is required.

Now, all the above-mentioned decisions are related to survival and connection to the earth plane.

This gives the impression that, if we make decisions between connection to spirit as opposed to Earth connections, most people incorporate into their life plan, connection to Earth rather than connection to spirit.

This might be a bit confusing so let us explain in greater detail.

As you should know, we are all pure spirit as we are all created by God, and God is pure spirit.

However, the earth plane was created in the 6th dimension and even though it is an illusion, it apes physicality as closely as possible.

Physicality is closely connected to the way plants and animals survive.

We are sure that you know that the average animal has incorporated into his personality the fight/flight emotion.

They fight for survival and for food. Also for mating rights, etc., and if danger rears its ugly head, they run away.

That is the way that animals survive.

Although most plants remain static, they fight to survive by competing for water, nutrients and sunlight.

Although they cannot run from danger, many plants have developed different mechanisms: thorns or toxins. These take the place of flight.

So, basic survival on Earth is connected to fight/flight.

With humans, although the survival mechanism might seem more complicated, people battle to get money or food to survive.

They compete to attract the best mate and, if danger looms, they defend themselves either through actual fighting or through litigation.

If you think about it, the way we humans survive is just an adaptation to the way animals survive.

We call that fight/flight instinct, common sense.

Common sense is used as a means of creating what we need in order to satisfy our desire to create what our life plan says that we should.

But there are others that decide to incorporate brilliance or genius into their life plan.
So, they have their personality rather split between the Earth sentiment of fight/flight, i.e., common sense, and a connection to the God force which is contained in the brilliance or genius plane in the 4th.
Now, it should be obvious that these two sentiments or emotions are rather opposed. It would be very difficult to have total common sense, the 'feet on the ground feeling', and also a total link to the genius plane which is directly connected to the God sphere.
So, people make a choice.
The vast majority of us ignore the genius plane. Indeed, before incarnating, when people are being shown around heaven and see the genius or brilliance area, once they have it explained to them the choice they would have to make when incarnating, they totally reject brilliance and settle for a degree of intelligence, usually connected to common sense, thus giving them a greater chance of survival on Earth.
However, there are some who decide to incorporate brilliance into their life plan at the expense of common sense.

Then these people have to decide to what degree they wish to incorporate brilliance into their life plan.
Please remember what we said above. You can't have both. In the degree that one incorporates brilliance or genius, one must reject common sense.
Equally, in the degree that one rejects brilliance, one can incorporate common sense - the feet on the ground sentiment.
But, thanks to personality, ego and DNA, etc., it is possible to incorporate a varying portion of this brilliance power.
How can we describe it?
Shall we imagine a See-Saw with brilliance on one seat and common sense on the other or shall we imagine it as a pair of scales, once again with brilliance on one pan and common sense on the other?
Whatever way we look at it, we have a trade-off. As brilliance is accepted more and more into a person so the common sense factor tends to reduce. And vice versa.
Of course, as we mentioned, there are occasionally those who are able to accept a measure of brilliance and still retain a good measure of common sense but, usually, the more brilliance a person decides to incorporate into him, by the law of trade off, common sense reduces.

The extreme case of someone accepting brilliance in his life plan and thus his personality, is the case of the autistic savant and, at the opposite end, we have people who accept just a small amount of the brilliance field within them and become a clever person able to cope with incarnation.
Those who decide to accept a large amount of brilliance into their personalities have two problems.
The first is an almost total trade-off with common sense, the ability to cope with life, and the second is that, generally speaking, at this stage of evolution of the human race, the person cannot incorporate more than a narrow part of total knowledge.

Thus they become brilliant at a chosen subject, very inferior at anything else and unable to cope with life.

Of course, we are generalizing, but that is what usually happens.

We will just say here that the destiny of man for the future is not to incarnate to Earth. It will not be necessary as man evolves beyond the need to test himself through incarnation. We have mentioned this before. Man will stay in the 4th and, as he evolves, he will be able, eventually, to incorporate, totally, the brilliance plane and, totally, be able to incorporate common sense because, even in the 4th common sense is very much required.

So, we hope that you can see that an autistic savant is a brave person who has chosen a very difficult incarnation path in order to experience what it is like to be a genius at a subject.

The price they pay, as do all that have a degree of brilliance, is heavy.

They are often rejected or mocked by society when they see a very clever person unable to cope with everyday common-sense matters.

We should not mock them. We should admire them for wishing to experience brilliance on a planet where the majority of incarnates have no idea either of their brilliance nor why they struggle with incarnation.

However, once their incarnation finished, they are welcomed into an area of Summerland where their genius is appreciated and their common sense is not tested. They are cared for by guides and angelic beings who look after them with total love.

Their brilliance, they are given free rein to express and expound, free from any constraints that incarnation put on them.

For those who choose to cease to be brilliant, steps are taken to free them from the link with the brilliance plane and they return to become normal people before their life plan was put with them. In effect they choose a different life plan.

We hope that you have understood this chapter which was not easy to explain and we hope that you will start to admire people who show signs of being autistic savants or even eccentricity.

They are different from you in that they are exploring a difficult path through incarnation, but they provide a valuable insight into what brilliance is and though they are different from you - and us - they are, nevertheless, part of us as we are part of them.

So, try to accept them as you accept yourself.

We will end this chapter and move onto yet another topic.

CHAPTER 21

ALTERNATIVE REALITIES

You may be getting tired of all the introductions that we put into virtually each chapter. It is not that we wish to pad out the chapters with words just to make each chapter longer. Far from it. We would much rather dive straight into the subject matter but we feel, quite often, that we need to preface each chapter with a warning about the dangers, or otherwise, of each subject.

After all, how many people have published information about astral projection and have described techniques for entering the etheric world but have failed to give the slightest warnings concerning the danger of encountering negative creatures that live in those realms? The result has been many people becoming ensnared, emotionally, with these entities.

We, on the other hand, have gone to great lengths to advise you not to go into the etheric without correct training and without being protected by guides.

We hope that we have saved many people from unfortunate encounters with negative etheric entities.

That is at least one reason that we preface descriptions of the planes or landscapes in the 4th with advice either asking you not to go to certain areas or, on the contrary, suggesting that it would be safe, under certain conditions, to do so.

If we can issue a general warning. The 4th dimension is astral. As such, only trained people can enter it.

We mentioned this in the preface of this book.

No one should attempt to do esoteric work or try to enter any part of the 4th until he has mastered, to a good extent, the art of projecting his personality into that area and has attracted guides who will protect him and guide him around the area.

For those who do not know, let us describe the path between the earth plane and the upper 4th.

We have the solid earth plane that you see around you. Then, as you start to do what is called astral projection, you enter the etheric realms. There are several of these realms or layers, each one separated by being encased in unique frequencies.

If you traverse all of these layers you enter the lower 4th.

That is the area where demons live.

We have described these areas before. There are a number of layers, once again, each one kept apart by unique frequencies.

Only after traversing the lower 4th can you enter the upper 4th and explore the heavenly realms.

So we hope that you can see that without a great deal of psychic training and without being able to have the protection of specially trained guides around you, the chances of you leaving, spiritually, the earth plane and arriving safely in the upper 4th without being interfered with by entities from either the etheric realms or from the demonic planes of the lower 4th are slim indeed.

And yet very few people who laudit the virtues of astral projection explain all this to you. We do because we do not wish any of you to fall victim to negative entities.

It is up to you, either to pay heed or to ignore our warnings.

As a last statement on this subject let us mention frequencies.
The earth plane vibrates to a certain frequency.
The etheric plane vibrates to a slightly higher frequency.
Then the lower 4th vibrates to a higher frequency and, finally, the upper 4th vibrates to a yet higher frequency.
Anyone who has no spiritual training vibrates to the frequency of planet Earth.
It is only after much meditation and application to spiritual work that one can commence to vibrate to the frequency of the upper 4th.
So, if a person who has done little or no meditation attempts to enter the upper 4th he fails miserably because he does not have the ability to vibrate to the frequency of the upper 4th. Nor will he have attracted the special guides who will guard him from harm and guide him safely to the upper 4th.
So, if he manages to leave his physical body at all, the best he can hope for is to land in one of the etheric realms or, if he is really unlucky, he might end up in the lower 4th.
That would be bad news indeed.
Anyway, the moral of this story is do not attempt to do any form of astral projection without long months of training, and only train with a qualified and respected teacher.
Do not fall for giving money to online psychics and never fall into the clasp of fake mediums who charge money.
Spirituality is freely given by God and all spiritual training should be free.

We will warn any psychic that he or she feels has enough knowledge or skill to teach others, not to fall into the trap of asking money for passing on their knowledge.
God's gifts are freely given and must be freely passed on to others.
If money becomes involved, God reserves the right to withdraw those skills and then any teacher who has no skills left has to improvise to maintain the illusion that he/she still has psychic skills
It will, in effect, become the case of the blind leading the blind.

Now, once again, we have spent several pages warning you about astral projection, unless you have correct training and protection and we hope that it will not fall on deaf ears.
We do not wish for anyone to fall into the snare of evil entities.

Having said all that, let us turn to the next subject that we have selected for discussion.
You may think that we are presenting chapter after chapter at random but, effectively, we try, as far as we can to link each new chapter to the previous ones.
This next chapter may, at first sight not seem to follow on from the last ones but, in fact, is connected.
We wish to consider alternative realities, a subject that we have mentioned before.
Although we have given you some information previously about alternative realities, we did not explain everything we know about them.
This chapter will give us the chance to give an expanded overview on the subject.
We do not promise to give a total explanation as the subject of alternative realities is extremely complicated and it would take a book in its own right to explain.

We will also say that it will profit you little, because it is not within the gift of many people to explore alternative realities. Most of us have quite enough to do exploring our reality without wondering about other realities!
However, curiosity about other aspects of life is natural, so we are happy to explain at least some of what we know about alternative realities.

Let us start from the beginning and mention a subject about which you should already be aware.
We have mentioned that each and every one of you lives in your own particular universe. This also applies to us, by the way.
We have mentioned this a number of times but will do so again in order to bring everyone up to the same level.
What we are going to say will have a direct bearing on the subject of alternative realities.

The simple fact of the matter is that you, if we may mention just you in order to keep things simple, are God. Now, God is an invisible life force that is real, but is outside of any means of locating with it.
This God force created, with the help of his archangelic friends, a means of you being aware of yourself, as opposed to anything or anyone else.
We call this your 'sense of awareness', or 'self-consciousness', 'ego' or 'personality' amongst a number of other things.
You, it turns out, are a singularity, a minuscule point of life. But you live in a world that is exclusive to you that your ego has created.
You are the only thing that exists in your world that you create with your imagination.
We do realise that we have flown through a mass of complicated information in a few lines but you should know all this. If you do not, please stop here, go back and study the information we have previously provided.

If you think about it, every person who has ever lived, is living or ever will live (because future people are alive already) is living in their own universe - their own alternative reality to yours. It is only the fact that the people you know have similar thoughts to yours that make them seem almost part of you. But, if you could link to their minds you would be amazed at how different, how unique they are compared to you.
Even the people close to you - immediate family for example - have hopes, aims and objectives that are completely different to your hopes, aims and objectives.

However, this is not what interests you. You wish to learn about life forms, humans, in different areas that are invisible to you.
We understand this and we will do our best to describe what we know about alternative realities and the people - and animals - that live in them.
We only prefaced this talk by mentioning that you and everyone else live in their unique universe to open your mind to the fact that you already live in a world full of alternative realities.
However, let us try to explain the sort of alternative reality that interests you.

This, as always, is going to be a bit difficult to explain, as to understand what we are going to say supposes that you have already read and understood our previous works and have a knowledge of the esoteric worlds and the life forms that live in them.

As we mentioned above, each and every one of them live in their own, unique universe. This is because all is one. What you are, everything is. We have repeated this ad nauseam but will do so again and again to try to drum into you that there is only one and that one is God.

All else is just the logos given to all living things to enable them to have experiences and to grow in wisdom.

We also mention this to remind you that your ultimate destination is to rid yourself of ego (personality, if you will) and return to God from whence you came.

You are on an endless cyclical journey from God back to God.

Everything is on the same journey as all is one.

However, with plants and animals the path from God back to God takes a different journey to the journey humans take.

Humans are God's chosen people.

This also implies that the beings we find in alternative realities are also human and are following the same path as you - from God back to God.

They may or may not live in strange worlds compared to the world we all live in but the path is the same.

Let us try now to delve into the nuts and bolts of this subject of alternative realities and slowly and calmly unravel the mystery as clearly as we can.

But we do warn you that parts of what we must say might be difficult for you to digest but, as always, we will do our best to simplify our explanations whilst, at the same time, ensuring that what we will tell you is accurate.

So, where do we start?

We have already mentioned dimensions and have said that each dimension, or aura, is divided into to a plethora of sub-dimensions, each one separated from any other sub-dimension by a coating of thin gravity, the whole dimension kept separate from any other dimension, or aura, by a coating of thick gravity.

If you do not understand this, it is not our fault.

We gave you a complete book called 'Auras' in which we clearly explained all this.

Now we need to look into which part of this plethora of dimensions and sub-dimensions alternative realities are to be found.

We will say that this is going to be difficult to answer as they are actually all (for there are many alternative realities) contained in the 8th dimension where our existence started.

Once again, we have told you of the progress of life from the 8th to the 4th, where we all end up, and we hope that you have read and understood that progress.

We also mentioned the kindergarten area where life is first created and nurtured before being transferred to the 8th dimension to start its long journey back to God, who created life in the first place.

All this refers to our creation. The whole of this immense work (creation) refers to life as we know it, or can know it, if we investigate it enough.

But now, the Master God (for it seems that there is an overseeing God) is very creative and very careful. He thought to himself, 'What happens if life' - as we know it - 'Ceased to be for any reason?'

So he created, based on the same system as ours, an almost infinite number of alternative realities but that were created around the model that we live in.
So, somewhere, there are a large number of creations that follow, more or less exactly, the system that was created for us: the kindergarten planet, the 8th dimension, the 4th and so on.

This is where it starts to get a bit complicated because we have to realise that our multiverse, which is immense and extremely complex, is only one of a virtually unlimited number of identical creations.
They are all back-up plans for if any - or many - realities should fail. There will still be more carrying on.
When we mention identical, we refer to the construction.
The life forms may differ widely from the life forms in our reality, as they were created by the wishes and desires for experience of the various Gods that oversee each reality.
For, yes, each alternative reality has its own God following a theme and these themes may seem very strange to us but are, nevertheless, as important as our life forms seem to us.

We don't know if you have understood this?
We have previously mentioned that elsewhere in our creation there are areas that form parts of personality, and we further mentioned that each one of these areas had a God overseeing it. But this is a different form of reality, virtually identical in its construction and that there are many of them, each one of which has a God in command just as our reality has a God in command.
So, we wish you to realise that the 8th dimension is subdivided into a large number of areas, if we may use that inaccurate term to describe an endless number of alternative realities. Each one is identical to the part of the 8th dimension that concerns us and each sub-dimension is coated with a thin gravity, the whole dimension being coated with a thick gravity, as are all dimensions and sub-dimensions. All is one, as we keep reminding you.
Then, as you should know, each sub-dimension has its own unique frequency.

So, the multiverse that we live in is only one of a large number of other multiverses, all following the same form of construction, but each one housing life forms either similar to ours or widely differing according to the instructions the God force gives to the archangels creating the life forms in any particular sub-frequency or multiverse.
We will go on to explore some of these sub-dimensions - alternative realities - not from the point of view of the construction, because each alternative reality is virtually identical in its construction to ours, but from the point of view of the lifeforms that live in them.

Each and every alternative reality, we remind you once again, is virtually a carbon copy to ours in that it has 8 dimensions, each one with countless sub-dimensions, and all the events that we have going on in the 7th down to the 1st dimension.
They are all identical because the Master God decided that it was a perfect concept so he put in charge of each one of these sub-dimensions a God and told that God to explore a certain life theme. Therefore, each God created archangels who, in turn, created the various life forms that God decided should be in accordance with the instructions of the Master God.

We don't know if you can understand this? It implies that our multiverse is just one of many and there is nothing special about our multiverse. It just so happens that we all live here in this multiverse.

At the same time that we are exploring our multiverse there are countless other beings in countless other multiverses - each one separated from any other by thin gravity - scratching their heads and wondering what life is all about just as we wonder also.

It also implies that the 8th dimension is not reserved just for us.

In other books, where we might have mentioned the 8th dimension, we may have given the impression that life in the 8th was exclusively ours. This is true up to a point because all life, as far as it concerns us, was or is contained in the 8th, at least at first.

But, to keep things simple at that time, what we did not mention was that in the same 8th dimension, separated by thin gravity, was an infinite number of alternative realities. They all start off from the one, unique 8th dimension.

It is only after that, that each group of entities (humans, animals) follows its sub-dimension down to its own 7th, 6th, 5th, 4th dimensions etc.

Can you understand this?

All life starts from the 8th dimension but within that dimension it is all kept apart by being in its own reality (sub-dimension).

From then on, life, as it develops, follows its own path in what is called alternative realities.

So, in a way, the 8th dimension is huge. It is also multi-dimensional. Each sub-dimension has its own God who creates the life force under its command and then its archangelic forces create the beings that suit each sub-frequency. We call each sub-frequency an alternative reality.

As we said, each one of these alternative realities are created as backups in case any one or any group of realities should fail.

So, in the unlikely event that our reality should be exterminated, there are plenty more to carry life on. So, life will never cease. Our life might cease or another alternative life might cease but life will always continue. This is difficult to comprehend but it is so.

Generally, beings from any one reality should not contact beings from any other reality, but it can happen that very advanced beings from our reality learn how to enter other realities and, equally, advanced beings from another reality might learn how to enter our reality.

Curiosity pushes people to do this sort of thing but we must advise you that it can be very dangerous to enter an alternate reality and no one incarnate should attempt to do such a foolhardy thing.

We have mentioned before that it occasionally happens that in large forests people come across staircases just standing alone.

This can happen if a person from another dimension (reality) wishes to visit us and creates what we perceive to be a staircase as a passage between their world and ours.

Now, such a person would be a very advanced being and has learnt how, successfully, to traverse dimensions and create this staircase. These are strange looking things. The lower end stops on the forest floor but the upper end just stops in the air.

Although one cannot see the connection the upper end has to an alternative reality, nevertheless, it is there and the whole staircase forms a path between an alternative reality and our reality - a portal.

It has been known for people to climb such staircases and when they reach the top they disappear, never to be seen again.

Quite simply, what happens is that the person from our reality climbs the staircase and if he reaches the top, he enters the alternative reality to which the top is attached.

So, he enters this alternative reality and is gone forever from our reality.

The entity from an alternative reality that created the staircase, when he has finished exploring our world, climbs the staircase, returns to his reality and allows the staircase to dissolve because it was constructed from etheric matter and is under the control of the mind of the visitor.

So, let us now turn to what we would experience if we were to visit an alternative reality. Before we start may we say a big 'thank you' to our angelic colleagues who have provided us with most of the information we are going to share with you. Even we who are in the 4th, hesitate to enter these realms because we are not sure of our ability to be able, successfully, to return to our reality, so we rely on angels who have much more skill than us. Even these angels can only traverse a few of these alternative realities as the further one penetrates, the stranger they become.

Let us start by saying that our multiverse is not the starting point as regards the totality of alternative realities. There are many on either side of ours.

The easiest way to imagine them is as a circle. A circle has no beginning and no end as a straight line would have.

If we select any point on a circle, there are points on either side of it. That is the nature of a circle.

Parallel universes are similar. We do not know where they start nor where they end. We only know that there are many of them.

Now, the interesting thing from the point of view of exploring them is that, if we were to visit any parallel universe (alternate reality) the next one to it would only be slightly different from the original one. Then the next one would be only slightly different from that. The differences become more and more marked from the original one to the point that, if we go far enough out, the universes are completely remote from the original one. But the change from each parallel reality to the next is slight.

Can you understand that? Let us explain again.

If we take our multiverse and compare it to another alternative reality - and here we mix universe, multiverse, parallel reality, alternative reality and so on but they all mean the same thing. We are mentioning a creation that looks, physically, more or less like ours in all aspects, dimensions included.

It is not so much the creation in a physical or astral sense that alters, it is the life forms that live in them that change.

But let us explain how they alter.

Let us call the first reality A. If we move from reality A to reality B, there would not be much difference and the beings that inhabit reality B would not differ very much from the beings that inhabit reality A.

That is why, by the way, that some people from reality B (if we live in reality A) can integrate and live with us for a while.

They might be more or less intelligent than us, speak our languages or not, but would pass amongst us unnoticed.

But now, if we move from reality B to reality C, the beings in reality C would not be much different from those in reality B but would start to show a difference between those in reality A.

If we may labor the point, if we go to reality D, the beings would be similar to those in reality C but show a marked difference from those in reality A.

And so it goes on. Each parallel reality being similar to the one next to it, but the difference becomes more and more marked the further one progresses from reality to reality compared to those far away, reality A, for example.

So even angels can only progress so far down the chain of parallel realities before the differences become so bizarre that they cannot comfortably proceed.

Therefore, we are aware that for the first few parallel realities close to ours, the humans and animals that live in them are instantly recognisable as such, but, eventually, the angels reach a point where the life forms are totally 'alien' if we can use that word without confusing strange life forms to true aliens. At variance to us would be a safer term to use. Now, if we are human and all is one, are the beings that live in parallel realities that look human really human? Logic would say they are. Equally, cats, dogs, sheep, horses, cows, etc., that one might find in a parallel universe close to ours should be very similar to those we find in our reality.

But, if we were able to glimpse into a parallel universe (reality) far from ours and if all the life forms looked totally different from those found in our reality, would, for example, what we call a human still be a human even if he looked nothing like us? Once again, logic would suggest yes but let us turn to our kind and helpful angelic comrades and see what they can tell us, because they are the only ones that we know of who have the skill and courage to enter some of these realms and have the ability to return safely back to our reality.

The next paragraphs are what we were told by the angels.

Although we will present the information in our words, the wisdom comes from the angels. When we return to us talking, we will tell you.

So, here is what we were told.

'The first thing is to learn how to change realities. This is not easy because we are meant to remain in our reality, so we have to invent a portal to move from our reality to the next one closest to ours. Then, if we wish to move on, we have to learn to invent a different portal to move on yet again. Inventing portals is not a simple thing because, as we said, we are not designed to change realities, so a lot of spiritual work has to go into creating a portal. Further, a portal will only transport one person so if several wish to change realities, each person has to learn how to do this.

Finally, of course, portals have to be recreated in order to move back again to our reality.

Portals are actually created by altered etheric material but this alteration has little or no connection to what you call astral projection. Astral projection uses etheric material but that normally would be used to move from one point of our reality to another.

Obviously, we are aware of how to do this, but changing realities is a different order of complexity altogether.

We know that everything is vibration (frequency) so we realise that each and every reality vibrates to a unique frequency just as our reality does.

The problem is finding the frequency of the reality next to ours and then finding the frequency of the one after that and so on.

This is not easy and took us a long time to discover the different frequencies of the parallel realities close to us.

We will not describe the frequency nor the technique because readers of this book could not emulate the technique and it would be futile and dangerous to try.

Suffice to say that after much trial and error we managed to discover the key to creating the frequency of at least some of these parallel areas, and as we already knew the frequency of our reality, we were able to create an etheric portal between our reality and the next one closest to ours.

What one has to do to change realities is to concentrate totally on the desired frequency. If one can do this sufficiently, one creates a portal between our reality and the desired frequency.

This links to the desired destination and so we can project ourselves from our multiverse's frequency to the desired multiverse's frequency.

We move on to our experiences in a parallel dimension closest to ours.

The first thing we noticed is that it appears very similar to ours geographically.

There are fields, mountains, lakes and forests. The sky looks much the same as our sky. The animals seemed to be much the same as ours but we noticed that there were a lot less farm animals than in our dimension.

But what interests us - and you, no doubt - are humans.

We wish to break off here to correct a common misconception.

There are people who think that parallel universes (realities) are some sort of copy of ours and the humans that inhabit them are just different versions of us. This is not true. Each and every parallel reality is a separate, unique creation under the control of its own God who, with the help of his trusted archangelic colleagues, creates totally new and separate life forms - separate from us, that is.

So, if a person from a parallel reality looks human that is because the Master God told each multiverse's God to create humans but they are unique humans and are not copies of you or any other human in our reality.

They are all different people created expressly for that multiverse.

We approached a group of humans and introduced ourselves. This did not seem to shock them in the degree that people from a parallel universe would shock many people on Earth. They seemed just to accept us.

Now, we noticed, as we toured the planet we were on, that they could speak verbally just as we can but their spoken languages were not familiar to us.

Fortunately, they all had the ability to communicate telepathically and thus, as we can communicate telepathically and as telepathy is a thought process, we could communicate.

Another aspect of telepathy is that mixed with the actual words are the emotions of what the people, the communicants, are. So, we could tell that they were peaceful people and they could tell that we meant them no harm.

We should perhaps mention that, being human angels, our normal state is a spiritual sphere of energy, but we are able to create with our minds a physical form, which we did, and, as these people had a physical form, we looked similar.
The people we spoke to as we toured their world looked very similar to Earth people and we could easily be mistaken one from another.
Clothing was different to what the average human tends to wear, being of much brighter hues, many people wearing toga style robes of somewhat rainbow colours.
In the colder areas they wore thicker versions of the same robes but no animal products were used.

We discovered, in our communications, that they were somewhat more advanced, spiritually, than the average human and their diet was vegan. They ate no animal products and the few farm animals we saw were kept as pets and were cared for with all the love and attention that we share on our loved pets.
They had no armies and killing, stealing, etc., was virtually unknown. They live in peace and harmony together and have respect for all life.
They believe in God but, although they knew about religions from their past history, they did not follow any religion.
There were men, women and children just as there are on Earth. The children seem to be loved and cared for and were free to play together without supervision as there was no concept of child molestation.
The whole atmosphere was of peace and harmony.

Some of them had heard of the concept of parallel universes and they told us that there were people who could traverse universes but we never managed to find one as it is quite a rare event in their universe.

Their homes were different to ours as the houses were built from a material which does not exist on Earth. We were informed that they did not wish to harm nature so they had invented building materials that did not contain any products taken from nature. Quite what the building material was, we never discovered. It was not that they wished to keep the building material secret, it was just that it was created using a technique with which we were not familiar.
But their homes were somewhat similar to ours with tables, chairs, beds, bathrooms, etc.

Their entertainment was more advanced than ours with a lot of 3D projection. They did not have televisions nor computers. They did not need them.
If they required entertaining, they thought of a concept and a holographic film would appear, the theme of a creation of their desire.
If there were a number of people in the room all projecting with their minds aspects to add to alter the film, this would be a cause for much mirth amongst the viewers.
None of the films would show violence as violence does not exist in this alternative reality.

It is all very innocent, one might almost say childish, but causes happiness to all who watch the film.

Similarly, if they need any information, they simply consult their equivalence of the akashic record and retrieve the required information.

They have no parliaments as such but they do have groups of wise people who make decisions for all the people of whatever country they represent. The people have the right to question their decisions but it is all done very peacefully.

As far as we could tell, all of the humans on their planet were vegan and their food was very simple. There were no complicated meals. They ate a lot of vegetables raw.

They did not seem to eat a great deal and we saw no lavish banquets.

The monetary system was similar to ours but was used to help all people rather than a few hoarding vast riches while others starved.

People often shared what they had, so all benefited.

In that respect, life was much different to that on Earth and more closely followed that experienced in the upper fourth dimension of planet Earth (heaven).

Moving onto the next parallel reality, things started to change somewhat.

Once again, it followed the previous one as far as being vegan and their democracy, but the humans started to look different.

They were all quite tall and their heads were more bulbous than Earth humans.

They seemed extremely 'brainy', if you see what we mean, and were very quick to pick up thoughts and reply to them.

Once again, although they had languages, telepathy was their main means of communication, certainly with us.

There was no conflict and we got the impression that the earth plane was the Nadir of alternative realities.

We could not visit many alternative realities but we never found one that was as primitive as planet Earth.

All the planets we visited, the humans and animals altered in appearance but they all lived in peace and were clearly more advanced than Earth humans.

This gives us food for thought. Why should planet Earth contain such primitive people compared to what we encountered in other parallel realities?

Were there realities that contained people more primitive than us? Perhaps, but we never came across any.

So, as we could not progress very far because of the difficulty of selecting appropriate frequencies to create portals, we will stop here.

We will end by saying there have been, from time to time, people who claim to have come to Earth from other dimensions.

Some just fabricate the stories but the genuine ones all seem to be more advanced than Earth humans.

If what we experienced is true for most of the alternative realities, it would seem that most, if not all of them, are more advanced spiritually than us.

We are not in a position to say why.'

That is the end of what the angels told us. Obviously, they could have explained a lot more about the daily lives of the people in parallel realities but the angels tailored their remarks specifically for this chapter and just gave an overview.
We think that they said sufficient to enable you to comprehend that most, if not all, parallel realities seem to be more advanced spiritually than us, which is interesting.
Why this is we cannot say.
We could guess but guesses are not facts, and if we are not sure we do not like to speculate.

However, if there are other realities and their lives are more advanced in a positive sense than ours, it gives us hope that our planet and the people on it will follow the same path.
So, we consider that this short chapter about parallel or alternative realities has reached its conclusion and we hope that you have learnt something from it.
We will stop here and turn to yet another subject.

CHAPTER 22

CATASTROPHES

We have given you a lot of information in this book and we are pleased to share our knowledge with you.

There is so much more that we could talk about. You may not realise it, but there are hundreds of aspects to life and each one is interesting and each one connects to the others to form creation. Creation is endless, so the number of topics we could describe is endless.

If you go back to book one and carefully read all the books, and if you read all the lessons and watch all the videos we have given you, you will see that we have already described a fair number of elements of life, but what we have said so far is just a drop in the ocean of what is waiting for you to discover.

So, we cannot possibly cover all the aspects of life before we end this book by telling you how to enter the upper fourth dimension. But, we will cover a few more aspects.

This next one concerns the way life reacts to problems

This may seem nonsense and we would agree that we do not refer to the petty concerns that occupy so much of people's time.

We are talking about the major decision's life has to take as and when catastrophes occur, the worst being ELEs (extinction level events). Fortunately, these are few and far between, but there are lesser events that can cause problems: volcanoes, earthquakes, forest fires, major floods and so on.

These, generally, effect a relatively small portion of planet Earth at any one time and, when they occur, the cost in human lives lost is counted and people mourn the demise of their loved ones.

But, all is one. The tiniest microbe and you all contain the totality of God. It is only the logos that denotes the difference. There are angels and the Directors of Life that are deeply concerned when there is a catastrophe because of the vast number of life forms that perish. Not just humans - with which you concern yourself - but also the plants, trees, animals, insects and so on that also lose their lives.

Each and every one of these life forms is as precious as you are to God and to his servants.

They mourn the suffering and demise of everything that is alive when something happens that destroys vast numbers of God's creatures.

Now, why do we mention this?

It is because, when something happens that destroys, prematurely, huge numbers of life, it upsets the balance of power that is so important to keep life in balance.

By power, we are not talking about man's political shenanigans. We are talking about the balance between all the life forms that were created by God's archangels to keep life in balance.

Each and every life form is essential, otherwise the archangels would not have spent the energy to create them.

We can afford to lose a few creatures but the sudden demise of huge numbers of life forms, some of which only grow in selected areas and climates, can cause major knock-on effects throughout the world.

God's archangels and the Directors of Life (who are another form of archangel) are constantly monitoring all life and are altering the DNA of all life to keep pace with the constant changes to planet Earth. This happens billions of times a second. The reason they do this is because it is essential to keep all life going in order to keep all life in balance.

Angels do not waste energy, so you can see that it is of vital importance that these angelic beings spend so much energy doing what they do, because it is of the utmost importance to keep life in balance.

However, catastrophes happen from time to time. Some of them are promoted by man and some of them are natural.

Although we heartily condemn the man-made catastrophes and assure you that, once the incarnations of the instigators of such events are over, they pay a heavy price for their crimes, we will not dwell on them as, man-made or natural, the loss of life is the same and it is that loss and how it is dealt with that interests us.

If a catastrophe hits a part of the world, the devastation can be much greater than you can possibly imagine. The devastation to towns or cities, which promotes worldwide news is comparatively harmless in the terms we are considering because, although the loss of human life might be severe and cause much heartache to the relatives and loved ones remaining, generally speaking, the actual numbers of life forms lost is not that great.

But, if there is a catastrophe that affects a forested area, for example, the loss of the number of life forms will be considerable.

As we said, each and every life form, whatever it is, is God taking the form of that life form, so even though humans are considered to be more important by man to plants and animals, in fact they are all God taking whatever form their logos created for them.

So, they all play an important role in the balance of nature.

Can we possibly imagine the number of creatures that live in forests, for example, that would be exterminated by a catastrophe?

We mentioned plants, trees, insects, animals and humans but we would have difficulty in counting the number of such entities that would be lost to nature.

Fortunately, in any catastrophe, the loss of human life is limited but there might be thousands of trees destroyed, millions of plants, thousands of slow-moving animals, millions of insects and billions of microbes. Each one is alive and each one is God in one form or another. So, each one is as important as any other life form, human or otherwise.

Then we might consider the nature spirits. These delightful creatures cannot be physically harmed as they are etheric but the effect on them to see their habitats destroyed would be severe.

The only creatures that might be happy might be the goblins who are part of the negative forces involved with the demise of plants.

All the rest of the fairy realm would have to set up home elsewhere in areas where there are already similar creatures living. Whether newcomers into their home lands would be welcome or not, we do not know.

Do not forget that even nature spirits are God in the form of a nature spirit and so are essential to the balance of life in that area.

The problem is what can be done about it?
If it is a flood, generally, the flood waters recede after a while or are soaked up by the Earth.
So, although huge numbers of plants might be destroyed and a large number of slow-moving animals drowned, not to mention the earthworms and other entities that live underground, the damage is limited and life soon returns to normal once the flood waters recede.
However, in the case of huge forest fires, whole areas of forests and all the life forms that could not escape the fire would be burnt.
Fast moving animals such as birds, deer, elk and even rabbits might be able to escape but other creatures such as tortoises, snakes, mice and worms, etc., have no chance and get burnt alive.
If such a fire was created by man deliberately, the crime against nature is immense and anyone responsible for all that suffering pays a terrible price in hell once his incarnation is finished.
No right-minded person should provoke such a fire. The price in retribution that he pays is the equivalent of every sufferance he caused to any of God's creatures. He pays until the last debt is resolved.

Earthquakes, once again might cause major upsets and can alter the landscape permanently but, generally speaking, there is no irremediable damage to life.
Life (fauna and flora) is very resilient and with the help of God's archangels and the Directors of Life, balance is usually restored.
Volcanoes erupting can cause a lot of damage because, from the point of view that we are considering, it is not only the immediate destruction of fauna, flora and humans caught unaware, but if lava covers an area, although other fauna and flora might eventually cover the area it is lost permanently to the original fauna and flora that lived there.

Now, we have mentioned all this and we are sure that you agree with us that catastrophes are most unfortunate, you may be wondering what it has to do with this book which is about the areas in the 4th concerned with us.
Well, in a way, we could say nothing, as we could go through our lives and not give a thought to catastrophes unless, by bad luck we happen to be involved with one - in which case they very much come to the forefront of our thoughts - but we know of two reasons why we should concern ourselves.
1. By leading good lives we create positivity which reduces the chances of catastrophes, and
2. We can, spiritually, play an active role in praying for peace in the world as a whole. Not only making sure that we never involve ourselves in negative thoughts and actions, but by doing all that we can to help all life, when appropriate. You would be surprised of the degree that you can help peace come to all areas of life, no matter in what degree we try and in what degree catastrophes might start to take place.
By surrounding ourselves with peace and love, we can change life.

You must remember that you live in your own universe, created by you and so, by refusing to give way to negativity, your world stays peaceful and so all of life stays peaceful.

This sounds like gobbledygook and we would be the first to admit that we might keep our lives peaceful but others, who live in a more violent world, would provoke catastrophes that could harm innocent people.

Now, although we have mentioned that we all create and live in our own unique universes created by us, and have given quite detailed explanations as to how the singularity we are, in conjunction with our logos, DNA, and other parts of us create the world that seems so real to us.
But what happens if there is a catastrophe, for example, that seems to affect huge numbers of humans, fauna or flora? If we are alone, how can others be affected?

We are gradually working our way towards the area in the 4th that governs all this, but we need to explain in much greater detail this concept of you living in your singularity - just you, alone - with no one else existing in your reality.
We will attempt to explain but we are not sure of how great a job we can make of the explanation, nor of how much you will be able to understand.
As usual, however, we will do our best and hope to make this topic understandable.
It will not be easy because although we have mentioned this topic many times and although we have mentioned alternative realities, in fact this topic - that you are the only one that lives in your reality - will be just about the most difficult and counterintuitive subject we could ever discuss and yet it is quite simple once one understands.

Let us first repeat the point that is hardest of all to comprehend.
You are the only human that lives in your reality.
If anyone told you this before you had read the many thousands of words we have written explaining this fact, we are sure that most, if not all, would reject that concept.
Indeed, even now we know that there are many who cannot accept this, and we don't blame you.
It does seem obvious that we are surrounded by countless people, animals, plants and minerals. The sky is full of planets, suns and stars (points of light in the night sky).
This is obviously, incontrovertibly true as you look around you.
You go outside your house and are instantly in contact with all that goes on in the outside world.
You turn on your TVs and you see countless people presenting entertainment of one sort or another.
And yet we tell you that none of this is real.
Please notice that we did not say that it didn't exist in your imagination. We said that all you see that seems so real is not real.

Let us try to examine what the word real means.
A dictionary gives the impression that the word real implies physical as opposed to imaginary and yet we tell you that nothing is real. All is created by your imagination, aided and abetted by your logos, ego, personality, DNA and a number of other aspects.
So how can we resolve this conundrum?

If you look at something you 'see' it with your eyes and your brain translates the image into a form that you consider to be real.
If you touch the object, another aspect of your five senses confirms what your eyes - or rather your brain - saw.
And so it goes on.
The only link to the object is what your five senses transfer to your brain, and thus you form an image of the object.

But, if we were able to link to the brain of someone else, how could we be sure that both people were seeing exactly the same thing?
The truth is, we couldn't. We just accept that one person's description of an object conforms to ours, and thus we call the object real.
We have stated before that if, for example, a crime is committed and the police ask a number of witnesses to describe the event or the culprit, descriptions can vary widely.
We could go on to discuss religions. Some people are convinced of one version of a religion and another believes something quite different.
Politics is another example that we are sure that you are aware of.
We could go on and on pointing out the differences people have in a whole variety of topics.
If we question a number of people about a variety of topics, some physical and some intellectual and we carefully note their replies, we have to come to the conclusion that no two people see, or think, the same thing.

We could go on and examine relationships.
Someone might love his husband or wife, mother or father, son or daughter, and that image would be coloured by his/her love for the person and forgiveness of faults. The person who loves someone would tend to overlook physical blemishes and see the loved one as handsome or beautiful, with a nice voice and a nice comportment (manners).
But, on the other hand, someone who hates anyone would see them in a diametrically opposed fashion. And yet it is the same person.
If we have a pet dog, for example, we might love that dog, find it beautiful, gentle and loving but anyone who was scared of that dog - maybe he has been bitten by the dog - would have a totally opposite view of the animal.
We are sorry to labor the point, but we wish to point out that our image of something or someone depends entirely on our opinion of the person, animal, object or scene and can vary widely. We form in our minds and our brain an image, not formed by fact but by emotion.
So, what is real?
What is reality?
This is the point we are making that reality is just the image we form of something, not the object itself. That is because the object does not exist. We create it in our minds and personalities.
We do appreciate that we have made a leap from saying that we form an image of something to saying that the object does not exist, and it is difficult to understand this fact.

If you think about the subject dispassionately, no matter what image you form of the object or subject, it can only be exclusive to you. Each and every person forms an image of what they are thinking about and that image can, and is, only relevant to that person.

Let us go on and hammer home what we are trying to describe to you and then we will expand to try to explain why nothing exists.
Let us imagine that we go to a shop with someone close to us to buy something. It matters not what the something is. It might be a house, a car, clothes, furniture, kitchenware - absolutely anything.
You know from experience that, initially, no two people will agree instantly that what is being considered is the correct choice.
A whole plethora of factors might be brought into consideration depending on what the object is.
If we take a simple example - a tea service (which we have chosen out of the blue) - can you imagine the number of factors that come into play?
For example, one person might think that enough cups and saucers for four people might be correct. The other person might think that enough for six or more would be correct.
Then the types of cups, modern or more traditional? Is it in china or porcelain?
How many plates and ancillary ware - cake stands and so on - should be considered?
Does the service include cake stands? The price? Is it unique or does everyone have a similar service?
On and on.
The two people might go from shop to shop before settling on a compromise.
A compromise usually pleases no one totally, as each person has an image of what he/she really wants, and either cannot find it or has to settle for second best.
The moral to this is that the tea set the person wants does not exist and what is finally purchased is not what was imagined by either person.
Now, this story may not, at first read, seem to be connected to the fact that nothing exists, but look at it this way.

In a factory somewhere a designer draws a tea service that he hopes will sell. He may not like the design himself, but he feels obliged to draw it.
Then a craftsman makes the molds. Then others create and fire the actual cups, saucers and other things. These people may like or dislike what they are obliged to make.
This goes on until the buyer for the shop looks through a catalogue and selects that tea service, hoping it will sell.
He also may like or dislike the service but he hopes that his customers will like it.
Finally, as we said, the customers, after much deliberation, settle for that tea service.
Once again, what has this got to do with the fact that it doesn't exist?

The answer lies in the emotions of the various people who were involved with the design, manufacture, sale and purchase of the tea service.
We have told you that you are pure spirit and you are one with God, which implies that there is only one and that one is God.
Whether you believe this or not, there is only one life form in reality and that is God pretending to be you and everyone and everything else.
This is the fundamental truth about life.

If you refuse to accept this, there is no point in reading this chapter. If you can accept this, we will continue to explain.

Everything is made of atoms combining in some way to produce all that exists. We hope that even the most skeptical reader can accept this.
Atoms contain the force of God. In a way they are God using his archangelic colleagues to produce objects through atoms combining under the logos that is given to all things.
But, atoms create objects: animal, vegetable, mineral or human as spirit forms because God is a spirit form, so atoms are spirit forms.
They appear to be real due to the fact that they are placed in the illusionary world we call the 6th dimension (or part of it) but that you call reality.
It all seems real to you because you are also part of the illusion.
However, atoms contain auras and auras contain personality, ego, etc., as we have often explained. As all is one and as you have personality, so everything has personality.
Thus, when you look at an object, a teacup, you are not really looking at the object, you are looking at the way your personality thinks about the object, and that object thinks about you. That is why you are drawn to some things and not others.
That is why there can be so many points of view about a simple tea cup.
If you consider this, if there can be so many points of view about a teacup, can it be real?
If reality is how we think about a teacup and there have been dozens, at least, of points of view concerning the mining of the clay up to the point that someone sips tea from the cup, whose point of view is the correct one?

Further, as all is one and you and the teacup are one, only your point of view can be valid for you.
Think about this and try to feel the connection between a teacup and you.
That connection is there because the cup and you are one.
There is no other 'one' involved. All is one, so that cup and you is all that exists as far as you are concerned.

If you take the logic on, it should lead you to the conclusion that you - your thoughts, etc., - are all that exist.
Everything else is your imagination creating what we have called background people and objects, popping in and out of your creation.
It is all very much like a play or a film as Shakespeare and us have often explained.

As we said, if you cannot accept this truth, so be it.
We understand, as it is counterintuitive of the worlds we all live in, but it is a great truth and by understanding and accepting this, it can change your life.

Now, at long last, let us turn to the 4th.
There is an area in the 4th that contains the emotion to do with the connection of all life and how we can help reduce catastrophes through the realization of our oneness to all life and that, as all is illusion, we can cast our emotions into that area, which is connected to catastrophes, and reduce or negate them.

We spent a number of pages trying to explain how and why you are all that exists in your world - which you are free to accept or reject. - and we assure you that it was very difficult for us to explain the basics of it in simple, easy to understand terms.
If that part was difficult to accept and understand, this next part will be equally difficult but we will do our best as always.

Now, planet Earth is alive, just as alive as you are. We tend to term her 'she' because she is the mother of all incarnate and, even though mother Earth is an illusion, to all those incarnate, you live on her and every aspect of your life comes from her. You are made of atoms that come from earth. Your food, clothing, housing and heating come from earth. But there is a difference between earth and Earth.
The earth provides all that we need but mother Earth is a living entity. She is you, as you should be aware of now, and you are her. All is one.
But mother Earth, like all living things, has personality.
As such, she takes the decision, from time to time, to react and cause changes to her morphology.
We will ignore man-made catastrophes and just consider the catastrophes that mother Earth decides to make.
The reason that she decides to make changes are difficult for us to comprehend, but the fact is that, from time to time, she decides to take actions that can affect us.
Let us use some childish examples taken from human life to explain.

Your whole body is covered with bacteria of one sort or another.
Some people seldom wash but the majority of people take showers or baths and those actions cause the demise of countless bacteria which, we remind you, are alive and are God taking the form of bacteria. So, each time we wash we are killing millions of life forms, but we consider it necessary in order to remove the smell created by bacteria on our skin.
Equally, we might cut our hair or trim our finger and toe nails. Once again, numbers of bacteria are eliminated.
We could say that to protect all life we should, perhaps, never wash, brush our teeth, trim our hair and nails, never wash our clothes and there are certain holy people that protect bacteria by never performing any acts of hygiene but we think that you would agree that although protecting all life is a laudable act, we would have some difficulty in being accepted if we never washed, never brushed our teeth and never washed our clothes.
As far as the bacteria are concerned, they have no idea why we performed the hygiene acts we do. They only know that by living on human bodies they are regularly affected by catastrophes occurring to them that we call hygiene.

We apologise to you for using this childish example but we hope that you can see the point we are making which is that, for some reason unknown to them, millions of bacteria are destroyed through drowning, scrubbing or poisoning them with hygiene products, etc. In a similar way, for some reason incomprehensible to us, people, plants and animals are harmed by the dramatic actions taken by mother Earth.
No doubt, mother Earth is aware of the living creatures living on her skin, or just below it, but just how much she takes their destruction into account before she performs any violent action, we don't know.

However, the point of this chapter is to tell you that in the 4th is an area that connects to mother Earth. After all, if all is one, it would be logical that we, plus the animals and plants should be connected to Earth.

This place in 4th provides that connection. However, it does more than that.

As we humans have quite strong personalities, through this connection to Earth in the 4th, we can persuade her to reduce or stop catastrophes.

We repeat that mother Earth is alive just as you are and is, in fact, you in just another form. Just as you in incarnation have moods - happiness, sadness, illness and health, the desire to move, scratch, clear yourself of unwanted microbes, so mother Earth has similar feelings.

This may seem strange to those who think that Earth is just made of earth and is there to be exploited in any way, shape or manner anyone desires, if and when we can realise that Earth is the same as you, the picture changes.

You may remember us saying, 'Never do anything to others that you would not like done to you.' And, equally, 'Always do to others that which you would like done to you.'

If we can include mother Earth in those statements it implies always treating mother Earth as you would wish to be treated.

Now, in the 4th there is an area that provides a link between us, and all living things, to the mind of mother Earth.

We should perhaps say that we constantly use the term 'mother Earth' to denote the difference between a living object that is just as alive in all respects as you, compared to a dead sphere of earth, rock and stone that people feel free to exploit and destroy.

We want you clearly to realise that mother Earth is as alive and as sensitive as you are and should be treated with the same respect as you would wish that you would be respected.

Gradually, as man advances in ascension, so all animate life will be respected and, we hope, mother Earth will be treated with the respect that she deserves.

We will also mention at this point, that new forms of manufacturing vegan food will come to be - the same system that is used in alternative realities - so that it will not be necessary to destroy vast areas of nature in order to allow livestock to grow, nor to grow the huge amount of vegetable food products to feed livestock.

Mother Earth is aware of this terrible, primitive method of feeding the world and we can tell you that she does not approve.

Man must learn to live in harmony with nature and not exploit and destroy it.

We have spent most of this chapter explaining to you that physical life, as you know it to be, is actually the result of the way non-physical aspects, personality, ego, etc., play out in physicality, and this area in the 4th deals with the way that our spiritual aspects of personality link with the personality of mother Earth. It is all non-physical, but plays out on Earth in physical events.

So, if we link to this area, as it is non-physical, even in an astral sense, there is nothing to see. It is yet another area that is purely mental as opposed to physical.

But, the important point is that, as all is one, our attitudes can link with the non-physical aspects of mother Earth and by impressing on her our feelings of love, peace, acceptance of her as a respected being, we can reduce catastrophes that mother Earth feels inclined to create in order to rid herself of unwanted interference, just as we wash in order to get rid of unwanted bacteria on our bodies.

Mother Earth is quite a gentle, tolerant being and she allows man to abuse her to an extent that few humans would tolerate, but she does protest from time to time.
Who can blame her when we consider the way we have treated her over the millennia?
But the levels of abuse that man has imposed on her over recent years is too much.
Coal and oil mining. The emptying of the seas of fish. Atomic explosions and, finally, fracking have reached such proportions that she protests.
She has no intention of causing harm to us but she is warning us, in her own way, that enough is enough.

To reach into this area in the 4th normally requires knowing the exact frequency of that area, but this matter is of such importance that advanced guides and some angels have volunteered to help good people send our loving thoughts out. They - these advanced beings - will pick them up and transfer them to this area in the 4th where mother Earth can pick them up and thus reassure her that we are not all bad people which, we hope, will calm her and help her decide not to create catastrophes.

There will always be some catastrophes as mother Earth moves and adjusts her body (planet Earth) but, by the simple act of prayer and adjusting our lives to live in peace with each other and with the planet, we can stop many of the catastrophic events that devastate us from time to time.

So, what should we do to help?
The first thing is to have the desire to help mother Earth and, by the same token, help all life.
The second thing is to become, gradually, vegan. This act, which we remind you should be done slowly to help your body adjust to the change, will help planet Earth enormously.
We will remind you that you must take vitamin B12 (cyanocobalamin), in one form or another or you could become very ill. Humans have been carnivores for so long that our bodies have adapted to the meat diet, which naturally contains B12, and so you must augment your vegan diet with regular doses of B12 to replace the B12 contained in animal products.
We should also advise you to survey your health. Not all people can accept a vegan diet and if this applies to you, stop and return to your normal diet.

The next thing is to meditate regularly, if and when you can. We have described the technique frequently and will do so again at the end of this book. As you meditate you are sent the power of God and, at the end of each meditation, you should send, with your mind, that power out to the world. It will be picked up by the aforementioned guides and angels and will be transferred to this area in the 4th and mother Earth will receive it and it will help her reduce her desire to react to man's negative actions.
Lastly, never harm by word or deed anything or anyone.
Always stay calm and loving.
Those emotions will fly around the etheric realms and will help bring peace to Earth.
These acts will spread and will be noticeable in a reduction in the number of catastrophes inflicted on us by Earth's retaliation to the way we abuse her.

We feel that we have explained enough about this plane in the 4th and our relationship to mother Earth and we hope that you will join the ever-growing throng of people that recognise that mother Earth is a living, sentient being as sentient as you are, with feelings as deep as yours.
We hope that you will help us live in peace with our mother so that she can live in peace with us.

So, we will end this chapter here and move onto yet another topic in the 4th dimension that has relevance to us all.

CHAPTER 23

CHANGING LIFE PLANS

This chapter will deal with another aspect of the areas in the 4th that connect, not only to the last chapters, but with the way that it connects to you in your incarnation and on into the afterlife.

We wish to mention actions that occur as you progress through life.

As you live your life day by day and follow your life plan, you may think that you have control of your life and, to a certain extent, you have.

Others feel they are almost victims of their life plans and, once again, although we would not use the word victim, you are obliged, to a certain extent, to follow your life plan.

Your life plan you decided on before you chose to incarnate and, thus, you were born male, female (or otherwise), into a certain family, in a certain country - with all that this entails - and follow a certain path.

However, this is not the whole story by any means.

There exists in the 4th an area which, if you can link with it, enables you to change your life plan and thus your destiny as you progress through life.

Changing your life plan is not something that one should undertake lightly as, unless it is done with the greatest care and with serious and prolonged consultation with one's guides and mentors, could be catastrophic.

The incarnation that you first decided upon - with prolonged discussion with a number of guides - was designed to help you deal with at least one facet of incarnation and, we will be perfectly frank with you, is most unwise to change.

However, this area in the 4th that helps people change their life plans exists, and for the sake of completeness of this book, we feel obliged to discuss, but do not think that we are recommending you to follow.

We are merely mentioning it to you as it exists and, obviously, is a link between the 4th and incarnation, which is what this book is really about.

So, for those who do not fully understand about life plans, let us go back and start at the beginning.

You are a spiritual being which means that you are not a physical human as you probably perceive yourself to be.

You were created by God and, as we have said countless times, contain the totality of God, not only in every atom that creates your spiritual and physical (on Earth) body, but is also connected to your personality, ego, DNA and logos.

You are God taking the form of you.

Do not think that this is blasphemy - which is a concept created by religious leaders to keep you a slave to them and their religion.

You are God. Every aspect of you is God. There is no part of any of you that is not God. Every atom of you is God. Every aspect of your logos is God taking the form of you.

Every grain of sand, plant, insect or other human that connects with you, including the air you breathe and the water you drink is God.

That is all that exists. God is everywhere and is everything. You need to understand this deep in your soul.

You and God are the same thing.

That is the first and very important point we wish to hammer home to you. You are God.
Do not be ashamed of thinking this. It is not blasphemy. It is the truth.
Until you can accept this, much of what we and other sages and mystics, going back for
thousands of years, have told you or tell you now will not make sense.
Indeed, it is an insult to God for anyone to suggest that all is not God.
Those who tell you that God is some psychopath waiting to pour hellfire and damnation
on you might well be describing themselves and the destiny that awaits them for the lies
that they have spread, but it does not describe God at all.
God is the force of pure love and, as you are God, your natural state is that of pure love.

However, as you are no doubt aware, your personality that you gradually created and
finally adopted as a result of the information you learnt in your tours of the various
information centers in heaven before incarnating, alters your natural form as a being of
love and allows you to accept other flavors of life into your personality.
This is important because physical incarnation, which allows you to meet all sorts of
people, acts as a protection if you can be loving but also have degrees of - not hate
exactly - but degrees of emotions that are less than pure love.
Indeed, coping with incarnation in its present form would be almost impossible if some
of us just had pure love while the rest of people lived with selfishness and violence
upmost in their personalities.
We will also say that on our side of the veil, many advanced souls project love but they
still retain a degree of other emotions in their personalities in case they need to deal with
people or situations not based on pure love.
As we said, in the future, as ascension progresses, things will change for the better but
planet Earth was designed as a melting pot for many different people with many different
points of view and attitudes and will always remain so to a small extent even in the
future.
There would be no point in incarnation if there was not this mixture of personality types
for us to test ourselves against.
That is why you come to Earth and why we, in turn, came to Earth. We suffered,
probably, much more than you do today at the hands of evil people and it was only when
our incarnations were, thankfully, finished and we returned home to our oversouls in the
4th that we could look back at our incarnation and see the point of it.
And the point was that both we who suffered and those who caused our suffering learnt
valuable lessons of dealing with each other and learning the lessons that incarnation
presented to us so that we could learn, either through being the perpetrators or the victims
of wrongdoing, that it was incorrect and that love for each other was the answer.
This information was and is presented to the next generation preparing themselves for
incarnation and so these next generations incarnate with the knowledge in their higher
selves that hate, cruelty, unkindness, etc., is not the way forward and that kindness, love
and care for all is what matters.
Of course, as this information is hidden in the higher self via the akashic records, not all
people realise this love for each other and so terrible deeds still occur but, generally, such
acts are frowned upon nowadays whereas, years ago, not only was cruelty and

unkindness accepted as normal, it was actually encouraged by states and religions - with the possible exception of Buddhism.

We see, as time passes, that, less and less is the opposite of love in all its connotations acceptable and we see, at least in most civilized countries, systems where the weak and poor are cared for whereas, years ago, poverty was looked at almost as a crime and poor people summarily dealt with.

There was no sympathy for the weak, the poor, the disabled and those who did not fit into the dog-eat-dog societies. To be rich and powerful was all that mattered and those who could not be rich and powerful were treated dreadfully.

People did not realise that they incarnated to learn compassion for others. Self preservation was all that mattered.

But, life progresses and, generally, things are improving.

What has all that we have mentioned got to do with this place in the 4th where we can change our life plan?

The answer, of course, lies with those who feel that they have chosen the wrong life plan and wish to have another stab at having a different one.

As we have said, everyone, whether they intend to have an Earthly incarnation or not, is given a long education in the 4th and are shown a multitude of different aspects of personality.

This education, before a physical incarnation is even considered, is thorough.

Virtually every aspect of life is presented to the student, and his mentors take careful note of what the student is drawn towards and what he rejects.

We just mentioned that a physical incarnation is a choice people make and many young students in the 4th decide not to have one. It is not through cowardice, being unwilling to face the rigors of incarnation. It is because, quite simply, they are not attracted to it.

But many people who are shown what incarnation is and the part they could play in incarnation decide to incorporate that option into their personalities.

And so, gradually, a sort of list of options builds up and forms the personality of the individual.

This happens to everyone whether they decide to have an incarnation or not.

In your case and ours, we decided to have an incarnation and so, as we have explained, decisions are taken as to the sort of incarnation we wish to have.

We will not discuss the pros and cons of our decisions as we have already discussed this many times and even gave you a book called Personalities in which incarnation choices were discussed and described at length.

Of course, as we go through our incarnation, often feeling lost as we are battered by the negativity flooding around us through the thoughts of evil and lost souls whose thoughts go into the etheric realms and affect us all through all sorts of negativity.

We do not realise that we chose that type of incarnation and we wish we could change life, usually by winning a lot of money but, as we have said, the rich are not necessarily happy. They exchange one set of problems for another.

The life plan a person chose ensures that, whatever his bank balance, he has to have certain experiences.

No matter what we do, our life plan pushes tests to us and we have to learn to react to those tests.

If we change our financial situation, the changes might alter but these tests, which to a certain extent are preordained, will be presented to us.

Perhaps, to make the point clear, let us imagine a child who goes to school.

Towards the end of each year he will sit examinations in a variety of subjects.

Now, imagine that the parents of the child win - or lose - a lot of money. This might result in the child going to a different school, one private, or if the parents lose their money, a state-run school.

In either case, at the end of each year, examinations are held. The fact that the child changed schools does not alter the fact that tests are held to find out how much the child had learned.

Life is the same. No matter what one does, life will present the tests already programmed into his life plan.

So, there are some people who wish to change their life plan.

The area we are going to describe is created for these people.

As we said, changing one's life plan is not a simple thing to do as it involves not only a change for the person concerned, but it also affects each and every person the individual knew and each and every event that occurred.

This part is going to be difficult to explain and, no doubt, difficult for many to understand and accept because it involves going right back to the moment the individual left the 7th dimension and moved to the 4th.

It is not just a question of adding a new life plan to the end of the previous one. Life does not work like that.

Each and every experience, from the moment the person became conscious, is recorded for all time in his personal file in the akashic record. These records, normally, are a permanent recording of that person's life and should remain as a permanent record for all time rather like a diary written and carefully conserved.

It is by the method of conserving people's diaries, for example, that scholars can refer to them and discover how the person who wrote the diary lived. The record in the diary never changes. It is a permanent record of how the person lived in whatever detail was recorded.

The akashic record is much the same. It is a permanent record of that person's life as controlled by his life plan and his personality.

However, if someone wishes to have a new life plan, his file in the akashic record has to be erased and a new one created as if the person was a totally different individual.

Can you imagine just how complicated this is to erase each and every event, conversation, encounters and actions of the person since he was created?

Equally, someone has to go through the files of the huge number of people, guides and angels the person had contact with and eliminate all of it from the files of those he encountered.

Not just in incarnation, if the person had an incarnation, but from his long life in the spiritual planes.

What, for instance, if the person had an incarnation, happens to his life in incarnation?

His family into which he was born?
Any children he had? Any grandchildren?
All of this has to be altered as if the person had never existed.
All of his school and work history has to be erased as if he never went to school or work.
The memories of those who knew him have to be modified via their files in the akashic record.
It is an immensely complicated thing to consider changing one's life plan. It is possible to do but is an immense amount of work, as you can imagine.

By the way, we spoke of erasing from a person's memory the existence of someone.
We will tell you how it is done. It is not difficult once one knows how but it is something that should not be done. We will mention it just for those curious about modifying memory, safe in the knowledge that no one incarnate could do it.
First, it has been noted that certain quasi military people have developed techniques through drugs and hypnosis and have been able to suppress or alter memories.
This is not permanent as the real memory of an event is stored in the person's file in the akashic records, and merely blocking the event does not make it permanent.
The real memory can be recovered.
No, what we are talking about is getting access to a person's file in the akashic record and eliminating, not only that file, but the same event that is stored in the personal file of anyone connected to that event.
This would be impossibly complicated for anyone to do and only specially trained angels - very advanced beings - are permitted to go into the akashic record and perform such actions.
When we say 'permitted', we are not implying that there is any police force in heaven controlling things. We are implying that people's sense of right and wrong would prevent them from taking such a step.
The memories in the akashic record are connected to the God force and are considered sacred.
It is rare that they are tampered with.

But what happens if someone insists on changing their life plan?
Before we deal with an actual person let us take a look at the place in the akashic record that concerns these changes.
First, let us say that it is not physical. It is a frequency.
But, associated with it are a number of angelic beings who, if someone insists on this change, have to enter the akashic record and make all the adjustments. These angelic beings are wise and powerful and, we will say, courageous when you understand the tasks they perform.
Anyone changing their life plan is, fortunately, extremely rare so, no doubt, these angels occupy themselves with other duties until required to come together to perform this special duty.
So, this place in the 4th concerned with life plan change is difficult to describe as there is nothing to see nor, if we visit this place, do we have the desire to change our life plan.
It is only when a person wishes to change his life plan would it 'wake up' and send a message to these special angels to meet and decide what to do.

Now, the individual concerned makes it known that he wishes to change his life plan. Initially, his guides and helpers all meet with him and discuss with him why he wishes to do this and what sort of new life plan he desires.
These guides and helpers do not take sides to prevent him from following his desire to change. They discuss the pros and cons of such a decision and, quite often, the person concerned changes his mind and retains his old life plan.

However, assuming that the person insists on changing his life plan, the above-mentioned angels swing into action.
Erasing the old life plan of the person concerned is a relatively simple affair but erasing all knowledge and the consequences of, perhaps, long years of connection to others is a matter of a different order of complexity altogether.
Erasing the memories of people that only vaguely knew the individual is not difficult.
The difficulty comes in sorting out those who knew the person well.

Let us examine what happens if the person had an incarnation.
In that case, he would have parents, grandparents, spouse, children and, possibly, grandchildren all of whom knew the individual well.
Some of the family - and friends - might still be in incarnation and some would be in the 4th dimension somewhere.
So, how is it possible to deal with all those situations?
Logic would suggest that all the children, for example, would have to be eradicated as, if the individual who changes his life plan would have a completely different life, his descendants should no longer exist.
However, the angels would not conceive of eradicating countless people who knew the original individual, so another course of action is practiced.
The angels change the life plans of all those that were close relations of friends and link them to a volunteer who takes over the role of the original person.

This is a complicated thing to do, but by going into the akashic record and altering the events stored there, it is possible to do.
This may sound crazy because the spouse and children, for example, one moment have a spouse and/or father or mother and then, in a flash, have a totally different person as a relation.
As crazy as this seems, this in fact, is what is done.
The new person will play the role of the relation until his or her incarnation ends and the person goes to the 4th. From there, it is easier to control events.

We will repeat just to make it perfectly clear.
For those who only slightly knew the individual who wants to change his life plan they have their memories of contact with that person wiped from their memories in the akashic record.
But for those closely related to the individual, another person plays the role of the original person until his/her life on Earth ends. The memories in the akashic record of all those who knew that person are altered and the family and close friends suddenly find themselves with the new relation that they are convinced is the original person.
At the same time, any official documents are altered to correspond to the new person and no one notices the difference.

We do appreciate that this sounds like make believe but, fortunately, changing life plans is such a rare event that it can be achieved successfully.
If it were a common event, it would be difficult to control and it might be possible for a slip-up to occur
Due to the fact that it is an extremely rare event - a change of life plan - great care can be taken to ensure that every eventuality is covered and the new person plays the role of the first person while incarnate.

All this is possible due to this area in the 4th that is a place of a certain frequency that sends out a signal if a person wishes to change his life plan, and enables certain angels to take charge of the event.
We repeat that this life plan change is an extremely rare event and we explained it just for the sake of explaining yet another area in the 4th.

We hope that you have found this chapter interesting as it gives an idea of the power that angelic beings have and the incredible dedication and skill they demonstrate to assist someone who desires to change his life plan.
But, we insist to remind you that this is a very rare event.

The person who decides to change his life plan, of course, has his memories wiped from the akashic record and he starts again with a new life plan of his choice, made in conjunction with a new set of helpers.

So, we will end this bizarre chapter here which, we do understand that many will have difficulty in believing, and turn to yet another area in the 4th connected to life both in and out of incarnation.

CHAPTER 24

DEATH AND ETERNAL LIFE

This new chapter will deal with yet another aspect of life in areas of the 4th that can concern you but that some might find difficult to accept.

You may have noticed that, as this book progresses, we have been moving from fairly down to earth, easy to understand topics into rather stranger areas.

We do this deliberately for several reasons.

Firstly, we know that there are some readers who are very curious to learn about topics that are rarely or never discussed, and if they are, are usually just guesses and have no connection to reality.

Then, there are other readers who have not yet incarnated but, when they do, although much is hidden in their higher minds, we hope will jog their memories and help them to remember their lives before incarnating and will thus enable them to recreate the link between themselves in incarnation and the lives they lived before incarnating.

We want, eventually, all people to have this link to the 4th which will help those in incarnation to be fully connected to their friends and guides in the 4th.

Thus, will planet Earth change and peace be restored.

Imagine a life where you could live in peace with all people and also have a daily link with your friends in the spirit realms.

Would that not be a better life?

That is the object of what we do and the information we give you.

However, we give you the information and leave you to decide what to do with it.

So, let us go on to describe yet another area in the 4th that exists and deals with people who think, either that life after incarnation doesn't exist or, for religious reasons, think that they are 'dead' until some being comes to wake them up to eternal life.

Although these are different subjects and we will talk about them separately, let us describe what happens when people's lives first come to an end in so-called physicality. We have talked about this subject many times and we know that there is a video in which our Earthly instrument described at least two different methods of transitioning from Earth to heaven (the 4th dimension).

We will just briefly repeat them.

1. The first is that, as a person prepares to transition (die), a member of his/her family will appear psychically and remain until the person dies which means, quite simply, that the silver cord which transmits energy from the spiritual aspect of the person - the real person - into the so-called physical body and, once this cord separates, the physical body ceases to function and the person is declared dead.

At this point the family member guides his charge safely to the 4th dimension (heaven) and the newly liberated person is met by an advanced individual who explains to the new arrival that he/she is in heaven.

2. The other method is the famous tunnel of light.

If, for some reason, the individual who is to die does not have a family member arrive to assist him, in the case of a violent accident for example, the higher self opens a portal between the spiritual aspect of the individual concerned and the heavenly spheres and the individual finds himself floating down this beautiful tunnel of light, as it is called.
Once again, we use the masculine when describing things and events but this is just standard literary convention. We include females or any other gender, of course, in our intentions and mean no offence to anyone.
Once again, the individual steps into the light of heaven and is met by an advanced person who explains that the individual is now liberated from his physical body and is in heaven.

This is what normally happens to a newly released individual. Released from incarnation either through old age, illness, accident or suicide. We will discuss suicide cases separately.
So, we repeat, in one way or another, all people should transition from Earth to heaven in a calm and dignified manner.
What happens after that - the life review and so on - we have already described in other chapters.
But there are two cases where the person either does not go to heaven or does not believe heaven exists and he is, quite simply, 'dead'. Believing that there is nothing after the physical life.

We have already mentioned the unfortunate individuals who finish up in limbo but will briefly mention it again.
It can happen that a person, for some reason, is not met by a family member or does not have the tunnel of light open.
Once released from physicality, the spiritual person has to go somewhere so he goes off to a place called limbo.
Now, limbo is a sort of storage area although, to those who are there it appears real, and with their imaginations they create buildings of various sorts and try to construct a life as best they can.
Limbo is an unhappy place.
It is not heaven and it is not hell. It is an area made available for those who, for whatever reason, did not make it to heaven. That is why we called it a storage area because the people there remain so until they accept to be guided to heaven.
Guides of various sorts volunteer to spend long periods of time trying to persuade the denizens of limbo to be guided to heaven.
But, unfortunately, the very nature of limbo promotes distrust because there are a number of negative beings of various sorts who get pleasure from misleading victims and so the people there learn to be distrustful of anyone and any advice, including that given by well-meaning guides.
We have been asked why people end up in limbo and what sort of people end up there.
Let us say, and here we are taking care not to insult or criticize anyone, but there are a number of people who, shall we say, have never considered what happens when we die.
This, of course, includes those who feel that life ends with death of the physical body, but even these people have considered the possibility of life after death, even if they have rejected the concept.

These people, having sowed the seeds of life after death, usually end up in heaven.
No, we are mentioning those who are so wrapped up in incarnation that they have never
thought about life after death and so have not sown the seeds, if we may use that
expression, that there is a heaven. It has not crossed their minds to think about it.
This might include some teenage children and a number of middle-aged men and women,
in the prime of their lives, who suddenly die but have not made the connection to heaven.
Their spirits have to go somewhere and so some of them end up in limbo where they still
live, not realizing that heaven exists and they could make the transition if they would
trust the guides to take them there.

Young children, obviously, may not have heard of heaven but, when the demise of a child
occurs, guides quickly come to assist them to make the transition.
It is only when the person concerned has reached what we would call adulthood and can
make decisions for himself that he is left to his own devices until he accepts to be guided
to heaven.
It is all part of life's rich pageant, as Shakespeare said, and we allow them to have that
experience, safe in the knowledge that, sooner or later, out of desperation they accept that
heaven exists and they link with a guide who assists them to the light of heaven.
Elderly people, generally, as they approached the day that their incarnation will end, turn
to thoughts of what happens when they die and accept that heaven exists. Thus, it is rare
that elderly people are in limbo.
It is mainly occupied by people ranging from teenagers to late middle-aged men and
women.
As we said, young people and the elderly nearly always end up in heaven.

You are never alone, as each person, whether in incarnation or not, has a guide who looks
after the individual as best he can.
However, this guide has no right to interfere with the life of the person he has charge of
and, if the individual has no concern with esoteric matters, being totally involved with his
incarnation, the guide can only look on, helpless to assist the person to go to heaven.
This guide will stay with the individual even if he goes to limbo and can only wait
patiently until the person decides to go to heaven.
This guide will work with the guides who try to persuade people to go to heaven but, as
we said, has no right to interfere with the person's choice.

Limbo is found in the upper portions of the etheric planes just below the lower 4th
dimension and is thus influenced by that dismal area.
Thus, limbo is a horrible, dull, dismal place and the denizens of that area are usually lost
and unhappy, wondering where they are and why they are there.
Some people try to contact them using specially modified radios.
Usually, they connect to other areas of the etheric realms and other entities who inhabit
them.
We consider it most unwise to use these devices as they can open the doors to be attached
to evil entities.
The spirit realms should be left to those who have been trained to enter them safely.

But let us return to the subject of this chapter, which is what happens to those who enter
heaven firmly believing that they are not there and what they are seeing is an illusion.

We said that we would deal with the two types of people who refuse to accept that they are alive after physical death separately.
1. Those who are convinced that there is no life after physical death, and;
2. Those who are convinced that they remain dead until a person (Christ) comes to give them eternal life.

Let us, however, consider first suicide cases, that we said we would mention.
Now, it should be obvious to all people that, having taken the decision to have an incarnation and having decided on a life plan, no matter what that involves, they should see their life to its natural end.
Unfortunately, there are a number of misguided or evil people promoting the idea that suicide is acceptable.
Some of these people might be promoting this concept out of humanitarian sympathy for those struggling with their incarnation, while there are evil individuals promoting suicide in the hopes that, not only the person who takes his life will suffer terribly but also their friends and relatives will also suffer.
The object is to make the atmosphere that surrounds planet Earth in the etheric realms full of unhappiness, which allows them to spread misery to all people.
These people, when their incarnations end, will go to hell where they will suffer greatly, but we are concerned with what happens to a suicide victim when he leaves his body and his incarnation ends.

We are aware that there are many who wish and hope that the person who ends their life prematurely suffers in the burning depths of hell for all eternity, and, indeed, many religions portray this horrible fate for those who terminate their lives prematurely and at their own hands.
Now, we have to proceed carefully here.
We wish to state with all the force at our disposition that no one, and we repeat, no one should commit suicide for the simple reason that even the nastiest of people are surrounded by those who care about them. No one is an island. We all have family, acquaintances and friends and the object of life is to put others first and ourselves last.
For those who can understand this, it should be obvious that anyone who commits suicide causes great unhappiness to all those who cared for and/or loved the individual. We have no right to cause suffering to others.
So, we repeat, no one has the right to cause others suffering and so no one has the right to end their life prematurely.
We hope - indeed, require - all people who are thinking of committing suicide because of some trauma in their life to step back and consider the effect, not only upon themselves, but upon the people who care for them.
Suicide is a selfish act.
We are given life by God and we choose an incarnation to have experiences.
Some of these experiences might bring us joy and some unhappiness but they are all part of our life plan and should be faced with bravery.
No one should consider suicide as a means of escaping the trivial ups and downs of life.
We can assure you that, no matter how heavy a burden you think that life has placed upon you, others in the past endured, bravely, much greater hardships and lived to tell the tale.

No unpleasant event lasts forever and, sooner or later, we will move into peace and tranquility again so we just need to take life day by day until the storm passes.
So, we formally forbid you to commit suicide.

As for those who are actively pushing others to commit suicide, the destiny of such people once their incarnation ends doesn't bear thinking about.
To push someone to terminate his incarnation is one of the most heinous crimes it is possible to do and the punishment in hell for these people is commensurate with the level of that crime.
However, having explained that no one should commit suicide, let us consider what happens, in reality, to those who do.
As we said, most religions describe a dreadful fate for such people and we can understand this as God creates life and only God has the right to decide when it should end.
Also, we must say, normal people might have a difficult time - from time to time - but do not consider suicide.
It is a natural thing to want to cling onto life for as long as possible.
Even animals and plants cling to life until the last moment.
Mention has been made of Lemmings leaping over cliffs but that is not really based on truth.
Life is considered sacred by all life forms.
So, religions try to dissuade people from committing suicide and we formally forbid it.

But, we see, increasingly, young people - perhaps influenced by the evil ones - that for apparently, to others, simple reasons, decide to commit suicide.
This is very sad and if they had ridden the storm their lives would have settled down and given them both joy and a reason to go on, but no, we get the impression that, at the slightest upset in their lives they find a way of ending it.
As you should know, life is immortal and you, once you were created by God can never die.
Your so-called incarnation will end one day, but the true you will live forever.
So, what happens to someone who commits suicide?
We wish that we could say that you would burn forever in the pits of hell as a punishment for committing suicide but that would be a lie.

The truth is that someone who commits suicide, generally, find himself transported to heaven as do virtually all people who die of natural causes.
Some, of course, might end up in limbo as we described earlier but the vast majority of suicides go to the heavenly spheres.
They are met with an advanced being who explains that their Earthly incarnation is now terminated and that they have returned home.
Why should this be?
The answer is that God is love and heaven is based on love. Even what we call hell is designed to enable people to come to terms with the wrongness of causing harm to others and to reject those concepts and turn to love.

A person who commits suicide is, usually, deeply confused and depressed, so that person, generally, would be placed in one of the hospital areas until he is cured of his depression and then he has his life review and understands, not only that he has committed suicide

and the reason why he did it, but also understands the pain and trauma he caused to others.
According to his reactions he may go to one of the levels of hell but if he is truly repentant, he remains in the light and picks up life again.

That is the simple truth concerning suicide but do not think that we are condoning it. We are obliged to present you the truth but we severely condemned suicide and formally oblige you to see through the pros and cons of life bravely and we formally forbid you to take your own life.
We hope that we have made this abundantly clear. No matter what your circumstances are and no matter how much you think that you are suffering and how black the future looks, we formally forbid you from considering suicide as an escape.

Let us now turn to the real purpose of this chapter which is to consider the reasons of those whose incarnations come to an end but who are convinced that their lives should not continue in an unbroken chain from incarnation into the afterlife, which is in the 4th dimension.
Like the vast majority of people, once the silver cord is broken, they find themselves in an area of bright light and are greeted by an advanced being, usually dressed in white, who not only greets the individual but pours pure love out to him.
Actually, if someone thinks that life does not continue after physical death, if it were not a serious matter it would be quite amusing to observe the reaction of the individual.
He suddenly finds himself with the appearance of a physical body, more awake and alert than he has ever been before during his incarnation, being greeted by a noble spirit who also has a physical body, but every fibre of his being tells him that it is not happening.
He does not think that it is an illusion because that would imply that he must be alive to observe the illusion. But he is convinced that there is nothing after physical death so even an illusion cannot occur.

So, he stands there while his mind battles with what he observes.
One part of him can see, and feel, that life is continuing while another part of him tries to convince him that what he sees cannot be.
The advanced guide who is, of course, fully aware of the internal battle the newly deceased is going through, stands in front of the individual, pouring love towards him, but says nothing.
He waits while the individual completes his internal battle knowing that the person must, eventually, start to question the guide.
It can happen, on rare occasions, that the individual patently refuses to accept the guide and the area of light in which he finds himself, and on those rare occasions the new arrival is placed in what you might term a deep sleep or even an artificial coma and is placed in a hospital area until, one day, he wakes up believing that life does, indeed, continue.
The way this works is that while the person is in a deep sleep, energy is poured into him by healers and this energy can be directed towards the areas of the individual's mind connected to what we might term 'common sense'. This is not actually true and is used as an illustration.

Eventually, when the individual has begun to accept that life continues after the demise of the earthly body, the person slowly awakens and is introduced to the world in which he finds himself.

We mentioned that this is not exactly what happens because, in heaven, no one has the right to influence anyone else. It goes against the law of free will. So, in effect, the individual, during his deep sleep is shown dreams, if we may use that word, which reach into his subconscious and presents him with possibilities that, perhaps, life continues after the death of the physical body. As time does not exist in the 4th, it matters not for how long these dreams last.

The point is that, sooner or later, the person awakens and accepts the possibility that life does continue, and from that point forward the individual can gently be introduced to his loved ones, and life in general in the 4th.

We insist to remind you that at no time is the individual forced to accept that he is still alive. It has to be his decision and, obviously, some people take longer than others to accept that life carries on and so great patience is exercised by the healers until the person, by his own accord, accepts that life continues in the 4th.

That is the nature of life in the 4th: patience, kindness and love.

No one is ever pressured to do or to believe anything.

But let us go back to the moment that the newly deceased person is face-to-face with this loving guide.

The individual stares at the advanced guide who stands and says nothing.

Having the ability to master telepathy, he, the guide, can read the individual's mind and is aware of the internal battle going on in the mind of the newly deceased person.

His old beliefs convince him that life cannot continue once he is 'dead' and yet he sees that he is alive - clearly alive. How can this be?

It does not seem to be an illusion and yet it cannot be true!

The guide waits patiently until the individual starts asking questions about what is going on and where he is.

This gives the chance for the guide to explain that the person has passed to heaven and is still very much alive. Indeed, much more alive than he was during his incarnation.

He gently and patiently answers all the questions the newly deceased has until the individual can accept that he was mistaken and that he has entered the realm of eternal life.

As you can imagine if you put yourself in the shoes of the deceased person, this is no easy thing to accept - that after spending all his life convinced that life after death did not exist - to find that he was totally mistaken.

Not only was he wrong, but his ego has taken a blow.

He tried to convince anyone with whom he discussed life and death and, indeed, the existence of God, that it was all baloney but now he sees that he was wrong on all counts.

His pride, his opinions, his ego and his concepts were all wrong and he now has to reject all those wrong assumptions and has to accept that the opposite to his belief is the truth.

This is not an easy thing to do and causes much turmoil in the mind of the individual.

The guide, obviously, is aware of this and so, very gently, describes at least part of the truth about eternal life.

There would be no point in going into depths about how life works as we explain to you because it would be too much for the new arrival to accept.

So, the guide explains that life goes on and stops at that.

In all probability a house would be constructed by etheric means to allow the individual to have the sort of base similar to what he had on Earth.

Food and drink (vegan, of course) would be created to satisfy any feelings of hunger that the individual might have and great effort is taken to ease the passage between the old reality and the new one.

We are always very pleased to see a new soul opening himself to eternal life.

There are, of course, certain individuals who refuse to accept that they are still alive and accuse us of being hallucinations brought on by the fact, in his estimation, that he is still alive and we are just figments of his imagination.

We have no right to interfere with his beliefs and so we take him to a hospital and place him in a deep sleep while healers project rays to him which work on his mind until, one day, he wakes up realizing that he is still alive. Then can he be introduced to life in heaven.

In both cases, eventually and gradually, his family and friends who passed before him are introduced to him to help confirm that he is truly alive.

Gradually he is able to take his place in the heavenly spheres and take an interest in the educational work that goes on.

Let us lastly consider those who are convinced that they are 'dead' until God or Jesus or someone returns and wakes them up to eternal life.

As soon as they arrive in heaven, special guides are awaiting their arrival, and before they can see the light of heaven they are placed in a deep sleep.

Then they are transported to a hospital and are allowed to sleep deeply until, one day, they awaken of their own accord and accept that the long awaited moment of the arrival of their savior has occurred.

This gives them great joy because they are convinced that they are amongst the chosen ones who merit to be saved.

Who are we to disillusion them?

There are many such people who have left their incarnation with such beliefs and so there is an area reserved exclusively for such people.

This area, like all areas in the 4th, is a matter of frequency or vibration, so this area is kept apart from any other area by the simple expedient of its unique frequency.

The newly awakened person is instantly transported to this area by specially trained guides, which the people see as angels, and is welcomed into the group.

He or she is accepted as yet another chosen one and causes great joy to this relatively large group of 'chosen' individuals.

It may seem somewhat childish to those who know the truth about eternal life but everyone has free will and thus everyone has the right to believe what he chooses to believe.

Let us take a short tour of this area and describe to you what goes on there.

First, we notice that there are a number of buildings of various sorts that seem real to those who live in this area.

Of course, the buildings are constructed by thought and, although to us who realise that we do not need any buildings in order to live in this area, the particular vibration permits the construction of any buildings those who live there think they need.

So, there are houses for all people. Some people live alone in these houses and some live with their family members.

There are churches, meeting halls and courthouses where any who commit misdemeanors - in the eyes of the people who live there - are tried for their crimes.

There are no jails as such but there are judges who try anyone who oversteps the rules laid down by the elders and are sanctioned.

So, the people of this area have set up a system based on early life type rules and regulations and all who live there are obliged to conform to these rules.

They eat and drink (vegan, of course) food they produce and they either eat at home or eat in communal halls and gardens as many used to do in the past.

Church services are regularly held so there is a priesthood who wear special clothes to denote their status.

All people are required to do work of some kind, ranging from growing crops to writing religious texts. There are a number of leaders rather like politicians who create laws to which all must comply, and there is a complete civilization - if we may use that term - based on a hodgepodge of various Earth ways of living.

We cannot say that the majority of people who live there are happy because they are bound by so many rules and regulations that they are scared of failing to obey them in some way.

There are no punishments really but transgressors are severely criticized and made to feel guilty for not obeying the mass of laws to the letter.

This area has existed for a surprisingly long time because the concept of some God coming to give eternal life to the chosen ones far out dates Christianity.

This has given the inhabitants of this area the chance to set up a complex infrastructure of life, rules and regulations.

It must be appreciated that religions - all religions - are based on control, and transgressors of the rules laid down have to be dealt with.

It may seem strange to us who live freely, to observe these people living in permanent dread of transgressing any law invented by these people but we have to accept that this is their chosen path and they live that life of their own free will.

Now, we must touch on the rather delicate subject of racism.

In the world in which we live, we only see people with whom we live in harmony. This implies that those who do not live by the same concepts as us live in their own areas, areas full of people who live in harmony with like individuals.

These areas are not based on creed, colour or race but are based on harmony - like thinking.

The area we are describing is somewhat similar. The main criteria for being accepted is the belief that they are the chosen ones of God.

Now, this is more complicated than one might imagine.

Most people are aware of the modern Christian belief of being a chosen person - or not - but, as we said, it by far predates Christianity.

There are also other religions that embrace the same concept.

So, to be accepted into this group requires that each person believes that he or she is a chosen one, regardless of their religion they followed on Earth or their skin colour.

This causes a certain amount of confusion because, although each person believes that he or she is a chosen one, they may still have a desire to follow their own religion.

The elders, those who first came to this area, set up a certain type of religion far predating Christianity or Islam but, over the years, new arrivals appeared convinced that they were the chosen ones but may have followed, on Earth, a particular religion such as Christianity or Islam which, although often based on previous religions, differed somewhat from the earlier religions that the elders followed.

This has caused much conversation and confusion as you can imagine.

The elders recognized that all the new arrivals believed that they are the chosen ones but, when questioned, believed in a different sort of savior.

This might include Jesus or Muhammad or one of the plethora of Indian gods and so on.

Much discussion took place until it was decided to create a new religion that tried to incorporate the concept of a God, eternal life and their special place as chosen ones.

We will not describe this religion as it would take too long and, to be honest, is no concern to us.

But all new arrivals are obliged to follow this religion.

We do not criticise it because (a) we have no right to do so and (b) it is based on God so is based on truth.

It is just the cleverly thought out details that might seem bizarre to us but satisfies the people of that area.

So, there is no colour bar, nor is there any religious dissension, as all must conform to this created religion.

The only people who are sanctioned are those who, at first, refuse to accept this religion and they are brought before a tribunal of elders who oblige them to reject their old religion and accept the new one and are placed in isolation houses until they agree to accept the new religion. Then they are permitted to rejoin society.

Language, of course, is no barrier as the universal language of telepathy is used by all people.

Now, there are, from time to time, those who start to question the wisdom of living like that and wonder if there is not a better, freer way of living.

None of the people who live in that area, because of the vibration, are in contact with the rest of heaven anymore than the majority of you have the ability of contacting heaven where we live.

On Earth, you all live in an area of a certain frequency which keeps you trapped there.

We in the 4th live close to you but are separated from you by being of a different frequency.

In the case of the individuals we are discussing - the so-called chosen ones - they are kept apart from the majority of us by being in a world of a different frequency.

If someone wishes to escape, he has to learn to incorporate a different frequency into his being in exactly the same manner that you have in order to link with us. Indeed, we have to do the same thing if we wish to link with you.

The difference between us, you and this chosen group is that we explain to you how to contact us whereas, as in the chosen group, no one explains how to contact the other dimensions that surround them.

Therefore, it is rare that anyone escapes from the area that he finds himself in - the chosen one's area.

So, it is rare that anyone could remove himself from that area and any such desires would be quashed by the elders and leaders who are convinced that they are the only ones in heaven and nothing else exists.

They have no idea of the enormous world that surrounds them and they have no concept of the type of information that we give to you.

They would be horrified if they could glimpse the real world outside of their enclosure, and they are quite content to live in their little world and keep it as it is.

No angel or advanced guide ever visits them to try to open their eyes to the greater reality the rest of us live in.

They have free will and their free will decision is to live in their little world, safe in the knowledge that God has chosen them as his special people and they will live forever, one assumes, following that belief.

So, we have described yet another area of the heavenly spheres and we hope you found it both interesting and informative. We will end this chapter here and move on to yet another area which we hope you will find instructive.

CHAPTER 25

HATE

We are somewhat hesitant to give you this chapter because some of you might deduce that we are insulting you personally. We are not. We explain the faults that we are all subject to, no matter who we are, but if what we say in this chapter applies to you, we say it with the best of intentions. Not in any way to criticise, insult or harm you but to point out the temptations that can affect us.

We are no different to you, having all had incarnations at one time or another and so we, too, were tempted by the subject of this chapter.

Some of us mastered it to a certain extent and some of us did not.

It is only since we have been in the heavenly spheres and are thus removed from this temptation that it fades through lack of opportunity.

So, what are we talking about?

The subject of this chapter will be about hate.

What do we mean by hate?

First, let us say that we are sure that you have a concept of hate just as you have a concept of love.

But the subject of hate is quite complex and can involve righteous indignation or dealing with people who do not think like you.

It can involve people of other religions or skin colours, and a whole variety of topics, many of which are considered normal and even acceptable to many people.

So, as we said in our opening statement, if we describe any attitude that might apply to you and that you accept as your right, please do not be offended.

Step back and allow the information to flow over you without reacting, as if it had no connection to you. In fact, it does not have any connection to you.

We are merely describing attitudes and do not wish anyone to think that we are criticizing their personal attitudes, which they have a perfect right to hold.

Of course, if someone finds that it does apply to them and resolves to correct that attitude, so much the better, but the aim of this chapter is just to describe some of the ways that hate can affect and damage our lives.

So, where to begin?

We must start by saying, once again, that planet Earth was designed exclusively for animals and so all the personal attributes given to planet Earth were to enable animals to survive in the dog-eat-dog environment that was necessary.

Let us say that the archangels who work for God are neutral in their attitudes.

God creates life. We have said this many times but must repeat it once again as it applies to this chapter.

God creates life and stops at that.

He is not at all as described in religious texts as an old man with a long beard, sitting on a cloud pouring hellfire and damnation on us all.

God is the force that creates life. However, God has intelligence and the ability to learn.

So, God created archangels and tasked them to create all that exists, not only on Earth, but in all the dimensions and areas that we have mentioned in this and other books.

This must have taken a vast amount of intelligence, wisdom and trial and error on behalf of these archangels and we must say that they are still hard at work keeping the whole system going.

Perhaps we should mention at this point two things.
First, there is no physical life anywhere in our galaxy above and beyond anything that we have described in our books, with particular mention of what goes on in the various dimensions. And those seeking life elsewhere are wasting their time. Planet Earth is the only one with physical life on it.
Second, we must say that God's archangels have no sense of emotions as we would know them to be.
This leads back to Earth and the animals that were created by these archangels and placed here.
The fact that some are herbivores and some are carnivorous seemed appropriate to these archangels who saw no difference between an antelope eating grass and a lion eating the antelope.
They, the archangels, do not have any appreciation of that type of emotion, emotions that shock, sadden and horrify us if we see lions attacking, killing and eating antelopes for example.
These are human emotions and we humans were never intended to incarnate to Earth originally. Planet Earth was created for animals and even now animals have almost no human emotions, so if one antelope saw another being killed by lions, apart from being relieved that it was not he that was attacked, thinks no more about it.
Of course, a mother animal, if one of her young offspring was attacked, killed and eaten by a predator, might be sad for a while but she would not show the sorts of outrage that a human would if her baby was attacked and killed.

The archangels did not introduce human emotions into animals.
So, what emotions do animals have in the wild?
Generally, they are fairly basic; the desire to eat, to mate and the feeling of fight/flight.
It is this last feeling, that of fight/flight that interests us because it is the basis of this chapter which is about hate
We will ignore, in this chapter, the wonderful love that some animals show towards humans that adopt and love them and we will ignore the horrendous cruelty some people inflict on animals.
Nor will we mention the love that most female animals shower onto their offspring. We will concentrate on what feelings wild animals have as and when it is transferred to us humans.

Eventually, as you know, humans were introduced to Earth and thus were given a variety of personality traits exclusive to humans, with the exception of fight/flight.
Now, we must say that no animal has the emotion of hate. He might show fear, aggressivity and the desire to fight but that comes from the fight/flight concept.
Animals do not know hate.
And yet humans do.

This may seem strange because in heaven, where we all came from before incarnating, the overriding emotion is love. The theme of our God is love, and in heaven, we are all surrounded by loving beings.

So, where does hate come from?

This is difficult to explain because hate does not exist in heaven except, perhaps, in the hellish regions, but certainly does not exist in heaven. We will explain the one exception later.

But, when we incarnate, swirling around in the etheric realms is the emotion of fight/flight.

This also links to fear. All animals have a feeling of fear.

This may be fear of being attacked or fear of not finding food to sustain the animal.

A mother with young might be frightened of her young being attacked.

So, closely related to fight/flight is fear.

Once again, fear is unknown in heaven. There is nothing to be frightened of. No one is going to attack us and no one is going to insult us as we are surrounded by like-minded people and so we can discuss topics without fear of anyone disagreeing with us. Someone might suggest a modification of a topic but no one insults anyone else. We all live in peace and mutual harmony.

The only possible exceptions are those in hell and those who live in the area we explained in the last chapter - the chosen ones!

All the rest of us live in peace together.

But incarnation is a whole different concept.

Before incarnating we are taught about all the disagreeable attitudes that exist - attitudes we have described in other works - and so we are taught about fear and about fight/flight.

So, we are born with these two aspects added to our basic personality that we have developed before incarnating.

These two additional aspects are vital to our survival on Earth, and yet they are unknown in heaven.

They are animal instincts.

So, let us look at this again.

Humans may have a variety of personality traits but they have no concept, in heaven, of fear or fight/flight.

Animals have these concepts - fear, and fight/flight upmost in their concepts.

So, we humans are born into incarnation with fear and fight/flight added to our personality.

But we still have not discovered hate!

Hate comes from the inability not to be able to reduce to fight/flight in a situation of stress.

We humans, given the chance, will run from a dangerous situation, or if trapped, might be tempted to strike out to defend ourselves but there are many situations where we can neither run nor fight.

So we are trapped, so to speak, and so that frustration, based on fear, creates hate.

Hate is unknown to animals and it would be a sad day if it ever was introduced.

They know fear and they know fight/flight but their defense mechanisms stop at that.

We humans, trapped in uncontrollable situations in which we have fear but fight/flight is inappropriate or impossible have developed an emotion termed hate. It comes from feeling trapped in a horrible situation.
This chapter will deal with some of the situations with which we can be confronted and why we hate these situations or people.

Hate is not an easy subject to talk about because there are many degrees of so-called hate ranging from expressions such as, 'I hate this or that', meaning that one dislikes the subject under discussion, to genuine, almost phobic dislike of something or someone.
Who can say what hate can describe in its most intense form?
Many people say that they hate someone or something but we have difficulty in finding an example of ultimate hate to describe to you.
There have been, from time to time, throughout history really dreadful and cruel people and their victims no doubt hated the individual but that hate was often tinged with fear.
So, to what degree of fear the victims had compared to pure hate is hard to say.
We told you that animals can fear but do not know the meaning of hate whereas, before incarnation, hate can be introduced into the personality palette of a human whereas fear is unknown before incarnation.
Therefore, fear and hate come together in an Earthly incarnation but are separate from animal emotions and human emotions in the different spheres; earth and heaven.

Why are we mentioning this?
The answer lies in a strange area in the 4th that contains the frequency of hate.
It is there in order that potential incarnation candidates can get a taste of real hate in order to recognise it once the incarnation starts in order to be for-armed, so to speak.
We will take you on a mental tour of this area to explain to you what it is like but, as we said to you above, we have no example to compare this area to you and words do not exist to describe absolute hate.
But we will try.

Now, the first thing we have to do is to separate fear from hate.
Fear does not exist in the 4th dimension, with the possible exception of certain levels of hell, and even there, our explorations have never felt fear except as brought by us after having an incarnation and thus having a knowledge of fear.
The denizens of hell have no fear of the suffering they experience because, strange as it may seem, the vast majority of those in hell are there because their personalities accord with the area that they find themselves in, and thus they are perfectly at home with whatever they are suffering, and that they can inflict similar suffering on others also in the same place.
They find it normal to be like that and who are we to criticize them?
To use an old expression, 'They have made their beds and must lie in them.'
Many of the people in hell do not have much time for being in bed as they spend their time either being tormented by others or tormenting those people in return.
So, the expression is not very accurate with regards to hell, but we hope you can understand why we used it.

But let us return to the area in the 4th that contains the emotions of hate.

As usual, it is of a particular frequency to keep it apart from any other area and students have to learn to connect to that frequency.

Also, it is non-physical. It is yet another area purely mental. We wish we could find another word to describe non-physical areas because the word mental has connotations with folly or madness but we use the word in the sense of it being non-physical, just an emotion.

So the student, always accompanied by an experienced guide, links to the frequency of hate and transports himself - or rather transports his mind - to that area.

So, what does he experience?

We need to search for words to describe the emotion of hate which bombards the mind of the student.

What can we say?

Pure detestation of all things. Pure desire to cause harm. Disgust for everything and everyone. The desire to cause as much revolt as possible.

We could look in a thesaurus to try to find words that truly describe pure, unreasonable hate but there are no words to describe pure hate.

It is an emotion without reason. It is not a question in this area of hating a person or a situation. It is pure, unadulterated hate. That is all we can say.

The student is bombarded with this incredibly powerful and negative emotion, something that he has never experienced before, always being in a world of love, but this is, if we may say, the total, complete and absolute opposite of love.

Hate is the ultimate negative force and yet it is a force that many use on Earth either in a half joking sense or slightly more realistically in terms like, 'I hate my job.' or 'I hate my school.' etc. But we consider that no one has ever incarnated to Earth with the full power of total hate in his personality. Even the worst tyrants and psychopaths have, or had, a watered down version of hate as expressed in the area in the 4th we tried to describe. And just as well.

If someone incarnated with the total force of pure hate in his personality, and rose to a position where he could exercise that degree of hate, life for others would be unimaginable.

As it is, there have been a number of tyrant psychopaths that have caused immense harm through exercising hate, but what they accomplished is a pale shadow of what someone expressing pure hate would exhibit in his actions.

So, we apologize for not being able successfully to describe the emotions of pure, unadulterated hate, but as we said, words do not exist to explain it and, to our knowledge, it has never been exercised to its full extent on Earth.

All we can do is to give a few examples of hate as expressed through people's personalities and leave it at that.

So where shall we start?

Let us start on a humorous note and ask, 'Hands up all those who have never used the word hate?'

We don't see many hands going up. Don't forget that we, too, had incarnations and for many of us, particularly those of our group who incarnated in the past, had much more reason to use the word hate than we do today. But we also used the word hate lightly although, when we realise its true meaning, it is no laughing matter.

Hate, on Earth, is invariably linked to fear.

Those who lived long ago and fell foul of some authority suffered terribly, rather as the description of what Jesus went through, as recounted in the Bible, was inflicted. Sometimes this punishment was inflicted just once but often it was repeated several times and so the unfortunate victim feared what was in store for him as well as hated the suffering he was repeatedly going through, so he hated the people who condemned him as well as those who inflicted the punishment, many of them thoroughly enjoying inflicting such pain.

So, invariably, in real events, hate and fear are linked.

This hate and fear come together when a person, faced with a difficult or unpleasant situation, cannot use the animal instinct of fight or flight.

We accept that Jesus, assuming that what happened to him is a true account, accepted his fate bravely and did not exercise either fight or flight.

We will just say at this point that even if the Biblical account of the fate of Jesus did not really happen to him, it happened to countless others, so it comes to the same thing.

But let us not get too morbid at this point.

We are talking about those who use the word hate lightly.

We have all said that we hate someone. We have also said, at school, that we hate some subject or some teacher. Or we hate our school uniform, for those obliged to wear one.

We go on into adult life and say we hate our job or hate our boss or hate a work colleague.

But none of these situations really apply to the word hate as we have tried - and failed - to describe it to you in the hate area in the 4th dimension.

What we really mean is we dislike some person or some situation and, possibly, we might fear someone or some situation, but on no account can our dislike conform to the true meaning of hate.

Now, what are we really talking about here?

It is obvious, and we are glad to say this, that we misuse the word hate. We should more properly use the word 'dislike' which, although one can say is connected to hate in a watered-down sense, is also, usually connected to fear and, to be honest, is often connected to fight/flight.

For instance, if we can avoid meeting someone we dislike or fear, we tend to do so by, for example, hiding if we see the person coming or taking an alternative route in a building if we see the person heading our way. That is flight.

If we are on a relatively equal status to the person, we might violently disagree with what he says and a shouting match ensues. That is fight.

These are simple examples, but we are sure that most of you understand what we are saying.

But if a person truly hated another and that second person approached, what would the first person do?

What action would his absolute hate for the other push him to do?

What action would he take?

Well, we really can't answer that question because we do not hate anyone, but it would not surprise us if the first person tried to eliminate the second - murder!

Now, unfortunately, murder happens all the time by all sorts of people in virtually every country and by using a variety of methods.

Does this mean that the murderer is full of hate?

Once again, we cannot answer this but we doubt that anyone contains, on Earth, the full measure of hate as found in the hate area in 4th.

There have been a number of fictional stories of people full of hate. The story of Dr. Jekyll and Mr. Hyde comes to mind, Mr. Hyde being the epitome of ruthlessness and evil which could translate to hate for humanity, and there have been other stories, true this time - Jack the Ripper - for example, where a person was overcome with hate for a certain class of ladies.

Now, these sorts of examples we gave, one fictional and one factual get pretty close to pure hate and we have no doubt that similar cases happen frequently. But in general, very few people push their dislike of someone to that extent.

However, murders are frequent for a number of reasons.

Couples living together can disagree and one murders the other.

Religious people of one faith can be indoctrinated by evil leaders to encourage gullible followers of that religion to kill others because of belonging to a different faith.

People of different skin colours can develop a form of hate and murder each other.

Occasionally, someone might dislike his business associate to the point that he will take violent action.

At the time of writing this book it occasionally happens that school children kill other children and teachers for no apparent reason.

And lastly, wars have been going on for generations for very flimsy reasons, resulting in the deaths of millions of people.

These are all terrible acts and we wish with all our hearts that they would stop, but to what degree does blind hate play a part?

These are difficult questions to answer and, certainly, we can offer no reason why these things happen, but if we compare what does happen - these terrible murders - and compare them to the emotion of pure hate we felt when we visited that hate area in the 4th, we can see little correlation.

If we link in the akashic records to the files of those who have committed murder, we can usually link the murders to the fight/flight or fear motives rather than just pure hate.

Most murderers target individuals or groups whereas hate acts indiscriminately. Hate doesn't care who gets hurt nor by what means. True hate implies hate for everything and everybody. It doesn't target individuals or groups. Hate targets all life.

We must mention two groups of individuals who have been vilified and not without reason.

1. Reptilians

2. Archons

We will say that both groups have their agendas to cause unhappiness in the world, but in their defense, we must say that from our investigations of these two groups they are not driven by hate.

It is quite simply that their way of living is not based on love as we should live and though they do cause immense harm, neither the reptilians nor the archons are hate driven.

They live in negative worlds and their negativity pushes them to create chaos, which gives them pleasure.
In true hate, there is no pleasure. True hate is a strange emotion that exists as the opposite of true love.
There is no other emotion involved except this rather enigmatic emotion of hate.
It stands apart and is not connected to fight/flight or fear nor any desire to cause harm.
These are animal and human emotions mixed.
Hate, true hate, exists on its own with no rhyme or reason. It just is.

So, we have presented to you this bizarre area in the 4th called hate for the simple reason that it exists and the object of this book is to relate to you a number of areas to which we hope you can relate.
We do not suggest that you try to contact this area because you would need to know the frequency and if you did enter it, the emotion of pure hate would shatter your mind.
We have enough problems dealing with dislike, and fight/flight and fear concepts without trying to introduce pure hate into our lives.

You might have found this chapter, the way we have presented it, rather strange as we have actually suggested that this area of pure hate exists but that it is not present on Earth.
As we said, we explained what we know about it and what we know about human/animal emotions in relation to what we call hate, but the bottom line is that, in fact, true mindless hate does not exist on Earth, thankfully.
What we call hate is really levels of dislike and are often based on fear and thus fight/flight.

So, once again we end another chapter and we'll try to find something else to talk about which we hope you will find interesting.
We do feel that some of you might feel a bit disappointed by this chapter entitled hate because it is, in a way, a misnomer as hate does not truly exist amongst the beings on Earth.
But this area exists in the 4th and we felt obliged to mention it.

CHAPTER 26

FAMILY

Shall we make this book much longer? We are torn between ending the book so that it can be made public and continuing into the future, because there are countless areas in the 4th that some of you might find informative.

We have had a short discussion with our Earthly scribe - he who kindly writes the words we transmit - and his opinion is that we should continue to describe as many of the areas in the 4th that apply to you all, because he is aware that there are a number of followers of our channel that are interested in learning as much as they can about the areas in the 4th that apply to you in incarnation.

After all, the only way we have of informing you about these areas is to describe them in books.

We took the decision, as we said at the beginning of this book, that we would correct the error we made in a previous book about auras of not giving you much information.

We are correcting that error by describing a number of areas that, not only exist in the 4th, but also enter your auras and directly affect you whether you are aware or not.

This is the purpose of this book, and you may have deduced that there are a huge number of areas in the 4th that transmit, if we may use that word, information constantly into your auras and, despite your personality, affect how you behave in your incarnation.

Some do more than others but all that we have described so far in this book play a role in the way you proceed through your incarnation, influenced by these areas.

As we said, there are countless more areas that play a role and, though we cannot describe them all, we have made the decision to continue to provide at least a few more of these areas and make a quite large book which will become a sort of compendium of the areas that broadcast out into the auras of all people and influence their behavior.

So, we will continue with this book, chapter after chapter, dealing with a specific subject that enmeshes with your auras and, via your higher self and other aspects of your makeup, influence your thoughts and your behavior in incarnation.

So, we crave your indulgence if we create a large volume.

We feel that if you have a knowledge of these areas, and that they are influencing you to some degree, it will enable you to consider your path through incarnation and permit you, by allowing some aspects to become more prominent in your life and by reducing others that you consider are harming you, to become a better, wiser and more noble person.

Without knowledge we are all lost.

This book, if carefully read, will give you the opportunity to mould your life in a more positive fashion, with you in control rather than the whims of life pushing you this way and that.

You may become, thanks to the information in this book, to be the captain of a fully functioning ocean-going vessel rather than a refugee floating on a raft blown this way or that by tides or wind.

We apologise for that childish metaphor but it describes how the information we give you will help you to become the person you were created to be.

Knowledge creates wisdom and wisdom is the key to becoming the powerful - in a spiritual sense - person God created you to become.

Thus, we continue the book.
The next subject will be about the area that creates the desire to belong to a family.

The first question we must answer is what exactly do we mean by the word family?
The word family is used in many ways to describe people or objects that are similar.
We all, in incarnation, have a family, whether we are aware of it or not.
Even single mothers who have broken all ties to their parents nevertheless have parents, grandparents, possibly brothers and sisters, aunts and uncles and they are that lady's family.
Similarly, the father would have a family.
Then we talk about the families of animals and plants meaning fauna or flora that have a connection.
This connection is genetic.
Despite any emotional attachment one person can have for other members of their family, the connection can be traced back and out from generation to generation and to brothers, sisters, uncles and aunts through DNA.
Similarly, the same thing can be achieved if the DNA of animals or plants are compared.

So, we have confirmed that, to a large extent, family and DNA are linked.
This is in incarnation where physical bodies; human, animal or plant are compared.
But, what about family connections in the non-physical realms - the 4th dimension where humans live?
We have to ignore animals and plants in this chapter because, (a) this book is about the connection between areas in the 4th and how these areas affect humans via their auras and, (b) if we wrote about fauna and flora, this chapter would be too complicated.
So, we restrict ourselves to families as applied to humans.

Where does the concept of family come from because each individual was created as a stand-alone person and does not need a family?
Indeed, in the 4th, unless someone has had an incarnation and thus has family members from that incarnation with him, those who do not incarnate cannot have a family as such as procreation does not exist in the non-physical realms. Procreation can only occur on Earth.

So, each and every person is created as an individual and yet most people have an overriding desire to belong to a family and many people who have had an incarnation spend a lot of time and effort tracing their ancestors through photographs, paintings, letters and documents.
Some create a family tree and are proud to have created one.
Clearly, the concept of family is important.
We can trace the origin of this desire to belong to a family back to our oversoul.
We have described this countless times but will do so again and we will try to link the oversoul to our DNA (non-physical) and to our auras.

When we are in the 7th dimension, shortly after being selected to become humans, already, guides and certain angelic beings that work closely with humans start to take an interest in the chosen individuals to observe any particular interests or talents, shall we say.

This is not exactly true but we wish to explain things in an easy-to-understand fashion and you are aware of organizations that look out for young people who might show a particular aptitude to a sport, an art form, mathematics and so on.
A similar thing happens in the 7th.
Now, eventually, all young embryo humans descend to the 4th.
This descent is vital because it is the plane that will mould and develop the young, totally ignorant human concept into a fully-fledged human such as yourself who is reading this book. The fledgling humans are divided, in a sense, into two groups.
Those who have already shown an interest in life, as we described earlier and the rest who are human but just remain as embryo humans.

In the 4th are a number of what are termed oversouls.
These oversouls are of incredible importance to the humans and a person will remain attached to an oversoul for all eternity.
It is important that correct decisions are taken at the outset to ensure that each embryo human is placed within the correct oversoul.
Oversouls are not all the same.
They all have the same basic concepts of acting as a connecting point for its members but, after that, they play a variety of roles.
Some oversouls tend to collect young humans interested in art, others sport, others mathematics, others languages and on and on.
Then there are those who collect embryo humans that show no interest in anything for the moment.

They have been likened to houses in schools and platoons in the military.
We are aware that not all schools have the house system but, in fact, for those who did, they served a purpose. If we may paraphrase a statement from a book, 'Your house will act as your family while you are at this school.'
In the 4th your oversoul acts as your family throughout your long-life sojourn from the moment of your introduction into the 4th until the day, far into the future, that you reach perfection and your life as we know it to be ends as you become part of the God force.

So, the concept of family starts with your introduction into your oversoul.
We have mentioned oversouls many times and have stated that an oversoul has no buildings, no uniforms and no identification markers that tell a person that he belongs to any particular oversoul.
An oversoul is a group of like-minded people.
Some of the members of an oversoul might be newcomers and some might have belonged to an oversoul for many thousands of years. Time matters not in the 4th. The overriding concept is like-mindedness.
It has already been mentioned but we will repeat that no one is trapped in his oversoul.
If a person feels that he is in the wrong oversoul, he may change at any time.
The overriding concept of an oversoul is that it consists of like-minded people.
We hope that you can see that the oversoul is the starting point of the concept of family.

Now, it may seem strange but there is an area in the 4th that contains the beginning of the concept of family.

It may seem strange, because logic would dictate that there should be no need for such a place, but the truth of the matter is that virtually every emotion that is available for humans to incorporate into their personality is contained in an area that is the starting point, the origin, of these emotions.
We will repeat this to try to make it perfectly clear.
Virtually every emotion that a human might incorporate into his personality - and there are a surprising number of aspects - exist because there is an area in the 4th that contains the concept in pure form.
If you look back over the chapters of this book, with one or two exceptions, each chapter is about an aspect of personality and we have explained the areas in the 4th that are the origins of these aspects of personality.
Family is no different.
In the 4th, there is an area that contains, in concentrated form, the concept of family.
Once again, it is non-physical and is kept separate from everything else by having a unique frequency. In order to enter it, the student must learn to link to this particular frequency.

When one enters this place or area, the emotions one feels are rather pleasant. One is filled with an intense desire, not only to love all people rather as a mother loves her newborn baby, but one is filled with the desire to fill one's life by welcoming everyone into contact with oneself. It is the epitome of family pushed to a concentrated form.
Can you imagine being in this place of total love?
Love for all people, plants and animals for that matter.
This love is important because the theme of our planet is love, and though that love can be demonstrated in many areas and by many people, the family area is one of the areas where love comes together.
So, family equates, not only to like-minded people, but also to love. Love and like mindedness have a connection.

Now, we are going to say something here that might be difficult to understand.
Love can take many forms.
We are all aware of the meaning of true love and we have described it many times in our various books and documents.
But love, as we said, is connected to like-mindedness.
Think about this!
Unless you think in a similar fashion to someone else or to some group, you cannot have any connection.
If you think about the word 'love' you will realise that to love someone implies like thinking.
It is true that advanced beings and angels are able to love everyone despite their faults, but these advanced beings can see beyond the personality of the individual and can see the God spirit that we all share.
So, that is the connection of love. The advanced being can love all people because we all share a common connection - the God spirit.
So, even advanced beings can see a common connection.
Us lesser beings are still trapped in our personalities and can only love - using the word love in a much less powerful sense - people who think like us.

Now, where does this take us?

We are discussing family and have postulated that family is connected to like mindedness and that is connected to a form of love.

We should, perhaps, repeat that love can take many forms. Pure love is the most noble aspect of life that exists, but love can also be reduced to 'like'.

For instance, we have all said that we love to do this or that but what we really mean is that we like to do something.

Let us return to our oversoul, which becomes our family.

There is usually a connection between people who love or like to do certain things. Some like gardening. Some like painting. Others writing and so on. Yet others do not want to do anything but they all end up in an oversoul best suited to them.

But what about those with the tendency towards evil, cruelty, harming others, etc?

Such beings exist and so there are oversouls that welcome such beings into their midst.

All people have a right to exist, and unfortunately, there is a minority who have a penchant for unpleasantness.

Therefore, there are oversouls for such people. Can we relate this to love? Certainly not in the sense of pure love as we have described it.

But we have also linked a weak degree of love to like. Some people like to cause harm. Unfortunately, they have the right to do that. All people have free will and if someone chooses to cause harm, that is his right.

But in the spirit world, it is not possible to cause harm to others except under certain conditions.

In these oversouls that we are considering, it is possible to cause harm to others within the same oversoul.

This may seem strange but there exists certain oversouls that like-minded people belong to and if those like-minded people enjoy causing harm to each other they have that right. Obviously, such oversouls are kept far apart from decent oversoul groups.

If we were to visit such a group, we would find them hard at work thinking of ways of causing distress to each other.

Then, of course, like all people, they are offered the chance to have an Earthly incarnation.

They are made fully aware of the consequences of causing harm during their incarnations by going to a level of hell once their incarnation is over, but this is not a deterrent as they already live in an oversoul that has many connections to hell.

Not all such people choose an Earthly incarnation, but many do, and we see the results around us on Earth.

So, can we trace a direct line, in all cases, between an oversoul, a family on Earth and the behavioral patterns of individuals?

It can happen that someone from a good, loving family can take to evil but it is rare.

However, the degree that a family can display love varies greatly. It is not unknown for parents, under the pretext of obeying the laws of God, can be very cruel to their children, and in such a case, it is not surprising that the victim child, when he reaches adulthood, treats his children in a similar fashion.

But in truly loving families, the offspring usually turn out to be loving people also.

There are many oversouls and many family types.

The point we wish to state is that before we join an oversoul, we belong to a family.

We are created by and from God. So, our first family and the one that will endure for all eternity is the family of being part of and total God. That is our true and enduring family.

We are all aspects of God.

This is very important and we want to impress on you all, as we have stated many times, and, no doubt, will state many times again in the future, you and we are all God. God acting in a myriad of fashions to create all that seems to exist, but we are all this one God. Can we call God a family? We consider that all things; people, plants, animals and minerals are all God pretending to be those things and so we feel that everything is our family because everything has a direct connection to us individuals.

So, God is our original family.

From there it expands - or perhaps we could say contracts - to oversouls and then for those who have an incarnation, our Earthly families.

Now, we mentioned that there was an area in the 4th that contains the concept of family.

We, perhaps, may question why this should be?

What purpose does this area serve?

A moment's thought should provide the answer.

If it is true that we are all connected because we are all God, then we might consider that we are all one family.

Then we have a second family, our oversoul.

Finally, we have a third, our family through incarnation.

But there is more to the concept of family. There exist clubs, political parties, religious organizations and so on where like-minded people group together and form 'families'. These may not be true families in the sense of genetic connection but nevertheless, people are like minded enough that we might call them families.

All of these groups, these families, exist because of the place in the 4th that contains the concept of family and this concept is being broadcast out to our auras and give us all the desire to belong to a family.

Of course, there are families and families *(different sorts of families),* by which we imply that some families - like minded people - are good, kind people but there are also families, if we may use that word, that are less than noble.

There are groups of people who might be criminals of various sorts; robbers, drug dealers, pedophiles and so on. And yet they all group together to promote whatever agenda they might be involved with.

This seems bizarre to us because, as we said, if we visit the family area in the 4th we get the feeling of harmony, togetherness and a very positive emotion. The sort of feeling that one imagines if one considers the concept of family.

And yet there are groups of people who link together in a way that we might consider to be a family and yet they are very negative people.

So, what exactly is a family?

One would think that if this area in the 4th is positive when one visits it, and yet there are groups of people that we could consider almost to be families and yet are involved in negative acts, there seems to be a problem.

Let us explain further.

The area we termed family in the 4th is positive and is broadcasting its emotion into everyone's aura so, initially, our concept of family is positive.
And yet we know that there are groups of people, like minded people, that we could term families, that are involved in a variety of nefarious activities. How can this be?
Can you understand what the problem is?
The emotion of family being projected into our auras is positive but there are many people who form families that are negative.
Perhaps we do not fully understand what the word family means.

If we ignore the genetic aspect of family in the sense of mothers, fathers, brothers, sisters, aunts and uncles, etc., that we obtain through incarnation, and broadening the concept of family to include groups of like-minded people, we get a different meaning to the word family.
After all, when we consider plants and animals, for instance, we talk about families of similar plants and animals despite there being no direct genetic connection in the sense of families as in mothers, fathers, sons and daughters. We talk about similar groups of entities as in lions, tigers, dogs, cats and various plants.
So, the word family has at least two meanings.
One is the sort of family we are used to describing as in people of the same genetic group; mother, father, son and daughter but we also use the word family as in similar groups of animals and plants.

Now, it is true that, in the 4th, the emotion we feel when we visit that area is of togetherness and even a form of love, which we can trace back to the fact that we are all aspects of God and, thus, are all one. But, we invent, if we may use that word, a different sort of family as in humans, plants and animals of similar types.
It is the second understanding of the word family that allows us to include negative beings - like minded but negative - that allows us to use the word family to mean like minded people.
Animals and plants may have some concept that if, for example, they are dogs or cats, lions or tigers, monkeys or mice they belong to groups, but we think its fair to say they would not have any concept of the word family.
It is only humans that think in that manner.
So, it is only humans that can form families of good or bad people.
Animals might know that they belong to a certain group and, generally, only live and mate with animals of their own species, but they would have no concept of good or bad.
No animal is able to understand that it might have a choice of linking with other animals of its own species but, within that species there might be good, kind ones and/or evil members. Animals and, indeed, plants do not think like that. Good or bad in the plant and animal kingdoms does not exist. It is only among humans that we have the concepts of being good or bad.

Now where does all this take us?
To understand the word family, we must ignore plants and animals.
Although plants and animals belong to families both in the genetic sense of mother, father, they have no understanding of the word family. They act automatically and mate, generally, only with members of their own species.

We humans are different. We can not only be aware that we belong to the human race and also belong to the latest variety of humans (homo sapien sapiens), but we are also aware that we belong to families in the genetic sense of mother, father, brother and sister as we mentioned above.

But, finally, we have a third meaning of the word family as in good people or bad people.

So, despite the family concept being broadcast into our auras from this place in the 4th, we are able, because we are human and because we have strong personalities, to realise, when we think about it, variants to the word family.

We can realise that we are all one because we are all God.

Then we can realise that we belong to the human race.

Next, we realise that we have genetic families, or we do if we have an incarnation, and finally, we realise that through our personalities we are drawn towards groups of like-minded people.

To each one of these aspects we might attribute the appellation family.

The meaning of the word family changes somewhat depending on which aspect of us we are considering but each one can carry the word family, if we choose thus to call it.

So, we have done our best to describe the word family.

We have pointed out that family is a multifaceted word implying quite a variety of meanings depending on the implication we give to the word.

We wished to inform you that there exists in the 4th an area that contains the concept of family but the actual meaning of the word alters according to how we use that word.

So, having told you about yet another place in the 4th, we will end this chapter here and leave you to decide for yourself the meaning you attribute to the word family.

We will turn to yet another aspect of the countless areas in the 4th that broadcast their message into our auras and influence our lives.

CHAPTER 27

THE GIVING PLANE

Let us jump straight into the next chapter.

This one will be about giving.

Once again, what do we mean by the word 'giving' and why is it important enough to devote a chapter?

In fact, learning to give is of vital importance, as we hope to demonstrate throughout this chapter, and is one of the differences between us humans and the fauna and flora of Earth.

It is important enough that there is a place, a landscape in the 4th that contains the concept of giving.

Giving is a rare act in nature and the only time we see in practice is when a female mammal gives milk to her young or when a bird, for example, regurgitates food for its offspring.

Nature is surprisingly selfish and this is due to the fact that virtually every animal and every plant devotes its energy to surviving by getting the most food, the best shelter and the highest protection for itself at the expense of leaving weaker members of its species to survive if it can and to the best of its ability.

Although most animals, for example, live in relative peace together, the concept of giving or sharing is unknown.

No animal, except for a mother, would even consider giving part of its food or giving its shelter to another of its species.

Strangely enough, there are two exceptions to this rule: ants and bees.

Within reason, and depending on the type of ants, they, for example, will gather a variety of food, transport it to their nest, produce the fungus that ants eat and all the nest participates of this stock of food.

But do not think that ants share their stock of food through any desire to give in the sense we understand.

There is a design that ants have developed over time which has created the need for all ants to partake of the common store of food, not through generosity but in order for the nest to survive.

It is the fact that, from the mass of fauna and flora that ants collect and is transformed by a process that creates a form of mushroom, that has evolved into the concept that all ants eat of this produced food.

If ants could digest directly any food, they would do so without a moment's thought for their fellow ants.

As we said, it is the fact that the ants have to work together gathering a variety of nourishment and then fermenting it that creates a common stockpile of food the ants can digest.

Their DNA is programmed to do this, so they work without thought, each ant programmed to play its part in the production of the end product. There is no thought of giving or sharing.

Bees do much the same.

There are exceptions but, generally speaking, it is only humans who give or share. And not all humans do this willingly!

Before we get too involved in expanding this subject, we wish to explain something. We are aware that many of you would like us to concentrate on and describe the dramatic aspects of the areas in the 4th. We do understand that it is natural to wish for us to describe the gory areas that appeal to people's desires to know about the negative areas. Some of the subjects we explain you may find unexciting or boring but we take a different point of view. We would like to excite you by describing the negative areas and, if space in this book permits perhaps we will, but this particular book sets out to describe some of the areas that affect us all and not all areas are dramatic.
But all the areas we describe play a cardinal role in people's lives.
This chapter, although not dramatic, is important for humanity to understand.
So, we hope that you will bear with us and allow us to describe the important subject of giving.

Let us first enter the place in the 4th where the feeling of giving is to be found.
As always, it has its own frequency to keep it apart from any other area so the student has to learn how to link with this area.
It is another non-physical area by which we mean that there is nothing to see, but when we enter this area or landscape we are filled with a glorious desire to be generous to all life.
It is a magnificent feeling.
We forget about our own desires, needs and concerns and just have the desire to help all life.

The question is, of course, why should this area exist and why should we feel the desire to give any and all of our possessions to help those without these things.
The answer is that we are all one and we are all God. Therefore, by entering this giving area, we are not so much entering an area that contains the desire to get rid of any possessions but we are entering an area where the God force blasts us with the knowledge that we are all one and thus anything that we might possess, that another might lack, creates the desire to help that person.
Can you understand this?
We are saying that when we enter this giving place we have an overwhelming desire to become one with all life.
To become one implies total equality between all people. What one has, all should have.
But there is much more to this area than that.
It has been stated that you cannot give anything away!
What does this apparently stupid statement mean?
Quite simply, it means that God created everything and as we are God, we can create anything.
But the trick is that to receive, we have first to give. You cannot add more water to a flask already full. You have to empty it before being able to refill it.
The Master Jesus was aware of this giving area. He was asked by a rich man, 'What must I do to enter the kingdom of heaven?'
Jesus answered, 'Sell what you have, give it to the poor and follow me.'

By 'me', of course, he implied his Christ spirit.

Jesus used a different metaphor to us, but it comes to the same thing.

We need to locate and enter this giving area, or at least allow it to enter our aura.

The concept of giving what we have to assist the needy is a fundamental aspect of being human and realizing our oneness to God and to all life.

So, this giving area is very important, and in a fairer world, there would be no needy people as there is more than enough of everything for all people to be cared for correctly and humanely.

We are all receiving into one of our auras this area. We are all aware that we should be helping the needy.

But, unfortunately, it was decided long ago that the rich and powerful keeping the poor and needy in that state was a good political stratagem by the rich and powerful.

If everyone had enough of everything the power of politicians would lessen. But, by keeping the poor in that state gives power to politicians because, that way, they can get people to vote for them by promising to end the difficulties whilst, at the same time, having absolutely no intention of providing any real aid.

You may have noticed that politicians make extravagant promises but, in fact, change very little.

This situation will continue until people wake up, reject the false promises, throw the liars out and replace them with honest people who really do care for the needy.

We do understand the lure of fame, power and riches, but to lie is a sin. One should never lie. But, we also understand that no one would vote for a politician who openly said that he had no intention of helping the poor and needy. So the lies go on and the amazing thing is that many people believe that they are going to be helped if they vote for any particular politician or party.

Politicians only help themselves. This needs to be understood for things to change.

Everyone deserves a chance but once it is noticed that someone is not fulfilling his elected duty, he should be replaced.

Now, let us return to the concept of giving. We mentioned that we are at least two things in one.

(a) We are God.

(b) We are all one.

We are all variants of the same person, if we may express it in such simplistic terms.

So, if we followed the advice of Jesus and gave to the poor, in fact we are giving to ourselves.

Thus, it is that by giving we receive because, if we are all one and we give to another version of ourselves, we are giving to ourselves.

Unfortunately, the vast majority of the human population does not realise this.

The result is that huge numbers of people spend their lives chasing after fame and fortune.

If we realised that we were all one and that one is God and God is the creator - via his archangels - we would understand that if we meet someone who has less than us, that person is us in another form. Thus, if we give some of what we have to the person who has less than us, we are, in fact, giving to ourselves.

What happens, in reality, is that by helping any person or animal that needs help, in the short-term we might seem to have less of what we gave away. But, sooner or later, God gives us back what we gave.
This is the inevitable result of the fact that by giving to another we are giving to ourselves and thus, what we gave returns to us.

But, it is even more miraculous than that because, let us say we have a certain amount of money.
We give some of it away. Thus, one person receives but we have given.
Eventually, God repays us so there are two lots of money generated.
(a) The money we gave away and is now in the possession of someone else, and
(b) The new money God gives us.
So, there was extra money created by God's archangels. God is all powerful and God can create anything.
By the simple act of giving money to another, God creates more to replace the money - or anything else - that was given.
If we give help, in whatever fashion we feel we need to in order to help another and have faith in God, that help is always replaced.
That is the way this area in the 4th, the giving area, works.
We give and we receive.
But we must give before receiving. We cannot add more to a cup already full. We must empty the cup and God will refill it for us again.

As we give and find that we are repaid so our confidence, our faith grows.
The more faith we have the more what seems to be miracles work.
So, if you see any person, animal or even plant that needs help and you have the means of helping that entity, do not hesitate.
Give willingly, knowing that God will replace what you give.
But you must do it willingly knowing that God will replace what you have given. If you do not give willingly, the magic doesn't work.

However, as far as the area in the 4th is concerned, it sends out to our auras the desire to give. It contains no information concerning what we give will be replaced, which is why many people hesitate to give because the knowledge that God will replace whatever we give is contained in our spiritual aspects.
We have to learn to trust God and this trust develops in the degree that we can understand that all is one and that God always replaces whatever we give.

We have just attempted to describe how this works. Indeed, we have explained and talked about this many times.
But we will repeat it yet again in the hopes that anyone sitting on the fence with regard to God giving us back that which we give, will be finally convinced.

We have an area in the 4th that contains the desire to give.
But we are God. Everyone and everything is the one same God that you and we are.
So, if we give something, providing we realise that we are all one and that one is God, it is, in effect, God giving to God.
God, taking the form of us who give, and God taking the form of the receiver.

So, as far as God is concerned, nothing much happened. Something; money, help or whatever, has merely moved from one aspect of him to another.

But from the spiritual aspect of giving and receiving, an exchange has been made. Someone lacked something. So, one aspect of God felt he lacked something and that desire to obtain the missing something reaches into the giving area which has now become aware that someone lacks something.

The desire to give is permanently being sent to all people, incarnate or not, and so some people are aware that they should give and some just ignore the message, wishing to hold on to what they have accumulated.

For those who are aware and desirous of giving, the law of mutual attraction operates, and the person desirous of giving is made aware of the desire to obtain something by the needy person.

The person who has, gives to the needy person.

But then the person who gave has less of whatever it was he gave.

Unconsciously, he sends a message to the 'give' area that he now has less of what he gave.

Although he may not worry about it, the faith in God that he will provide sends a message to someone else who is in a position to provide, and the person who gave finds himself reimbursed of what he gave.

This goes on and on, giving and receiving.

There is no shortage of anything. Governments are always pleading poverty and find ways of making poor people poorer by increasing taxes but have you noticed if, for example, one country declares war on another, both countries find enormous amounts of resources to fund the war?

Imagine if that vast reserve was given to the poor, as the master Jesus suggested, poverty could be relieved worldwide. And wars ended!

So, we have two types of people. Those who ignore the appeal going into everyone's auras to give and those who realise that one may give and simple faith in God will ensure that the person will recuperate what he gave.

However, we must add a word of warning here. If, for example, one gives money, that money usually comes from a bank.

Banks are not in the habit of giving money away, so the bank will not reimburse any money given.

That money will be reimbursed one way or another, but when one gives, angels leap into action to repay the giver.

However, it may take some time for the money to be organised so it may take some time to organize the repayment. Also, that money may not be reimbursed in exactly the way that it was given. Money is not produced from thin air but you can be sure that what you gave will come back to you one way or another.

Equally, if you help someone by rendering some service, you can be sure that when you need help, it will be given.

That is why we said that you cannot give anything away. Money, articles or help will all be returned to you as and when it is organised and as and when you need it.

Although the giving plane is of vital importance, it is easy to explain, which we have done and we hope you have understood.
So, we will end this short chapter here and move on to the next area.

CHAPTER 28

THE EMOTION PLANES

We have taken note of all the messages that have been sent over time concerning the somewhat new and mysterious way that life really works, as we have described in our various books, etc.

But there is an aspect to which we devoted this entire book, but without explaining the modus operandi behind our descriptions.

Now is the time, as you who have got this far through the book to be reading this message might have guessed, to reveal to you all that for each and every emotion that man is capable of feeling, there exists an area in the 4th that contains the essence of this emotion and broadcasts itself into our emotions (personality).

One way of imagining this is a sort of 'one-armed bandit', a gambling machine that, every time the handle is pulled a number of images appear. If the images line-up, the prize is won.

Now, obviously, the real world is not a bit like that but we want you to visualise a vast number of emotions that are contained in the 4th awaiting the moment you choose to activate that emotion.

When that happens, the emotion enters your aura and starts to influence you.

This influence can be anything you choose. Think of the vast number of emotions, of desires that you could consider. This might be love, hate, friendship, jealousy, any emotion connected to the arts, anger, fear, addictions, etc.

If one were to consider, seriously, all the emotions that exist for us to choose, the list, though not endless, is vast indeed.

Well, we want you clearly to realise that every one of these emotions is contained in pure form in the 4th.

Further, these emotions are poised, ready at all moment to spring into action and send that emotion to one of your auras where, in a flash, it enters your reality via your chakras and you feel that emotion.

The degree that you feel that emotion depends on the amount of it you let into your personality.

We mentioned above a 'one-armed bandit'. Well, imagine such a machine but with a large number of wheels containing pictures that you could line-up.

Imagine that you pull the handle and a certain number of images line-up. You block those images and pull the handle once more and more images line-up. You continue until all the wheels show the same image. At this point the machine regurgitates your reward, usually money, although it could be some other prize.

We do admit that we have used a poor example but if you have ever watched people hooked on gambling (an emotion), frantically throwing their money away, you can realise how powerful an emotion can be.

Most of us, if we go into a casino, might try a machine but would quickly stop as the gambling emotion has been sent from the 4th into the auras of the person concerned, but that person has not accepted much of the gambling emotion and so quickly stops as he realizes he is throwing his hard-earned money away.

But the hooked gambler accepts a vast amount of this gambling emotion into his personality and remains at the machine until he has wasted all his money.
Gambling is considered by many to be an illness, a disease and in a way, we could consider it so, but it can be controlled by an effort of will.

If we may, we will devote this chapter about how all that we have so far mentioned actually works and we hope that it will enable you to control your emotions better because none of these afflictions, gambling, alcoholism, depression and so on are actually illnesses. They are simply someone accepting into their personalities that emotion. They can be controlled, as we hope to demonstrate in this chapter.
So, let us go back to the beginning and give a short overview of these emotions that people are subject to.

In the 4th, there are a large number of emotions, all separate one from another, that are in pure, undiluted form. Those of you who have read this book thus far will realise that we have described a few of them.
As we said, the list is vast but each emotion that a person can be subject to is contained in its individual area in the 4th.
Until it is activated by someone, each emotion remains quiescent but, if you think of all the billions of humans incarnate and add to that number the large number of us in the spiritual realms, because we also can be subject to emotions, these emotions are very active. Pushing their concepts out through the multiverse, influencing any and all people concerned by their thoughts and emotions.
All of us, all the time are thinking and feeling, thus those feelings are connected to emotions and so we can assure you that most of the emotion areas are extremely active pushing their particular emotion out into the personalities of people who begin to think in any direction.

Let us explain this again in other words.
We want you to imagine the vast number of emotions, even just humans incarnate are subject to, not counting those in the spirit worlds, nor animals, nor plants.
Each and every one of these entities are subject to emotions of one sort or another.
Now, God's archangels constructed an area in the 4th for each one of these emotions and placed, in pure form, these emotions.
Perhaps we can describe why we have these emotions and how they were created.

It was realised that in order for life to have any real sense, it was necessary for all things to have personalities and it was further noted that, unless each and every being (entity) had the chance to have variations in their personalities, people would all be like zombies.
The same applies to a lesser degree to animals, to an even lesser degree to plants, and to minerals hardly at all.
So, the concept of personalities was created and placed within the spiritual concepts of all life as we explained in a book entitled Personalities.
But the obvious problem was that if humans, just to consider humans, had now the possibility to have emotions, these emotions and access to them had to be created.

As emotions are non-physical, it seemed obvious that emotions needed to be created and placed in a non-physical area.

The upper 4th dimension was chosen and so, within that dimension, a large number of frequencies were created, one for each emotion.

Then these emotions were created and placed within these frequencies.

Just how God's archangels constructed all these emotions would be such advanced physics that it remains outside of the scope of this book.

Please accept that the spiritual concept of each and every emotion it is possible to feel was constructed in pure form and placed in one of the areas created to hold them.

So, we have a situation where God's archangels thought about and constructed, in spiritual form, all of the mass of emotions to what one can be subject, and placed them in the individual areas in the 4th.

This, as you can imagine, was no easy task and we salute these archangels for their incredible skills and talents when you think that they, collectively and individually, constructed all that exists in so-called physicality, and also the vast numbers of concepts and events they constructed in the non-physical dimensions.

It is truly amazing and what we have so far explained in our various books, lessons and videos is far from all that exists.

There is a lot more to explain and we hope we will have sufficient trained Earthly instruments to whom we can transmit the information.

Transmitting books and having someone sufficiently trained to receive them is no small affair.

It takes an immense amount of time and effort to train someone to receive, accurately, what we send, and writing a book is an immense amount of work as any author will confirm.

Our books are more difficult in that we have to be sure that the scribe on Earth is fully trained in telepathy so as to receive our transmitted wisdom without distortion.

But we have been tasked to transmit information to you and nothing will stop us.

Let us return to the places in the 4th where various emotions are stored.

It would already be an immense task of creating these emotion areas, but they would serve no purpose unless they were used in some way.

Therefore, as you must now be aware, links to our personality were made.

Now, this, actually, is quite complicated. We have explained it all once, but will do so again.

Before even considering if we are going to choose an earthly incarnation or not, the young person in the 4th is taken on a long and extended tour of all the emotional areas.

Although we mentioned this form of education, we did not mention that these were the emotion areas we are now discussing.

We did not mention this fact because we did not wish to confuse you by jumping ahead of our explanations. But now is the moment to bring all this together.

So, the young student's guides show him all these areas.

You may question how it is that, if we wish to enter one of these areas, we have to learn the frequency of that area and yet our guides can take us there with ease?

The answer is that the guides have already taken the time and effort to learn the frequencies and they can, quite simply, take us along with them rather as if someone has a key to a locked room and by opening the lock, anyone with the person with the key can also enter the room.

So, guides show us virtually all of these emotion areas and take note of our reactions when we are affected by the emotion contained in any space.

Some interest us and some do not.

Now, these emotions that interest us are placed - or rather a connection to these emotions are placed - within our personalities.

There are so many emotions that virtually no two people have identical personalities.

Thus, we are born into the next stage of our lives. We could consider this like leaving one junior school and entering a more advanced school.

The next phase might include an incarnation or it might not.

The point we wish to make is that, having taken an interest in some emotions, and rejected others, they help form our personalities.

What actually happens is that, via an aura, we maintain - or not - a link to a number of the emotion areas.

The process is, in this case that we have sown the seeds (the desires) to incorporate various emotions into our personality, so we reach out through an aura and connect with any one or any number of emotions and draw that or those emotions back down, through the aura and into our personality.

The degree of that emotion that we draw into our personality depends, to a small or to a large extent, on our ego.

For instance, imagine someone has an interest in a subject.

This could be almost anything. But, now the person has a choice. He might be only slightly interested in the subject, in which case he draws very little of the pure power of the emotion into his personality, or he might be totally devoted to the emotion, in which case he draws a lot more of the pure emotion into his personality.

His ego governs just how much he draws within his personality, and that, in turn, depends on how much his aura reaches into the emotion concerned and how much is triggered to be sent back to the personality.

The emotions, each and every one of them, are placed in their independent areas as pure emotion. They are the pure form of whatever emotion we might consider.

It is only the degree of any emotion that we select and draw into our personality that varies.

Very few of us select the totality of any pure emotion. The effect would be overwhelming.

So, the vast majority, incarnate or discarnate, select a small amount of any emotion.

Those who select more are those who chase after one subject, generally.

History contains the records of those who devoted their lives to the pursuit of one subject.

The explanation we have provided above gives an indication as to how and why this happened.

We have more or less covered this topic, and in conjunction with at least one of the other chapters we gave you, should provide you with an indication as to why you feel drawn to any emotion.

But before we leave this subject, we wish to reinforce something we mentioned earlier.

You may change or reduce any emotion by an act of will. You may reinforce the desire to study any subject that interests you by the simple act of concentrating on that subject, which is also an emotion.

Equally, and more importantly, if there is any emotion that you could consider is harming you; depression, addiction, etc., you are not a victim of that emotion.

By an act of will, you may reduce or eliminate it from your personality by the simple act of refusing to accept it into your personality.

This sounds simple - and it is - but, in reality, it can be an uphill struggle to reject any negative aspects from our personalities.

Please never forget that we, the members of the Great White Brotherhood, are just like you. We have all had incarnations and have all battled to remove negative aspects of our personalities and, indeed, many of us are still struggling.

Many of us had problems with depression.

Others had problems of alcoholism or drug addictions. We are not perfect. Far from it. We have had to learn to battle to reduce the desire for harmful things.

The fact that we know how and why these harmful emotions affect us has helped us, and we pass this information on to you in the hopes that it will help those who have drawn harmful emotions into their personalities.

We have struggled and we know what an uphill battle it is to eliminate harmful emotions from our personality.

If one suffers from depression, it is a horrible thing, that can be conquered by refusing to accept that emotion.

Equally, anyone suffering from alcoholism or drug addiction battles with his ego for a long time until the connection to those pure emotions in the 4th is severed.

It is hard but it can be done.

It takes an act of will and courage but, every day that we resist temptation, reduces the connection to those emotions that are harming us.

So, we will end this chapter here and move on.

CHAPTER 29

ADULTERY

We have been asked to show you some of the more unpleasant areas in the 4th, so we have chosen one with which you will all be familiar, even if you have not practiced it.
We are going to consider the area in the 4th that contains the concept of adultery.
Once again, most people consider adultery to be a self chosen act that a person may select if he/she becomes bored with the partner he/she has, and is attracted to someone else.
In reality, it is quite a complex matter, but we will do our best to unravel the complexities of it in simple language.

Now, the word adultery actually has a number of meanings, or at least variations of the word does.
The first and best-known meaning is the one that we described above, but another meaning is to corrupt something, usually food, by adding foreign or unwelcome ingredients into the food for various nefarious reasons.
The most obvious reason is to make the food object cheaper to produce to increase profits but can also be done in order, deliberately, to corrupt something to poison people or animals.

So, is there a connection between deviant sexual behavior and acts taken to corrupt food items for various reasons?
Logic would dictate no, but we wish in this chapter to point out connections between devious sexual behavior and devious corruption of food items either by directly changing certain items in a recipe, or by poisoning animals for various reasons. There is a link between these apparently disparate acts.
This link is yet another area in the 4th that contains, in pure form, the concept of adultery or adulterous acts or behavior.
This area, as always, is within its own particular frequency and is, once again, non-physical, by which we mean that, upon entering it, there is nothing to see. One feels just the emotion of this area.
The strange thing is that, upon entering this area, one is not overwhelmed by the desire to cheat on one's husband or wife but one is overwhelmed with the concept of cheating one's fellow man/woman.

We used the phrase man/woman to demonstrate that this area is non-sexist and can corrupt either men or women equally, but from now on we will return to literary customs and just use the masculine; he, him, man, etc.
But please accept that we include females in our talk. We are not sexist. It is just literary convention and makes it easier than having to write he/she/they and so on, especially when one regards the plethora of gender identifications that have been invented by misguided individuals.
Can you imagine how ridiculous writing a book would be if every time we referred to anyone, we had to put a hundred different supposed gender variants in order not to offend anyone?

Until this nonsense stops, we will continue to ignore it and, in our books, refer to the masculine. From that you may imply that we include all people, regardless of their supposed gender identification.

Indeed, the origin of all this useless and misguided gender identification can be found in the adultery plane. It is adulterating the identification of people in a nefarious way to spread confusion and promote discord.

So, we want you clearly to understand that this strange plane exists to spread discord and unhappiness and any sexual connotation is just one by-product of connection to this plane.

Therefore, let us try to explain how this area which we could consider to be negative works.   It will not take long as most of what we will say is already known to people incarnate. Evil and misguided people have been using this plane for thousands of years to corrupt the lives of many people willing to link to this plane.

This plane, as we said, deals with adultery in all its connotations. We should mention at this point that these planes that we describe do not have name tags attached to them.

There are no signposts directing one towards one of these areas.

It is we that ascribe the names we give you.

This particular plane, we thought long and hard about before ascribing the name 'adultery', because we could equally have given the name 'corruption' to it and it would have been just as accurate.

We chose the word adultery because that word, originally, described changing or corrupting one thing for another by human intervention.

We described how food was and is altered for greater profit. How animals are altered by the administration of drugs, and we could include how plants and cereals are corrupted by the addition of foreign material for increased profit.

All of this came, originally, under the heading of adultery.

It is only more recently that it has come to mean deviant sexual behavior.

So, before we consider actual individual cases of adultery, let us describe as fully as we can what it feels like to enter this plane to which we ascribe the appellation 'the adultery plane'.

It is a strange feeling for us because we live in a world of honesty, respect and complete open-handedness to each other.

Entering this area takes us back to the feelings we experienced during our incarnation, when we were surrounded on all sides and in all areas by people trying in one way or another to cheat their fellow man.

This is a horrible feeling.

We remember always being on our guard to avoid being cheated by someone offering to sell us some service or goods that failed to live up to their - the salesman's - promises and our hopes.

None of this exists in the spheres in which we normally live, and we have to enter a plane such as the adultery plane in order to feel, once more, that worrying sensation.

So, as we enter this feeling, this concept of changing, altering, corrupting or cheating is in pure form and it is, to us, at least, a most unwelcome feeling.   We had left it behind, in somewhat diluted form, when our incarnations ended and yet here we are again being bombarded with the pure force of cheating. Perhaps we could have termed this area the 'cheating plane' and that would have described it just as well.

In pure form, as we experience it, it is the ultimate feeling of everything that is the opposite of fair play - if we may use that old-fashioned term. We are not sure that all people understand the meaning of fair play, but it implies never doing anything underhand or dishonest.

This plane - the adultery plane - opens our minds to consider any and all ways of cheating others.

The meaning of the word, in its sexual connotation, is only one aspect of cheating, but it is interesting that the offended party, who inevitably finds out, is usually very hurt, disappointed and is left with a feeling of not only disgust, but of feeling unclean as if not only their body had been soiled by the cheating party but the love bond is broken.

The couple might stay together to try to heal the bond, but the relationship will never be the same. Something was broken that could never be fully repaired.

All of this is the work of the adultery plane that exists exactly to spread all those unhappy feelings.

It is a negative, evil area, and when we enter it and receive full blast its effects we, ourselves, feel unclean and deeply unhappy.

Not that this area is trying to heal broken relationships.

Not at all.

It exists to promote broken relationships. It is our reaction to these concepts that make us feel sad and unhappy as we realise that there are so many people on Earth who are victims of this plane.

It is pernicious and very few people escape some of its effects.

Just to consider a couple. Their relationship may start out very loving and caring but, inevitably, they link to part of this area and then they start to put a watchful eye on their partner for signs of cheating on their vows they made when they got together.

Some religions have accepted this plane into their doctrines and allow men to have multiple wives. Some rich people in certain countries are even allowed harems. But you will notice that is always men who are allowed multiple wives. It is never women who are allowed multiple husbands.

Many women are shut in their homes, and if they are allowed out, it is in the company with a male who guards them and, often, the women are clothed so is to hide their beauty.

All this comes from this dreadful plane, and in this case is designed to make women unhappy as it is natural for women to make themselves look as attractive as possible.

So, this plane leaps into action and denies women to look attractive and insults them when their husband has the right to shower his affections on other women.

Some accept this, but many feel insulted when a husband announces that he has chosen another woman to share his bed.

This plane exists to promote that unhappiness.

So, you can see how negative this plane is, and it is constantly broadcasting its negative waves into the auras of those susceptible to accept its negative vibrations.

We will talk about other things that this plane can harm in a moment, but first we need to explain how and why adultery as you understand it exists.

When a couple start a serious relationship and decide to live together and, possibly, have children it is because they love each other.
Love is a wonderful emotion and is the foundation of the galaxy created by God because our galaxy contains the emotion of love.
So, the couple love each other and enjoy spending their lives together in all senses of the word.
But, this negative plane that we have called adultery is never far away.
One of the couple may start to notice that the person that he decided to live with may not live up to his expectations.
When we use the masculine, remember that we include the feminine and any blend in between.
So, inevitably, he starts to consider his options.
Infidelity may come into his mind.
At that point, one of his auras links to this idea and sends a message to this horrible plane for it to interact with the individual.
Instantly, the adultery plane reacts by sending a part of its pernicious influence back to the person.
So, the trap is set.
Over the coming days and weeks, the individual battles. His natural sense of self dignity, of honour, etc., tells him that he should stay faithful to his wife or husband, while the adultery area is telling him that he should be infidel to his vows of love to his partner.
What decision he comes to is his affair. Either he resists and learns to love his partner as he/she is or he gives in and seeks another person.

What is being sought is the thrill of that first contact of love he had with his partner.
Inevitably, that love will fade as he learns that the new person is not perfect for him.
So, this adultery plane will push him to seek another person.
In some cases, it has been known for people to share their lives with a large number of people, one after another. Never finding happiness.
The trick, obviously, is to resist this evil plane, recognise it for what it is, a mechanism that will destroy marriages and can be resisted.
It can only be accepted in the degree that one allows it to enter one's personality.
It can be rejected by an act of the will because you are God and you are in charge of your body, not some emotion plane in the 4th dimension.

We encourage all who are in a relationship to do all that you can to preserve the love that you had at the beginning of your relationship, throughout the long years that you may live together.
It is delightful to see a happy family and it is delightful to see an elderly couple who have spent long years together walking along, hand in hand.
They will arrive in heaven, one closely behind the other and spend all of eternity together in a loving relationship.

However, what we have described is only one small aspect of this plane that we called the adultery plane.

We said, 'one small aspect', but, in effect, the way that the effects of accepting the
negative influences of this evil plane into the lives of so many people, causes great harm
to families.
But, this plane exists to cause harm.
Some planes are positive and some are negative and you have asked us to choose to
describe a negative plane. We have chosen this one. Although, until you realise just how
damaging this plane is, it is hard to imagine it affects, but we hope to describe to you as
you reach into this area just how harmful it is. It is truly negative and although we do not
like to use the word evil, because it is not connected to the lower 4th where demons live,
nevertheless, its effects on humanity can be severely negative.
We will explain by giving a few examples.

One of the most outstanding negative results of this plane is what has become known as
terrorism.
This is fast becoming a worldwide phenomenon and is causing great distress, not only to
all those who have been directly affected by terrorist attacks, but also the families and
friends of those so affected.
Equally, its effects spread as people have to decide if they should leave their homes and
walk the streets, never sure if they will become victims to mindless attacks.

The normal state for people to live in is peace. Even when wars were and are occurring,
it was recognized that it was considered 'fair play' for opposing sides to wear a uniform
so that they could be recognized as either friend or foe.
But terrorism is different.
Terrorists do not wear uniforms, but mix with the populations of towns and cities, waiting
for the moment when they can attack.
This is both dreadful and cowardly.
As people walk the streets going peacefully about their business, they might be attacked
at any moment by some misguided person who has incorporated a large degree of this
negative emotion into his aura.
The individual, as he links to this area we called the adultery plane, is filled with the
desire to destroy the peace and calm, which is everyone's right.
This area exists to corrupt, to cause damage by pushing people to think in a negative -
dare we say evil - fashion, destroying the peace and equilibrium that is the right of all
normal people.
Just as we mentioned in the previous example about adultery in couples, and how the
design behind negative behavior by one of the parties was there to cause distress, so we
can link the negative behavior of a person to act in the way that we called terrorism to
cause distress.

Adultery in a family affects a relatively small group - the actual family and then their
friends - but terrorism is an act that can cause fear merely by the potential threat of being
attacked by a complete stranger.
Many of these attacks are promoted by religious fanaticism.
We have often said that we do not approve of religions because they exist to separate
God's children, one from another.

Religions have always been connected to this adultery plane, and as the leaders of any religion accept more and more of this negative plane into their auras, so that pushes them to think of more ways of causing separation.

One of the best (or worst) ways up till now has been terrorism.

Terrorism is not exclusive to one religion although it is fair to say that, at the time of writing this book, many acts of terrorism have been promoted by the leadership of a certain religion.

It is not the fault of the religion as such, but by the effects that the leaders of that religion imbibe into their auras, which causes them to promote terrorism for some dubious end.

The effect of terrorism is terrible indeed, and those who promoted and those that cause it will face terrible consequences for their ungodly actions when their incarnations end.

If those promoting terrorism, whatever the cause, could see the fate that awaits them they would not cause these acts, but unfortunately, this adultery plane pushes them to shut their eyes to any consequences of their actions and just wish to cause separatism between people.

Terrorism is a negative act and in no way will cause people to convert to a certain religion, often the cause of terrorism.

On the contrary, it causes people to detest the religion and those involved with it.

This is what the adultery plane exists for. To cause separatism between people. To cause unhappiness, as one detests one's neighbour for belonging to a religion that promotes terrorism.

Those promoting these negative and mindless acts will never dominate decent people, and by harming them, is only causing more division.

It is a pity that the leaders of religions do not realise that violence will never succeed in bringing people together.

Violence comes from this adultery plane, and this plane exists to cause separatism.

Can we think of any other act or acts that exists to separate one group from another?

Actually, the list is endless. People accept this plane into their auras and thus feel separate from other people.

The next obvious one is politics.   Political parties have existed in one form or another for thousands of years.

The basic structure is always a number of groups of people who claim to have opposing views on how a country should be run.

We will not bore you with details as we are sure that all readers of this book will be aware of politics and how they divide nations.

This will continue until the public bring the political concept to an end, and promote good and wise people to steer their country in a peaceful way, providing for the needs of all people and working to bring world peace.

We are far from that in most countries, but it will come to be one day.

We could mention wars. Once again, they have existed for thousands of years and exist in the degree that leaders are filled with the concept of causing separatism, which we termed adultery.

Looking back, we are beginning to think that adultery was not a good choice to call this plane, which is devoted to the concept of causing separatism.

Perhaps we should explain something here.

Many of the books we have given you were written a long time ago and have become textbooks that students in the 4th study. We give them to you to enable you to be on as equal a level as our students in the 4th.

That way, as ascension becomes more evident, you will be armed to accept the changes to society that will come.

But this book we, the members of the Great White Brotherhood, collectively have written.

Some of us in the Great White Brotherhood are relatively recent arrivals but many have been members for long ages, as the Great White Brotherhood has existed for a long time.

This title 'adultery' was suggested by elders of our group who understood the original meaning of the word adultery as in altering, corrupting, changing, harming.

They suggested the title, and out of respect for these much admired and wise elders, we adopted it.

However, we do understand that adultery has become a more narrow meaning word and its current accepted meaning is connected to unfaithfulness in couples.

So, when you read the word 'adultery', please accept that we mean this in its old meaning of altering and corrupting.

Let us touch on food.

Now, in our opinion, we consider harming animals to be a sin - Thou shalt not kill.

Even if an animal has been murdered and is cut up on a butcher's slab, it is for us that the animal was killed so we are guilty of its death.

So, we would like to see all people become vegan, as you call it, but we do accept that this evil plane has pushed people to think it normal and acceptable to eat animals.

We will not argue with you - it is your free will choice.

But all people, whether they are vegan or not, have the right to have clean, unadulterated food that will nourish the human body.

This gives an opportunity for people to be influenced by this negative plane called adultery (corruption) to introduce poisons into plants and animals.

Once you understand that the adultery plane exists to cause as much harm as possible in an opposite sense to normality, it is easy to see that those in a position to alter food, filled with the effects of this negative and evil plane, will find a means of corrupting pure vegetables, fruits and animals.

Thus they have found means of genetically modifying plants and of introducing harmful hormones into animals in an attempt to destroy the health of people.

We find the same with injections. Originally, injections of bacteria into the human body gave protection from harmful diseases and was a good idea, so once again, this awful plane influenced doctors to find ways of corrupting the injections.

The result has been the rise in unfortunate health problems that could have been avoided by giving clean, uncorrupted injections.

Fortunately, people have made the connection between adulterated injections and are protesting.

We could go on.

We could consider, for example, how old-fashioned cars were created with a proper chassis and metallic bumpers (fenders) at each end.

This meant that in the case of an accident, the chassis held the car together and the metallic bumpers (fenders) protected the body work thus reducing bodily harm and costly repairs.
Now, of course, most cars are constructed of subframes, which fold up in the case of accidents, and plastic bumpers (fenders) which may look attractive but provide absolutely no protection in the case of an accident.
The result has been many people hurt or killed, trapped in crumpled up cars and costly repairs.

We could go on. Virtually every domain of human life has been affected in a negative sense by this negative, corrupted plane, influencing all and sundry that allow themselves to reach out and contact this plane.

The remedy is simple. Sit down and consider all the things that you think about, all the things you do that could be considered to be the opposite of good, kind, and peaceful actions or thoughts and resolve to stop thinking and acting in that fashion.
As we said in the last chapter, you are God taking human form and though you are being bombarded with this negative plane, it can only affect you in the degree that you accept it into your personality, your thoughts and actions.
Reject all thoughts of negativity.
Reject all thoughts of harm, revenge and self-protection against a supposed enemy.
Walk fearlessly about, surrounding yourself with the power of God, the power of goodness and never give way to anger, insults or any thoughts of revenge.
Live in peace with yourself and with all people.
In the degree that you do this, you will rid yourself of the effects of this negative, evil plane, and God's angels can come close to you taking the space that was once occupied by this evil force.
You cannot have both negativity and holiness in your personality at the same time. It has to be one or the other.
Make your choice but choose wisely.

This plane, that we called the adultery plane, is just about the most pernicious and evil plane in the 4th.
It exists because we all need choice. We need to learn either to be under the domination of this evil place or to stand in the light of God.
It has to be your choice.

We have informed you of some of the dangers of linking to this negative force and we'll leave you to consider your position in relation to it.
Remember that we have only given a few examples of how this adultery plane can affect you. There are many more examples but we leave you to consider them.
So, we will end this chapter here and move on yet again to something else.

CHAPTER 30

CRIME AND PUNISHMENT

You asked us to present to you a negative aspect of the areas in the 4th that influence people both incarnate and in the heavenly realms. This we have done in the last chapter.
Before we continue with a new subject, we would like to explain an apparent contradiction that has occurred between something we mentioned in another book and what we have stated in this book.
In another book about personalities, we mentioned that there were other galaxies, each with their own God, that gave us the possibility of accepting, or not, these personality aspects into our personalities.
So, each of us will examine all these personality aspects and incorporate some of them into us and some we will reject.
What we accept or what we reject become an integral part of our personality, and makes us, basically, who we are.

However, it was noted that in this book we have stated that there are areas in the 4th that also have personality concepts that we are free to accept or reject into our personalities, and this has, quite rightly, raised some confusion.
We would like, if we may, to take a few moments to describe the difference between the aspects in the various galaxies and the aspects in the 4th that we are currently describing.

First, let us say that the personality aspects in the various galaxies are there, under the guidance of their own God, to enable us to develop personalities.
These personality aspects are fairly pure, almost abstract concepts and we are free to accept or reject them and they will create our personalities in a fairly pure, natural and undiluted form.
These aspects form our basic personalities.
However, the aspects that we are describing in this book could be considered to be sub-aspects of personality, and if we accept them, they are added onto our basic personalities that we accepted from the galaxy planes.

So, to repeat and expand.
When we are quite undeveloped in the 4th - we could almost say childlike - we are gradually introduced into all the personality types that these various personality galaxies present to us.
They tend to be basic, pure personality trends, and we are drawn towards accepting some of them and rejecting others.
But they are basic, pure aspects of personality.
So, we start out with a certain type of personality which was found in the various galaxies that we described in the book on personalities.
However, as we have spent this new book describing, there are other versions, other aspects of personality, in the 4th that tend to influence us as and when we consider the basic, pure personality aspects we selected when we visited the various galaxies concerned with personality.

So, what we are suggesting to you is that there are a large number of galaxies, each one containing an aspect of personality in pure form. These aspects of personality you will be familiar with: love, hate, fear, bravery, harmony and disharmony and on and on into mathematics, science, etc. Every type of personality is contained in pure form and you may select or reject any of these. But we wish you to understand that they are in pure form.

But, in the 4th, there are similar personality aspects but they are present in a slightly different manner. Some of these are positive and some are more negative.

Indeed, some, like the one we described in the last chapter that we entitled 'adultery', we consider to be almost evil.

Equally, of course, there are other areas that are very holy.

But the thing is that we have, first and foremost, these personality aspects in pure form without any variations added to the personality concepts.

While we are in this state, we are fairly unthinking people, not really individuals, as large numbers of people will have incorporated into their personality space - if we may thus put it - identical personality aspects taken directly from the personality galaxies.

If we start to question any aspect of personality, we automatically send a signal to an area in the 4th that contains information related to that personality aspect.

Then, this place in the 4th sends back information which is not identical to the pure aspect we obtained in the galaxy on any aspect of a particular personality trend - whatever it might be.

So, this area in the 4th sends us a somewhat expanded version of the same personality aspect.

It awakens us to the fact that there is more to any personality aspect then just the pure thought.

For instance, imagine that we have incorporated into our personality the pure aspect of love. This is all that the galaxy will provide us with, the pure feeling of love.

But, if we reach out into the 4th and make contact with the aspect or plane of love contained in the 4th, this will provide us with a large number of variations to the feeling of love. Not just a pure emotion of love but all the possible variants to love that exist. Love as in a human relationship. Love for a hobby or work situation. Love for pet animals. Love of nature and on and on.

None of this was contained in the pure notion of love. It is the plane in the 4th that can provide us with all the types of love that can exist. Variants to the pure aspect of love.

The same applies to all the types of emotions that we accepted during our visits to the galaxies of personality.

The areas in the 4th help expand our concepts, knowledge, ideas and thoughts about any subject.

All this enables us to have a greater understanding of the pure personality types.

We hope that you have understood this. It is fairly easy to understand.

We will just recapitulate.

The galaxy areas give us a choice of personalities in pure form but the planes in the 4th give us the fine details about any personality aspect.

Some of these ideas might seem positive and some negative but the planes in the 4th give us an expanded concept of any pure personality that we have incorporated into our global personality space.

The areas in the 4th fill in the blanks, so to speak, and allow us to understand more fully what any pure personality aspect might contain.

The 4th permits us to have greater understanding and this is a very important area.

Having just the pure concept of something is all well and good but it is important for us to be aware of all the fine details of the aspect under consideration.

Having dealt, we hope, with that explanation of the difference between the pure aspect of any personality as given to us in the galaxy planes, and the greater explanations given to us from the 4th when we ask, let us move on to the next subject.

As we mentioned earlier, you asked us to mention the more negative, dramatic and gory planes that exist in the 4th and so we will describe one of the most horrible, after the adultery plane. We will talk about crime and punishment.

We warn you that some of what we will say will be quite horrible because we are going to use a member of the Great White Brotherhood who fell foul of the law long ago and how he was dealt with.

But first, let's just say why there is such a thing as crime and punishment. There have always been people who have committed crimes of various sorts.

We are sure that you do not need us to describe crimes because newspapers and TV journals describe, virtually every day, the various crimes that people commit.

However, not all crimes are detected, or should we say that not all crimes are detected or are reported.

There is a difference in the meaning of the word crime.

The vast majority involve theft of one sort or another.

These crimes happen because some people feel that they lack money, so they either steal money or they steal items that they hope to sell to get money.

Then there are those who commit murder. The reasons that one person kills another are many and varied and we find this deeply regrettable that a person takes the life of another, whatever the reason.

Most of the crimes we have mentioned are noted and the culprit may or may not be discovered and dealt with in one way or another.

But, in our view, the most serious crimes that can be committed are those perpetrated by rich and powerful people who think it normal to rob the poor to make them richer.

These sorts of crimes often go undetected or, indeed, may not be considered crimes at all, because the rich and powerful tend to be also the lawmakers, so they create laws that protect themselves, whilst punishing those who protest against such injustice.

Naturally, once an incarnation finished, any person who grew rich on the backs of the poor has to pay the price by a visit to the appropriate region of hell.

But the question is why we are addressing the subject of crime and punishment and why it is appropriate to include such a topic in this chapter, and in this book, which deals with areas in the 4th and how they relate to us via our auras?

Believe it or not, there is an area in the 4th that contains the topic of crime and another that deals with punishment.

Although they are two separate areas, and we will examine both these areas separately, actually they are connected because crime is an offence that creates what one might call Karma and punishment is a crime also because no one has the right to judge another. Thus crime creates, in the after life, the fact that one judges oneself and is suitably punished by a period in hell, if appropriate, but punishment is also similarly judged by oneself as a crime because to judge another - which is what courts do - is also a crime. So, the concept of crime and punishment, which exists on the incarnation plane, is really two faces of the same coin.

Both are crimes and are suitably judged by the individual once his incarnation is finished. There are many judges and law enforcement people who consider it normal to judge the crimes committed by a third party, but Jesus made it quite clear that we were not empowered to judge another.

We don't know if you have understood this so we will explain again in different words.

(1) No one should commit any crime because if one had faith that God would provide and, equally, we are all actually one person and that person is God, there should be no meaning of crime because, if we steal, we are stealing from ourselves and stealing from God.

If people understood this and had the faith that God will provide, there would be no crime. We are stealing from or harming ourselves.

Even those who harm animals are harming themselves, because animals are also God in the form of animals, and as we are God and as animals are God, when we harm an animal, we are harming ourselves.

(2) Punishment is dangerous, because if someone judges another, that person, who is God, is judging another aspect of God so it is God judging God.

One should never judge someone because, as we are all one, if we judge someone, we are not only judging ourselves but judging God.

Similarly, if we punish someone, we are, in effect, punishing both God and ourselves. This must be a rather stupid thing to do.

If people only realised their connection to each other and their connection to God, there would be no crime and there would be no punishment. Such foolishness will end one day, but for the moment it is forging ahead at great pace - crime and punishment. As we mentioned, the notion of both crime and punishment come from areas in the 4th that exist to promote these aspects of human behavior.

Let us enter these two areas. Although they are placed in separate areas in the 4th, in effect, they are so similar that they could be considered to be one area. As we enter them we are filled with a rather horrible emotion. The desire to commit crime is foreign to many of us in heaven and the desire to punish anyone is equally strange to us. We do not have crime nor punishment in our world. Even the area known as hell is not criminal and there is no actual punishment as such. The hell regions contain people that made serious errors during their incarnations and the people are drawn to areas that correspond to those errors of judgement. So, they find themselves in areas that correspond to how they lived their lives. It is not punishment but a continuation of how they lived but from the aspect of their victims rather than themselves.

For instance, if someone was a criminal, he would find himself in an area where he is the victim of crime.

If he was a judge and spent his professional life handing out punishments, he would find himself in an area where he feels the effects of such punishments.

The object of hell is not negative. It is an educational area where people learn not to commit crimes and not to judge others.

As we said, if people had greater faith that God would provide for all his children, there would be no crime and there would be no judges and thus no punishment.   That is why crime and punishment go together.

Both are crimes against God, as we explained earlier.

However, when we enter either the crime or the punishment areas in the 4th, we are filled with a strange, negative emotion.

Crime is a sort of jealousy. A person feels animosity against another, for whatever reason he or she thinks that the other person is separate from the criminal.

We have not said that very clearly so let us say it again.

A person feels that someone has, for example, more money than another and decides to steal that money.

Or it might be possession of works of art; jewelry, paintings, statues or whatever.

Equally, a person might feel that he loves another but that love is not returned and so that switches on a need to take action.

Others feel the need to rape or sexually abuse another. The list is endless.

All this is contained in fairly pure form in the area in the 4th concerned with crime.

When one visits this area, there is not a list of possible crimes from which to choose.

This area promotes this sort of jealousy feeling in its most intense form. It is this jealousy that promotes crime.

In effect, as someone lives and feels that he/she is lacking something - money, love or whatever - he reaches out to the crime area, which responds by sending him the desire to commit crimes to fulfill his desires.

By 'he', we are using linguistic convention again. Both men and women commit crimes.

These maybe petty crimes up to world wars. They are all provoked by the feeling of lack or of jealousy.

Petty crimes like stealing are easy to understand but major wars are a little more difficult, but even wars are provoked or started by people who feel the need to conquer another group of people in order to get something. This might be extra land, in which case the winning country will get money and wealth by taxing the loser country, or it might be to get control of resources; oil, coal, minerals, etc.

Slaves were captured by one group capturing another and selling them for profit to landowners, who forced the slaves to work to grow crops, etc., for profit so the slave owner could be richer.

There is always the desire to have more that is behind crime, and that desire is a sort of jealousy.

But now let us look into the punishment area. Once again, it is a strange feeling for us because, as we said, no one has the right to judge another.

Generally speaking, those who rise to the positions of being judges are those who have amassed a certain amount of wealth. This wealth is, of course, obtained from poorer people. So, the only difference between a wealthy judge and a poor thief is that the judge has amassed his wealth through what is considered to be legal methods whereas a thief has attained his bounty through illegal methods.

But, when we enter the judgmental or punishment area, the desire to punish others is very close to jealousy once again, as the judge does not want the person being judged to have what he, the judge, has.

It is not unknown for judges to be guilty of the most horrendous crimes that he, the judge, hopes will never be discovered whilst he is handing out punishments to those caught committing the very same or very similar crimes which he secretly commits.

Indeed, from our readings of the akashic record, the more a judge is involved with indecent or criminal activities, the more eager he seems to be to hand out horrific penalties to those caught doing similar things.

For instance, we would like to quote here the crime that someone was accused of and the punishment handed out. We will also, first, quote what the judge was actually doing at the time he judged a miscreant.

What we are going to describe are the actual, real events as told to us by the people involved.

First, let us say what the judge told us. We will not mention names but we ask you to accept that what we are going to describe are the genuine reports the people involved told us.

So, let us report what a judge was getting up to.

In this case, a judge, who was a highly placed dignitary, many years ago, was not only rich and famous but he had a liking for young, unmarried girls and he would have them captured and taken to his castle where he would rape them.

He had absolute power over the serfs who lived, not only on his vast estate, but on neighboring farms and villages.

He had absolute power of life and death over the serfs, who were virtually slaves and prisoners under his domination. His word was law and anyone who displeased him could be dragged before him and dealt with in any way this judge, who was also lord and master, deemed fit.

A case was brought to his attention.

It involved a man who was accused of raping a neighbor's daughter.

Now, you must remember that this lord was doing this very crime on an almost daily basis. Of course, no one was able to protest, and the serfs just had to accept that he would rape young, virgin girls without any regard as to the consequences.

If any of the girls in question became pregnant, their futures were marred for life because it was unthinkable, at the time, for a girl to be married if she already had an illegitimate child.

At that time, virginity was a requirement for marriage and so a female with a child born out of wedlock was a prohibitive bar to any marriage.

Further, at that time, the lives of unmarried females was very bleak and the only chance any girl had of living a decent life was to be married. The man was the breadwinner and no one would employ a female with a child born outside of marriage.
Naturally, the lord in question, declined any responsibility for the children he fathered.
So, for a number of girls, rape would act as a bar to marriage, as no decent man could consider marriage to a girl who was not a virgin.
Thus, rape was considered to be a very serious crime.

So, this particular man was brought before this dreadful judge and his supposed crime was revealed.
Of course, it was not a case of really trying to discern if the accused man was innocent or guilty.
As far as the judge was concerned, this was a girl that he could not abuse as she had already lost her virginity. The fact that the girl had consented to the sexual act was not considered.
The girl had lost her virginity, so the judge found the man guilty of rape.

In those days and in the main village square there was often a whipping post. It was there as a permanent reminder to all that any crime, whatever it was, would probably end up with the accused person being tied to the post and whipped in full view, and for the delight, of all the people that lived in that area.
If someone was convicted of a crime, and the sentence was whipping, notices would be posted in various places stating the name of the convicted person, his or her crime and the date and time that the punishment would be inflicted. Thus, all that wanted to see the punishment being inflicted could turn up on the appointed day, and at the appointed time, and witness the act.
In those days, public punishments or executions were regarded as attractive and large numbers of people would turn up to witness the punishment.
The crime would be read out by someone who could read and the number of lashes counted.
We must also say that in certain countries, public punishments are still being inflicted and is seen by the public as a form of entertainment.
It was seen as such at the time we are talking about.

Now, we will relate to you the events as seen and felt by the accused person.
He was accused of rape and was immediately found guilty by the judge we mentioned above who, we remind you, was raping girls on an almost daily basis.
The judge delivered a diatribe saying how dreadful the crime was that the man had been found guilty of.
Then the judge read the sentence that he considered appropriate for the crime of rape.
As we reveal the punishment decreed, we ask you, if you can, to put yourself in the place of this man and imagine that it was going to happen to you.

The judge ordered the following punishment.

1. The person would be locked up in the dungeons of the castle until notice of a punishment could be posted in the various villages, so that all who wanted to witness the punishment could attend.

2. The first punishment was 100 lashes, starting at midday, to be administered by the adult members of the abused girl's family: father, grown sons, uncles and so on.   Each member would administer a few lashes with all their force and take turns to use the whip.
   This was considered to be a sort of retribution for the damage inflicted on the girl and also prevent any one person becoming fatigued after a few strokes.

3. The accused person would remain tied to the whipping post until nightfall so that he could be mocked by the villagers. At nightfall, he would be taken to the dungeons again.

4. Then, the next day, at midday, yet another hundred lashes were to be administered exactly as before and the person left tied to the post until nightfall. Then he would be returned to the dungeons of the castle.

5. This was to continue for a week - seven days - and the person left in the dungeons until he had recovered sufficiently for the next stage of his punishment to start.

6. This was to be broken on the wheel.
   This punishment consisted of a cart with large wheels being driven into the village square and the accused person being tied to one of the wheels, and his bones systematically broken by someone smashing his bones with a huge hammer. This would continue until the person was dead.

7. He would be buried in unconsecrated ground, which was considered at that time to be a terrible act, because to be buried outside of holy ground and without the blessing of a priest meant that the person had no chance of going to heaven.

8. One of the older brothers would be forced to marry the abused girl to make a 'decent' woman of her.
   This, obviously, implied one of the accused person's brothers having to marry a girl he did not know, did not love and was considered to be soiled goods, so to speak. So it was a grave slight on the accused man's family. The family would become outcasts. So, this was a terrible infliction on the family.

Now, just put yourself in the position of this prisoner.
He listened to his sentence, realized that he was going to be terribly tortured, finally killed in a most painful manner and would probably never go to heaven. On top of all this, his family would curse him forever for making them outcasts.
There was no possibility of appeal. The sentence was final.
The final thing was that his meager possessions would be given to the aggrieved family as payment for his sins against them.
So, he was taken back to his cell in the basement of the castle to await the day that his punishment would commence.

This person explained to us how it felt waiting day after day with no information as to when his punishment would commence. His guards showed him the whip that would be used and flayed it around to scare him.

Finally, one day, after a long wait, his cell door was flung open, the guards barged in, ripped his shirt off and he was taken to the village square.
A large crowd had assembled to witness the spectacle and they shouted and cheered as he arrived.
The judge and his cohorts were on horseback awaiting the punishment.
The local priest was given the task of reading the crime and the approved punishment, presumably because he could read. Not many serfs could read at that time.

The prisoner was tied to the whipping post and the punishment began. Each member of the girl's family laid on the lashes as hard as they could and the poor victim said the pain was indescribable. He thought it would never end.
The priest counted the strokes as they were laid on until eventually one hundred was reached.
The poor victim vomited with pain and also his bowels liberated urine and excrement into his trousers.
Once the flogging stopped, the nobles rode away but large numbers of people remained to mock the man still tied to the whipping post.
They threw rotten fruit and vegetables at him and some even put salt on to his wounded back.
At dusk, he was released and returned to his cell where he laid on the floor of his cell gritting his teeth against the pain.
The next day the same process continued and this went on for seven days, effectively giving him seven hundred lashes.
At the end of this process he was more dead than alive and so he was cast into his cell and allowed either to recover or to die from shock.
In his case he survived and, after a few weeks he started to recover.
So, the next stage of his punishment could be inflicted.

Once again, messages were posted stating that this person was going to be broken on the wheel on a certain date
On the prescribed day, he was dragged from his cell, tied to the wheel of a cart in a spread eagle fashion and a guard from the prison appeared with a sort of sledgehammer and, at a signal from the judge, proceeded to smash the bones in his arms and legs and finally his ribs so that he could not breathe and his life expired.

Can any of us imagine what this man went through?
Once he was pronounced dead, his body was flung into a fosse or communal pit but, of course, the real him arrived in our world, his mind and spirit totally traumatized.
He was placed in an artificial coma and put in one of our hospital areas while healers sent rays to help him recover.
Eventually, he recovered, of course, and took his place amongst the heavenly throng.
All those involved with inflicting the torture, when their turn came to return to heaven, were shown the terrible deeds that they inflicted and paid the price in remorse.
This awful judge spent a long time in hell paying for the harm that he caused to countless girls and the harm he caused to be inflicted on the person we described and on countless others.

All that we have described, and worse, was considered to be normal punishment for crimes. Often, there was no fair trial. It was sufficient to be accused to be found guilty and terrible punishments inflicted.

We apologise for explaining this event in such detail, but you asked for us to deal with the gory areas and these two areas, crime and punishment, led to those events.
Today, of course, in most countries, crimes are not punished with such brutality but public whippings still take place in some countries.

As we said, the subject of rape was considered to be a very serious crime for the reasons we explained.
Before we finish this chapter, we would like to explain the real events that led to the false accusations.
In effect, the couple - the girl that proclaimed she was raped and the poor man that was tortured to death - had fallen in love and this led to them having sexual relations.
Such relations before marriage were strictly prohibited and great steps were taken to ensure that a girl was a virgin until her wedding night.
However, it was always possible for the couple to slip away and allow nature to take its course.
Unfortunately, in this case, the girl's family discovered the lover's tryst and were horrified that the girl was soiled or damaged goods.
The family insisted that the girl proclaim that she had been raped and a report was transmitted to the judge we mentioned.
The judge, for the reasons that we explained, namely that this was a girl that he could not abuse, proclaimed the terrible sentence we described.
The girl, of course, could not mention the truth, namely that she had had sexual relations with the man she loved, and the man, to protect the honour of the girl, could not state the truth either.
So, events unfolded as we described. The poor girl finished up being married to a man she did not love and that he did not love and had no respect for, so they led an unhappy life together.

This is a very sad story but is just one of countless tales we could recount. But we hope that this one description of what happens when one links to the crime and punishment areas in the 4th will suffice.

Once again, we will end this chapter and move on to a more cheerful area in the 4th.
We do hope that what we have described will give some indication of what can occur if one links to the crime and/or punishment areas and how true justice can become distorted by allowing jealousy to colour our emotions.
So, we urge you never to commit crimes and never to judge another.
Both emotions are, to a certain extent, based on jealousy and that is based on a lack of faith that God will provide.
By having faith that God will provide eradicates the need to commit crimes and thus avoid any need of judgement and punishment.

CHAPTER 31

THE CHEERFULNESS PLANE

After the rather sad area of crime and punishment and all the harm that those two areas have caused mankind, let us turn to a rather more light area of the 4th. This will be an area that promotes cheerfulness.

Cheerfulness, as we are sure you are aware, is an emotion that some people naturally seem to feel. As we have mentioned before relating to an area that concerned joy (the happiness plane), cheerfulness is a sort of fellow area.

Cheerfulness is not exactly the same as happiness as people can be experiencing deeply unhappy times and yet still remain cheerful.

There exists in the 4th a plane that we call the plane of cheerfulness.

It is an excellent area to enter because, although we live in a wonderful and peaceful area compared to the incarnation plane in which you live, not all of us are naturally cheerful. We carry our Earthly emotions with us when we make the transfer from the earth plane to heaven so, if we were not naturally cheerful people in incarnation, we arrive in heaven still not being naturally cheerful.

This does not mean that we succumb to being unhappy or miserable as there is nothing in the true heavenly spheres for us to be miserable about, with the exception of if we visit the hellish planes and we see how the people who have self provoked a visit to these areas to help them correct some fault live, we do not know what feeling unhappy is like. But that does not imply that we are naturally cheerful.

Cheerfulness is a state that anyone who is naturally cheerful, no matter what circumstances he finds himself in, remains positive.

So, cheerfulness is a separate feeling to being happy as happiness can come and go as the waves of life experience rise and fall.

A cheerful person remains so no matter what the slings and arrows of life fling at him.

We consider that it is important to be cheerful because that emotion can be infectious and can be transmitted to others that meet a cheerful person. Contact with a cheerful person can provoke that person to wish to become cheerful themselves, and so can attract that emotion through contact with a cheerful person.

Such an emotion can be absorbed and can be transmitted to others. This will infect (if you will forgive the word) more and more people and this will provoke a rise in frequency to all, or at least to many people, and thus will humanity incarnate rise in ascension.

Ascension is a state that incorporates spirituality, knowledge, wisdom and, also, cheerfulness. One cannot rise in ascension if one is miserable nor if one is subject to swings of emotion from happy to unhappy and back again.

It is essential to be positive and cheerful no matter what circumstances life presents to us.

To be like the wonderful people, those who have a near death experience meet, those people have to be happy, positive, wise and cheerful.

Those who have a near death experience always report meeting a person who not only exudes love in a total manner but also cheerfulness.

Can you imagine someone having a near death experience being greeted by a person emitting waves of depression? It would be ridiculous. Those having a near death experience always report being met by a person exhibiting cheerfulness.

So, cheerfulness is a requisite part of being an ascended being, to use a term that you tend to apply to an advanced person.

The term 'ascended being' that you often use when describing someone who exhibits signs of spiritual wisdom is not a term that we readily use.

Of course, in our world in the 4th dimension, we are often in contact with people much more advanced than the majority of us are.

Perhaps, at this point, we can give a short description of the Great White Brotherhood. We have already spoken about our group and our Earthly instruments have been kind enough to put what we said on the website that was created. But for those who have not read what we said, may we repeat some of it, and do so from the point of view of the difference in the degree of spiritual growth?

The person who contacts our Earthly scribe has not been in the heavenly sphere for very long and is not very wise.

This is necessary.

Our Earthly scribe has a certain degree of spiritual wisdom.

But he is not very holy compared to some members of the Great White Brotherhood who have been in the heavenly spheres for thousands of years and who have risen to great heights.

But, in order for us to contact our Earthly scribe, a person had to be selected whose spiritual growth - frequency - was not dissimilar to that of our Earthly scribe.

Had a person in the heavenly spheres been selected who was many degrees in advance to our Earthly scribe, the difference in frequency would have been so great that communication would have been difficult or impossible. Frequency counts when using telepathy.

So, a person in heaven not very different in spiritual frequency was selected and the communication works.

We mention this to demonstrate that, in the case of the Great White Brotherhood, some of us are not very advanced whilst others are so advanced as to be almost at the angelic state.

This is interesting because the very advanced souls may not speak any language that the rest of us are familiar with. Fortunately, telepathy, which is what we use to communicate, does not need language. It is thought transference.

This enables us to communicate and so we are aware of the thoughts of the most advanced and we can all work as one team.

There is a stream of thought coming from the most advanced members, linking to those slightly below the wisest ones, down and down until the thoughts enter the minds of the least advanced.   It is in this fashion that these books are conceived.

The wisest ones transfer their thoughts down to us, and in the process, the language used is modernized and turned into an English that we hope you can understand when it is transmitted to the scribe who attempts to report, accurately, what is sent to him.

We do not know if you appreciate what an honour it is for you to read words that were originally sent from tremendously advanced people, and couched in words understandable to you by intermediary members who received the thoughts transmitted by the wisest souls, and present them to you in plain English.

One of the conditions, requirements, that are necessary to be a member of the Great White Brotherhood is to have had an incarnation but another is to be a cheerful person. We do not accept into the Great White Brotherhood anyone who has swings of mood into depression.
All the members must be stable, cheerful people.
This gives some indication of how important being cheerful is.
You who are struggling through your incarnation can link to the cheerful plane and incorporate this emotion into your personality.

So, let us describe this plane. Like so many areas in the 4th it is non-physical, meaning that when we enter it, there is nothing to see.
We have to learn to link to this frequency and when we can do this we are automatically transferred to this area.
Thus do we link to the cheerfulness plane and, as it is in pure form, we are filled with what we call cheerfulness.
Now, this emotion - cheerfulness - is more difficult to describe than we think.
We all know, or most of us do, what it feels like to be cheerful. But this emotion is usually linked to other emotions: to receive lots of money, to fall in love and so on.
But the feeling of having enough money to face any financial difficulty that might occur may not, necessarily, make us cheerful. Indeed, there are many extremely rich people who are far from happy or cheerful. They might be rich but they lead empty lives chasing ... something!
Falling in love is a bit nearer to being cheerful but even that emotion can be tinged with fear that the relationship might not last.
So, even being in love might make us cheerful for only a short while.

The feeling of cheerfulness that we experience when we enter the cheerful plane is different.
We will try to explain the feeling but it will not be easy as we will have to link it to other emotions which are not actually the case in reality.
We are familiar with feeling happy. Certainly, this plane - the cheerful plane - gives us a feeling of happiness. But, as we explained, happiness is often tinged with fear so happiness does not fully describe being cheerful. Being healthy and brimming with vitality is also a good feeling but, once again, we may feel fit but not cheerful as our minds dwell on all the things that might be lacking.
Being in love, as we mentioned, is a wonderful feeling but, once again, can be tinged with fear over the uncertainty that the love will last.
So, no matter what we describe, usually one can find a negative aspect.
Riches may not last, so even amongst the richest of the rich there is the fear of losing their riches.
Also, we may say that vast amounts of money do not always lead to happiness as possessions and an extravagant lifestyle seldom bring lasting pleasure.
Possessions become meaningless, and buying endless items does not ever bring lasting happiness.

Without happiness, it is impossible to be cheerful. The two, happiness and cheerfulness, go hand in hand together.
They occur in this order.
1. Cheerfulness
2. Happiness
So, no matter what our situation in life, without cheerfulness one cannot find happiness.

The question is, how does the average person, beset with money problems, beset with problems concerning love and/or health and all the mass of unpleasant events that life presents, ever find cheerfulness?
Quite simply, it is a plane that anyone can contact but to contact that plane is not at all simple for the average person.
Uppermost in our minds is the endless collection of problems we mentioned: money or lack of it, wealth, generally, as in the endless accumulation of possessions, health or lack of it, love or the lack of it and on and on.
One has the impression that each time a problem is solved another problem rears its ugly head. It never seems to end.
So, how can one possibly be happy faced with endless problems?
We can assure you that money or wealth does not solve all problems. You can ask any rich person and they will tell you that, despite all their wealth, they are beset with problems.
So, one cannot be happy if one is beset with problems and yet we all seek happiness.

In the case of animals, they might be temporarily content if they have a full stomach and a safe place to sleep, but this contentedness only lasts until they are hungry again or where they sleep becomes unsafe.
So, even animals are seldom completely happy.
You may remember us saying that to be happy requires that one first acquires cheerfulness.
So, in our opinion, one of the most important aspects of life is to acquire cheerfulness.
Cheerfulness is not affected by wealth or lack of it, nor by health, nor by love or any other thing that we might seek.
They are all secondary and, if one acquires cheerfulness, one can be happy despite lack of almost everything that most of us considered to be so important.

We will go back to the cheerfulness plane and consider what it is connected to.
We have said that cheerfulness is not related to anything connected to incarnation - wealth, health, love, etc., - and we will also say that moving to the non-incarnation planes does not promote cheerfulness.
Cheerfulness promotes happiness, but they are two separate things, and cheerfulness, we will tell you, is connected to our link to the God force.
Someone filled with the power of God is cheerful. It is the most important link, so when we enter the cheerfulness plane we are, indeed, filled with cheerfulness but we are also filled with a link to God.
This is more difficult to explain.

We have all met people who claim to be 'God fearing'.
This is not what we are talking about at all. We are talking about 'God loving'.

We are filled, in this cheerfulness plane, with an intense love of and for God, which means that we feel an intense love for everyone and everything, because everything is created by and for God.

So, cheerfulness implies a profound love of God, which implies a profound love for all things; humans, animals, plants and anything made of minerals (houses, statues or whatever).

But true happiness is independent of possession of anything.

The cheerful person is detached from any desire to possess.

The strange thing is that, in the degree that we can detach ourselves from the desire to possess, we tend to get things.

This also is difficult to understand but we will try to explain

Those who have constant desire to possess happiness chase endlessly after possessions, thinking that possessions are connected to happiness. They also think that by having possessions will enable them to be cheerful as their problems fade.

This is not so. Life does not work like that. As we rid ourselves of one problem, another appears.

Therefore, seeking possessions does not bring happiness and without happiness one cannot be cheerful.

They, cheerfulness and happiness, are mutually dependent.

However, cheerfulness plus happiness, and then possessions, are mutually independent.

By which we mean, and we repeat, wealth, health, etc., does not make us happy and without happiness we cannot be cheerful.

Especially, love is dependent on the partner being cheerful. No one will love someone who is horrible, bad-tempered and constantly chasing something, the desire to possess ever more eating away at them.

The great gurus that history has noted, and indeed, the vast number that have never been publicly known, all had some things in common.

By gurus, we mean wise people. Not necessarily Indian but people with spiritual wisdom.

First and foremost, they possessed very little. They did not chase after possessions. It sufficed that they had sufficient clothing to keep them warm. They ate very little and generally, relied on other, kind people to provide food for them. This was important because those who provided food were, themselves, often not rich. Rich people are often selfish and would not wish to share their food with a guru.

Their attitude is that if the guru wanted to eat, let him get a job and earn money to buy food.

But there are many poor people who give food to gurus. To be poor and often close to starvation is an important lesson. When one has gone to bed hungry enables one to appreciate what hunger is. So, if a guru asks a rich person for food, he will often be turned away, but if the guru asks a poor person, quite often that person will share his meagre rations with the guru.

This sacrifice brings great blessings to the giver and not only brings spiritual growth but helps to promote happiness and this helps to be cheerful.

These are the very attributes that the rich person seeks but he cannot receive the gift of happiness and cheerfulness unless he first gives.

You may remember the lesson in the Bible in which a rich person asked the Master Jesus what he should do to enter the kingdom of God. Jesus told the rich man to sell all his possessions, give to the poor and follow the path of holiness.
You will note that Jesus told the rich man to give and then he would be in a position to be blessed by God.
So, to receive one must first give.

The function of a true guru is not to seek salvation for himself, but to encourage others to find salvation.
That is why a guru asks for food.
A true guru could quite easily create food, because if he is really a true guru or holy man, he would have already mastered the art of creating all that he needs by manipulating the etheric and astral realms.
But he asks for food - or for anything else for that matter - in order to give a chance for another person to rise in spirituality by sharing what they have. The person gives and by giving he receives. We have already explained this in other works but it is worth repeating.
We also mention this because there are a number of so-called gurus who persuade rich people to share their wealth with the guru and the guru himself becomes wealthy.
Such a guru should, in our opinion, be avoided.
The object, the goal of being a guru, is not only to teach spirituality but also to help others rise in spirituality by following the advice given by great teachers such as the Master Jesus.
There is no point in asking a poor person to share his small supply of food with the guru if the guru is immensely wealthy.
For the trick to work, the guru must be in a position that he is genuinely hungry and not have any food and then the person who shares his food - or whatever else the guru needs - receives great blessings from God.

Jesus, in his great teaching on giving to receive, went on to say if someone asks for your shirt, give him your coat as well. If someone asks you to walk a certain distance with him walk twice the distance.
It all comes down to giving to receive.
The way it works, in fact, is that we are all one and that one is God.
So, by giving to another, it is our aspect of God giving to another aspect of God.
This creates a Gestalt - the whole being greater than the sum of the parts.
By giving creates more God power in those who give. God is the source of all love and love is the source of cheerfulness and happiness.
That is why we must do our best to care for all life.
No matter what we do, if we do it with love and a genuine desire to help no matter how great the cost to us in personal terms, by giving we receive.
The power of God will look after us and give us whatever it is we need.
By helping one aspect of God, our God power grows and this God power is the source of all creation. So by giving we create more.
Whatever it is that we need, by giving we create more.
If we are short of food, by giving we create more food.
If we are short of money, by giving we create more money.

No matter what it is, by giving we receive.
By being cheerful, we create more cheerfulness.
By being happy, we create more happiness.
It is all connected to the limitless power of the love of God.
The power of God can be endlessly created and this creation brings cheerfulness into our lives.
If God is deeply loving us through our generous deeds, that love manifests itself through cheerfulness and happiness.

So, to sum up, there is in the 4th dimension an area that creates cheerfulness. This plane is also connected to the God power.
Happiness, which we have already talked about in another chapter, is closely connected to cheerfulness and thus to God.
The power of God is endless, but to create more God power we have first to give.
Therefore, to be cheerful, we must link to the effulgent, never-ending power of God and to contact this power we must give.
It doesn't matter what we give of us - who are God made manifest in whatever we consider to be us - we give to another aspect of God. This has the effect of creating more God power and this manifests itself in creating more God love.
To have the love of God manifest in us creates cheerfulness and happiness.
Thus, to be cheerful we need to be immersed, enfolded, in the love given by God.
To create this love and thus cheerfulness we need to give to God. In the degree that we give to God, God blesses us with his love in an endless manner. It is not a question of quantity but of degree. It is related to the quantity of whatever we have, and how much of that we give, that God bestows his blessings on us.
To be fully and totally blessed by God is a wonderful emotion and that emotion creates a person who is always cheerful.

We think that you can see that to be blessed by God is not hard.
By the simple act of loving all life - which is why we give when necessary - we create more love and this love creates cheerfulness and happiness.
Love is just about the most important emotion that is possible to have, and to be loved by God is the most wonderful of all the love emotions.
To be loved by God requires that one cares for all his creation.
So, we suggest you help all life; animal, vegetable, mineral and human.
In the degree that you assist God made manifest in all these things, God will pour his love into you and that love creates cheerfulness.

CHAPTER 32

GROUP A AND GROUP B

Let us now turn our attention to yet another subject.

We have described many areas or planes in the 4th, and you will be aware that for virtually every aspect of life that you might be aware of, its origin is contained in the 4th dimension.

In fact, there are hundreds of such areas, some relating to physical life and some relating to emotions.

Obviously, we cannot describe them all so we have concentrated on the most interesting and well-known aspects.

We do not wish to be accused of overkill so we will gradually draw this book to a conclusion.

But there are still a few topics that we wish to discuss and the next one will deal with what happens when we die.

Why should we go to a place called heaven?

Why is it that once our incarnation ends, we do not fade into nothingness?

We have talked about the afterlife at length over a number of years, and those of you who have followed our teachings might think that there is nothing more to say.

Whilst it is true that we have described the afterlife at great length and have described many of its areas, there is one topic that we have yet to discuss.

We have described as fully and as clearly as we can what the non-physical planes/landscapes are like, but we have never mentioned why they exist.

We have asked you to accept that once physical life on Earth ends, generally speaking, everyone ends up in a non-physical landscape but we have not yet touched on why this should be.

What is the force that creates the afterlife? What is the reason for it and who set it all up in the first place?

That topic is what this chapter is about.

Once again, in other books, we have talked about the eight dimensions and have described life first being created in the kindergarten plane and then being transferred to the 8th dimension. We have described how life advances until it reaches the 4th, which is where it remains unless it has an incarnation in the 6th dimension.

Then we said that those who have an incarnation on what you call the earth plane (contained within the 6th dimension) eventually return home to the 4th where they remain for virtually ever.

It gives the impression that whether one has an incarnation in the 6th or not, once that incarnation is over, we merely rejoin the other life who did not have an incarnation and life continues almost as if incarnation never happened.

This is not at all true. Or should we say that the consequences of having an incarnation are not without major effect on our continued life in the 4th.

Let us explain.

Those who do not have an incarnation follow a certain path and, hopefully, rise in spirituality. This affects their frequency. So, those who choose not to have an incarnation find themselves in a different part of heaven to those who do have an incarnation. This first group - those who choose not to have an incarnation - follow a totally separate education to those who do have an incarnation.

Let us call those who do not have an incarnation group A and those who do, group B. This is just to make explanations simple.

The only Earthly example we can think of is to imagine group A as children not wishing to follow a military career and those in group B being pushed into becoming boy soldiers by their parents.

Although basic education might be somewhat similar, group B would contain a lot of military training that group A would not need.

Although this might be a poor example of the difference a potential incarnation makes, we hope that you can see that, from the beginning, group B would need to have information that would not be in the least relevant to group A.

So, from the moment a person makes his choice either to have an incarnation or not, their paths split and both groups receive a totally different type of education.

It is not that one is better than another, it is that they are different.

Group A follows one path that excludes incarnation while group B follows an educational path destined to prepare group B for incarnation.

Included in group B's education is the fact that the incarnation will only last for a certain period of time and then it will end and we call that end death.

But, you will notice that, generally, although group B are taught that they will die, it is rare that anyone from group B remembers being taught what will happen after death.

This is because the teachers of group B do not know what will happen.

This sounds crazy but it is so.

The teachers, those chosen to educate group B, have never experienced death or, more importantly, they have never met anyone who died.

We must explain this more fully for you to be able to understand.

We will totally ignore group A, because that group have their own teachers and those teachers only know what they need to teach group A.

You must try to understand something about teachers and education.

If we go back to the example we used about students either having a normal education as opposed to those involved with a military education.

The teachers of normal education were taught about normal subjects when they were students. Equally, those involved with a military lifestyle were, when they were students, taught about military matters and that is all they are qualified to teach.

We want you to realise this difference because it is important to the subject under discussion.

We have two groups of students and we have two groups of teachers that we called group A and group B.

Those in group A know nothing about those in group B and vice versa.

Those in group A know nothing about death, because this has no meaning to group A students or teachers.

But let us concentrate on Group B, which involved us and involves you.

There comes a problem when teaching Group B students.
The teachers have, themselves, never had an incarnation. They actually come from group A students and have received special training to enable them to educate Group B students up to the point that they will be armed to face an incarnation.
Finally, they learn that the incarnation ceases eventually, and at that point their knowledge stops.
They have not had, themselves, an incarnation, so they have no experience of what might happen when incarnation ends. If the teachers do not know what comes next, they cannot teach it.
This may sound strange but it is so.

We feel that we should explain this further to make it quite clear.
For group B students, life is in three parts.
Part 1 is the education given before incarnation.
Part 2 is the incarnation, which is what you are experiencing now.
Part 3 is what comes after incarnation ends.
The teachers of group B are only qualified to teach about incarnation up to the point that the students actually start their incarnations.
At that point, the teachers lose contact with the students and never hear from them again.
Incarnation creates a clean break from the classroom - if we may thus describe the group B educational process - and actual incarnation.
It is all a question of vibration, of frequency.
Part 1 is of a certain frequency.
Then there is a change of frequency when incarnation starts.
Finally, there is another change of frequency when incarnation ends.
They are all totally different frequencies, so there is no possible connection between part 1, part 2 and part 3.

But it is important to realise that the teachers of group B have never actually had an incarnation themselves. They have only been taught about incarnation and as the frequency of incarnation ends with physical death, they cannot teach group B students what, if anything, comes after death.
We, who have had an incarnation have no means of contacting these teachers because we are all on different frequencies and thus are in the equivalent of being in different worlds.
Therefore, we who know that life continues after death have no means of passing that knowledge to the teachers of group B.
That is why everyone who has an incarnation is born with absolutely no idea of what happens once a person dies.

We are sure that you find what we have so far said very bizarre, but we assure you that it is so.
Indeed, this lack of knowledge of the continuity of life after death has caused great confusion.
There are many convinced that there is nothing after physical death.
Then there are those who think that only the followers of their particular religion will go to heaven. And there are a variety of beliefs in between.

But, the subject of this chapter is why is it that life does indeed continue once incarnation finishes.

After all, if the teachers of group B students do not know about it, was there ever a time when life did end once incarnation finished?

We may not be able to answer all the questions but we can answer some of them.

To begin to answer these questions, we need to look back over past information we gave and we will mention two things.

We apologise if what we are about to say is already known to you but we must consider all readers of this book, and so we will assume that there are some readers to whom what we are about to say is unknown.

We will mention two things as titles and then we will expand on both of them because they are connected together as topics, and will also help us to answer the questions we posed earlier.

1. Planet Earth was first designed just for animals and plants.

2. Humans were a later introduction.

So, let us discuss topic 1.

When planet Earth was first created, a decision was taken that it would be the place where life could develop in what is termed physicality.

Right from the beginning, long before any thoughts of physicality were conceived, there was life created in the non-physical realms. We are going back a long, long time here to the time before any planets, galaxies, etc., existed in physical form.

Already, at that distant time, life existed and it started in the 8th dimension - if we ignore the kindergarten plane.

We have discussed this at length in a previous book (the Path of Mankind) but we must briefly mention it again in order to push this chapter along.

God's archangels created what you see as physicality. You see this mainly from the point of view of planet Earth because, when the archangels created what you see as planet Earth and all the various planets, moons, stars and galaxies which, we remind you, are all created from your consciousness, your imagination in the imagination plane - the 6th - it was decided to concentrate all of what you refer to as physicality on just one planet, planet Earth.

This was so as to be able to keep all of physicality concentrated together.

Although scientists are scanning the universe - the physical universe - in the vain hopes of finding life elsewhere, they are wasting their time.

There is no life anywhere else in physicality. There is plenty of life elsewhere in the non-physical realms, especially the 4th where we live, but there is nothing in or on the various planet's scientists claim to have discovered in the so-called Goldilocks zone.

Just because a planet is discovered just the right distance from our sun to create conditions similar to those found on Earth, and just because there might be liquid water on those planets, does not imply that there is physical life.

We can tell you that there is not!

You may ask why it is that all life is concentrated on and in just one small planet we call Earth although, due to the fact that most of it is water, seas, lakes, rivers, snow and underground lakes and rivers, it might have been more appropriate to have named it planet water!

Anyway, you might question why it was decided to concentrate all life on one planet? The answer is all around you.

If someone decides to create a zoo, which is a large collection of animals from all over the world gathered together, they are trapped inside a sort of cage, a fence that keeps the animals in and the public out.

In this way, should anyone wish to control the animals or to study them, they can do so easily as the animals are at hand.

Of course, we are aware that this is not a perfect example as there are animals in the wild in many countries and people go out either to study them or to destroy them.

So, we ask you to use your intelligence to see the point we are making which is that when animals are brought together into one place it is easier to control them than when they are spread all over the place.

You have the same concepts in schools, prisons, military establishments and so on.

Lifeforms are concentrated in specific areas to make it easier to relate to them.

The same idea was taken by the archangels when a decision was taken to create an area where life that was present in the 8th and 7th dimensions could advance the desire of God to grow in wisdom and thus, in imaginary form, what you call the solar system, including planet Earth, was created.

This takes us on to what is known as the Big Bang. It is thought that everything that constitutes the cosmos was created at once. This is not exactly true

Planet Earth was created first and it was only when man was introduced and he expected to see things in the night sky, that the rest of the cosmos was introduced.

So, planet Earth was created.

This takes us a bit further along in the story. We know that we said that we would try to answer some specific questions, the topic of this chapter, but we feel that it would help to explain all this in relation to incarnation.

So, planet Earth was created and populated with sufficient plants, water, caves and so on for the next phase to be introduced.

This next phase was to introduce animals.

As you may realise, it took a vast amount of spiritual energy to create planet Earth and populate it with plants, water and so on.

That energy needed, and still needs, to be replaced.

Spiritual energy is created at a high level, but to create so-called physicality, a large amount of that energy was lowered in frequency to create physicality.

Everything is made of vibrations of one sort or another. This energy that we are discussing was almost at the frequency of God himself. We have described this as pure starlight although, at that time that we are discussing, with the exception of the sun (a star), stars did not exist.

We mentioned in another book that man and animals already existed in the 8th and 7th dimensions so a decision was taken to introduce animals into the 6th dimension which is where physicality was created.

This was an experiment by the archangels to see if life could be introduced into physicality and if that physical life would evolve to the point that it could pay back the energy that was used to create physicality.

After much trial and error, and a number of failed attempts based on the elements found on Earth, especially water and stone, the concept of transforming plants and water into flesh was created.

This used even more energy but was successful.

So, animals of various sorts were introduced and populated the Earth.

The object was two-fold.

First and foremost was to satisfy the God force in his quest to grow in experience and wisdom and also, related to that first answer, was in the hopes that animals would evolve to the point that they would repay the energy used to create physicality.

So far, this part has failed. Certainly, animals have, generally, being successful at breeding, surviving and populating the world, but the hope that they would rise in spirituality and repay the energy used to create physicality has not succeeded.

At this point we need to return to man in the 8th and 7th dimensions and try to answer the question of this chapter which is to find out if life after death continues and why - assuming that life after physical death does continue!

For those in any doubt, we assure you that it does!

We got to the point concerning mankind where we were talking about two sorts of humans; group A and group B.

Group A never have an incarnation and Group B do.

But let us talk about life before man was introduced into incarnation.

Now, animals and humans were, originally, all only in astral form in either the 8th (really only as basic life forms - singularities) and later in the seventh as defined life forms either animal or human.

In either case, they remained in astral form as physicality had not yet been created.

Eventually, physicality was created and animals introduced.

This created a problem as animals need to be born, grow to maturity, reproduce and then they must eventually die.

This four-fold process created enormous problems for God's archangels because the concept of physicality was new and the concept of birth, growth, reproduction and death did not exist in the astral realms.   They were new, and each phase had to be carefully thought about and created.

One of the major problems was what to do with life once the death phase was reached. Recycling the atoms of physical life so that the animals bodies did not pollute the Earth and that there would not be countless corpses of animals everywhere was one thing, but what to do with the spirits of animals once the incarnation was finished was a whole different level of complexity as the 4th dimension, although it existed as a carrier wave, did not exist in the form that it is today.

As far as animals were concerned, they started their existence in the 8th, moved to the 7th and remained there.

Once incarnation had been perfected, a third level was created - 8th, the 7th and now the 6th (incarnation). But the problem remained, what to do with the spirits of dead animals.

We will also say that, at some point in evolution, the concept of the 4th was created but it was done so in order that man - God's greatest invention - could evolve.

So, a part of the 4th was created, the part that we called part 1 earlier on in this chapter, and specially trained teachers were hired to teach young humans about the mysteries of life.

We hope that you will forgive us if we go back to an earlier part of this chapter and refresh your memories.

We said that there were two groups; group A and group B. Forget for a moment group B and just retain in your mind group A.

This was involved with just teaching about life before incarnation because incarnation did not exist.

These teachers still only teach group A students (those not intending to have an incarnation) about the endless evolution, which was done in the newly created area which was placed in the 4th.

We hope you have followed so far?

Before we move on, we wish to say that all that we have said so far, explained in the various chapters of this book, with the exception of anything to do with after incarnation, is taught to students of both group A and group B. This includes all that we have explained and much more.

As we said, we cannot tell you about all the aspects (emotions) of life, as we wish to keep this book to a reasonable size, and that the teachers of group A students do not know about incarnation and what might happen after incarnation.

To return to animals. A part of the 4th had already been created for educational purposes for humans and so another part was created to deal with the spiritual forces after incarnation.

So, the spirit forces of animals, once their incarnations had finished were and are taken to a part of the newly created 4th and, in the case of animals, with the exception of loved pets, gradually fade and the spiritual atoms recycled.

The really big problem came when it was decided to introduce humans into physicality and what to do with their spiritual part once physicality ended.

Eventually, once it was obvious to God's archangels that animals would never evolve to the point that they would repay the energy used to create physicality, human volunteers were called for, and in your case and ours, we stepped forward and said that we would be prepared to have a physical incarnation.

At this point, two things had to be created.

The first was to split humanity, pre-incarnation, into two groups; group A and group B as we mentioned earlier.

Second, was to expand the post incarnation part of the 4th to accommodate the spirits of humans that had an incarnation.

This was done because it was decided that humans were too important to God's great plan merely to recycle their spiritual atoms. God wanted humans to continue their journey as they could continue to grow in knowledge and wisdom and that could contribute to the endless creation of spiritual power so necessary for all life to continue.

So, let us recapitulate so far.
* At one point there were no planets and no incarnations. In what we call physicality, there was nothing.
* Then physicality was created in the 6th and planet Earth was created.
* Eventually, animals were placed from the 7th into physicality in the 6th.
* At much the same time humans were moved from the 7th to the newly created 4th where a long educational process of all the emotions created by archangels were taught.
* Once the point that humans were introduced into incarnation was reached, two groups of humans were placed either in group A or group B: those not intending to have an incarnation and those intending to have an incarnation.
* So, the area in the 4th which, before incarnation, contained all student humans was expanded to accommodate the two groups, and also so as to accommodate the returning spirits of the group B section of humanity once their incarnation was finished.

Thus, we hope that you can see that the answer to the questions posed at the beginning of this chapter have been explained as far as we know.
The questions asked were, paraphrasing, what happens when we die?
Where do we go?
Did heaven always exist?
Why do we not just fade away?
We have done our best to answer these questions.

Before we finish this chapter we wish to remind you and bring to your attention the vast amount of work and intelligence it took for God's archangels to create, not only the various emotions that both group A and group B students are taught, not only the amazing complexity of incarnation but the incredible, never-ending life available for you and us to study and to learn about post incarnation.
It was, and is, a truly monumental accomplishment and our eternal thanks go out, not only to God but to his unbelievably creative archangels that put so much thought into making what we accept as creation, scarcely giving it a second thought.
So, we will end this rather complex subject here and move onto yet another topic.
We hope that you found this chapter interesting. We wish, finally, to tell you that this is new information revealed to humanity and you are the first to know about it.

GROUP A AND GROUP B: ADDENDUM

It has been pointed out to us that what we explained in this chapter was not entirely clear.
We would like to add this piece to the chapter to clarify the situation.

We mentioned that there were two groups of humans, those intending not to have an
incarnation and those intending to have an incarnation. We called these two groups
group A and group B.
We further mentioned that once the decision had been made, the two groups split and
followed different paths.

Now, let us for the moment ignore group A and concentrate on Group B.
We mentioned that group B teachers were taught sufficient about incarnation to inform
the group B students about the incarnation they would have and said that these teachers
taught about incarnation and stopped at the moment where a person's physical life ended.
To avoid confusion we mentioned little else, but it was pointed out that the chapter was
incomplete because we did not mention that the group B students did have further
education. They were able to meet people who had returned from an incarnation and
converse with these people about their incarnation and their return to the afterlife that you
call heaven.
We will now correct that lacune (gap).

We must always remember that in the heavenly spheres frequency always plays a large
part.
So, in simple terms, let us state that the teachers of group B are on a particular frequency,
as are the students.
However, once the teachers of group B have finished their task of informing the students
up to the point where incarnation ends, the teachers say goodbye to the students and the
students move onto the next phase of education prior to having their incarnation.

Then, the frequency of the group B students is altered to align itself with the next group
of teachers which we will call guides to avoid confusion with the first group of teachers.
As this change of frequency occurs, the first group of teachers disappear and the students
find themselves in the presence of guides who take control of the educational process of
the group B set of students.
There is a clear break between the first set of teachers and these guides.

These guides teach, among other things, that once an incarnation is finished, the students
will return to yet another part of heaven, with another frequency, and when the time is
ripe, these guides alter the frequency of their students to align them with the frequency of
those people who have returned to heaven after their incarnation was finished.
Thus, the students can meet and talk to those who have had an incarnation and have
returned to Summerland in the 4th dimension.
And so, these students can learn that life continues after death.
We must say that the story is more complicated than that and involves oversouls but we
do not wish to complicate matters more than necessary.

Once the students have learnt all that they need to know about life in incarnation (given by the group B teachers) and then, following a change of frequency and advice given by guides and people who have returned from incarnation, that information is placed within the akashic record, which is connected to higher self, and the students prepare to have their incarnation which involves not only yet another change of frequency but also the students losing direct contact with their higher selves and thus not having any memory of their long education.

And so, the students come to Earth according to their Earth plan and have their incarnation.
Eventually, that incarnation ends, the students return, one by one, to Summerland - involving yet another change of frequency - where they can not only follow yet more education, but inform the next group of students about their lives after incarnation.

This may all seem a bit complicated, involving a number of changes of frequency and thus a number of changes of landscapes, which is why we did not mention it.
We will also say that we have only described the bare bones of what happens. We have just given an overview.
The reality is much more complicated than what we have described, but what we have said will give you some understanding of how life progresses and an idea of the number of different landscapes, all contained in separate frequencies, there are in heaven.

Heaven - the 4th dimension - is vast, endless and each area/landscape is kept separate by changing frequencies and each area deals with specific parts of life.

CHAPTER 33

HEADING INTO MEDITATION

The last chapter was rather complicated. It is sometimes difficult for us who live in the 4th dimension and live daily with events about which you, who are incarnate, may know little or nothing of the topics we describe to you.   We sometimes forget that it is necessary for us to be specific to avoid confusion.
However, thanks to the vigilance of one of our members who is incarnate, we have added the addendum hoping to clarify a situation that we take for granted.

This brings us to the next topic which will be about the different frequencies, why they exist and how to link with them.
This may be a short chapter because, although there are countless areas and thus countless frequencies in the 4th, many of them would be beyond your ability to reach and others, once you have had the technique explained, one explanation will cover all access.
So, let us try to explain in simple terms how and why all these different areas and different frequencies exist.

If we can consider the earth plane, you all have areas which are kept apart by various rules and agreements.
For example, generally, if you wish to travel from one country to another, with the exception of certain European countries, travel documents are required: passports, visas, and sometimes, other documents also.
People are not necessarily permitted to enter foreign countries.
Proof of goodwill is also required and those who have offended a country would be refused entry.
Also, closer to your homes, people have their own dwellings and a visitor is required to be invited in before entering a dwelling.

In the heavenly spheres we do not have passports nor do we have locks and bars but we do have a very proficient means of keeping unwanted visitors out.
These are different frequencies.   This does not imply any desire to bar people but some, indeed many areas in the 4th, have to be kept apart for a variety of reasons.
The only visitors we do not wish to enter the upper 4th are those demonic beings from the lower 4th. No doubt, some of them would very much like to enter our realms but they cannot and never will due to a simple device which is a change of frequency.
The lower 4th, due to the nature of the beings that reside there, vibrates to a relatively low frequency as do its inhabitants.
The upper 4th vibrates to a much higher frequency, once again thanks to the noble, peace-loving people that live there.
The demonic beings would find it quite impossible to raise their frequency to ours and thus our world seems invisible to them.

We wish you to understand that the concept of different frequencies, although simple, is a very effective tool for keeping areas apart.
This concept was first thought of, as far as we have been informed, by God when he first invented the eight dimensions that constitutes all that exists.

No doubt, the archangels that work for the God force were involved at some point but we understand that the genius behind this simple but totally effective idea was God himself. We should, perhaps, remind you that when we refer to God in the masculine, it is for literary convention.
We are not sexist nor racist and if you wish to think of God in the feminine (she) or in the neuter (it) we have absolutely no objection.
But for the sake of simplicity we will continue to refer to God in the masculine (he). God does not have a colour, so the question of racism does not arise.

We wish you to realise that everything in all of creation is created by and through vibrations.
Your planet Earth vibrates at a certain frequency and every object on the planet vibrates at the same frequency. That is why you do not notice it vibrating.
But in the case of the upper 4th, although there is a quiescent frequency for both the lower and the upper 4th, there are a vast number in intermediary frequencies.
This is interesting because it implies that all the people - or animals - that are entering our area (the upper 4th) in their descent from the 7th dimension, or who are returning to the upper 4th at the end of an incarnation, vibrate to two frequencies.
The first is the quiescent frequency of the upper 4th and the second is the frequency of whatever part of the upper 4th the person, or animal, finds himself in.
We will ignore the animal kingdom and just focus on humans.
As you should know, a human, assuming that he has finished his incarnation (and assuming he had one), either finishes up in a part of hell, Summerland or one of the higher realms.
This is because, when having his incarnation, according to how he acted he was already vibrating at a certain frequency.
This implies that on Earth, also, people vibrate to two frequencies: the quiescent frequency of planet Earth and the frequency promoted by their personality, their actions and their thoughts and desires.

On planet Earth, due to the fact that it appears physical and 'heavy' in terms of its secondary vibrations, people of all temperaments are mixed together. This is one of the reasons that planet Earth exists and is what makes it so different and fascinating compared to the upper 4th.
We apologise for so often saying, but we have spoken about this phenomenon before, but this book being about the frequencies, areas or landscapes that we find both in the 4th and in incarnation, we feel obliged to mention it again.

So, all of you incarnate are vibrating to two frequencies, one being the frequency of your planet and this involves your physical body vibrating at the quiescent frequency of the planet. The second frequency involves the vibration generated by your personality and it is your spiritual body that is vibrating to this second frequency.
At the end of your incarnation your spirit withdraws and returns to the 4th. But your second frequency continues and that, by the law of mutual attraction, draws you, as we have said, to one of the many areas in the 4th of either hell, heaven or the in-between part, Summerland.

In order to ensure that you are drawn to a light area of the 4th implies that you lead a noble, spiritual existence whilst incarnate.

Nobody expects you to be a saint, unless you want to follow that path, but we do suggest that you try to be a good, kind person, doing good when you can and avoiding doing harm.

This will ensure that you at least go to Summerland when your incarnation ends, and thus avoid going to one of the regions of hell.

This book, we hope you have noticed, has been mainly concerned with describing various other landscapes of the 4th, some just emotional and some more concrete (physical).

So, a person incarnate can, in effect, seem to vibrate to three frequencies:

1. The quiescent frequency of planet Earth.
2. The frequency of his personality, and
3. The frequency of one of the areas/landscapes in the 4th that he tries to link with - the areas that we have described in this book.

Now, we have said that you vibrate to three frequencies but this is not actually, literally so.

Certainly, your body vibrates to the frequency of planet Earth and that never changes but areas 2 and 3 can become somewhat mixed.

A person is born with the personality that he developed before incarnating and if he stayed just with that personality, he would stay with that frequency.

However, we humans tend to be curious creatures and we tend also to want to explore other features of existence; the topics that we have described in this book and many more that we have not described.

Some of these areas, we told you, you could not enter for various reasons, but others you can.

This is where things get a bit complicated.

Most people, in most situations, mix a part of one of the landscapes into their personality and thus divide, in a way, their personality into two, one part remaining with the personality they develop before incarnation while another part explores one of the landscapes concerned with other aspects of creation.

For instance, if a person has developed a personality in which he displays love and compassion, he could also link to the happiness plane or the cheerful plane and incorporate some of that into his personality.

However, it may be obvious that if a person is full of love and compassion, he would find it impossible to link to a plane that promotes hate. The person might get angry from time to time but he would not fill himself full of hate.

So, there is a limit, based on one's personality, that one can link to other planes.

But, for a very advanced person, it is possible to link to other planes, totally, while retaining one's original personality.

This is not easy to do. Let us explain.

All people have their basic personality, and depending on that personality, it is possible to link, to a greater or lesser extent, with other compatible traits, areas or landscapes.

But the degree to which one can develop or incorporate this secondary trait into one's personality depends on the level of spiritual advancement of the individual.

Very advanced people can keep their basic personality and incorporate, totally, a compatible trait.
As we said, this is not easy to do and very few people can achieve this.
It is not a case of sharing one's personality with another area. It is that the individual can totally retain his personality while totally incorporating a second trait, in its pure form, into him.   Then he has two aspects to him.
1. His personality
2. The trait or area he wishes to incorporate.

Further, for an advanced individual, he is not limited to that. He can incorporate several areas into himself in their pure form.
Such people are very rare at the moment.
It is very difficult to be able to have, totally, more than just our basic personality.
Certainly, it is possible to incorporate a greater or lesser degree of a second aspect of a plane into a personality but it is done at the price of the original personality being sacrificed, reduced. But, to keep a personality intact and incorporate, totally, another aspect is very difficult.
It is almost as if one can split one's mind. This is not so.
People with split personality, which is an illness, change from one personality to another. But they only have one personality at a time.
We are talking here of people who can have two or more aspects of personality, in pure form, present at the same time.

The question might be asked as to why anyone would want to have more than one personality?
The answer is that, in the degree that one can incorporate different areas into one, the person grows in wisdom.
We must say that the people we are mentioning here are invariably holy.   Evil people tend not to be able to develop this attribute. It is only very holy people that have the spiritual growth to develop the ability of incorporating more than one aspect into their personalities.

If we only have our basic personality, one can be a good, kind person or one can be an unkind person, but to incorporate more than one personality indicates that one grows in wisdom in the degree that one can achieve this.
This is because we have a greater understanding of life.

The question is how do we link to one of the planes/frequencies in the upper 4th that we wish to incorporate into our basic personality?
The answer is twofold.
Most people can naturally link, to a certain extent, to one or more of the sub-personalities that we have described in this book quite simply by having the desire so to do.
This might be any one of the aspects that we have described in this book, but in this case, it is done in a rather haphazard fashion.   One might be successful or one might not. In the degree that one desires to incorporate a sub-frequency and in the degree that one concentrates on that sub-frequency, one tends to draw it towards one.
But there is another way of doing this that is more positive and assures greater success.
This is through meditation.

We have described how to meditate before but will do so again, as we stated at the beginning of this book that we would tell you how to link with the many planes that we have described in this rather long book.
The secret is meditation.

Before we describe the technique, for those who do not know how to meditate, let us talk about why meditation is so important.
We wish to state also that we who are in the afterlife and who want to serve God, spend a lot of time in meditation.
It is not only a tool that you on the earth plane can use and develop. We use it too.
Indeed, the holier some people are, the more they meditate. One can develop this until one is in a permanent state of meditation.
One can use this concept that we have described above of having two aspects going on at the same time.
It is possible to go about one's duties, serving all life, concentrating totally on the tasks at hand, and at the same time being totally in a state of meditation.
This is a very privileged state and brings great peace to the individual who can develop this.
Meditation has existed for thousands of years, particularly in countries like India but has now spread all over the world and we encourage all who can to learn to meditate.
Meditation is one of the paths of ascension.

What happens when we meditate, its goal, is to still the mind.
Christ said,' Be still and know that I Am.' This rather enigmatic phrase implies that if one can still one's mind, one can link with the God spirit.
However, to still one's mind is no easy task.
The mind is not used to being still.   Ever since we were first created in the 7th dimension, long ago, our mind has been active, thinking, exploring and puzzling out the complexities of existence, first in the spiritual planes and now in incarnation.
You are a lot older than you think you are.
Your incarnation into your family on Earth may have started fairly recently, but you - the real you - came into existence long ago, and in all that time your mind has been active.
And now we are asking it to be still.
The mind does not appreciate this and will fight us for a long time.
Indian people who wish to learn to meditate call it, 'the monkey mind,' because it always wants to be active sending us endless thoughts.
These thoughts are important but form a barrier between us, who would like to take control of our lives and our thoughts, and the higher self which is linked to God.
This barrier is difficult to break through but is the secret of meditation.
We should say that, in our experience, it is almost impossible to be completely successful at stilling the mind, and to be honest, for the average person who does not wish to become a guru, it is not necessary.
However, it is important to try. We must concentrate, in meditation, on trying to push thoughts away and, gradually, we will have short moments - seconds - when we will be successful.
These are startling moments.

To sit and be totally without thought is a strange experience and its effect can be - not alarming - but surprising at first.

Gradually, over time, as we become accustomed to these moments of stillness of the mind, we can accept them and they bring great peace into our lives.

Eventually, two or more things happen.

1. We see, with our eyes closed, a bright white light. This is the light from God flooding our mind with his power. We told you that God is pure starlight and this light that shines on us is an aspect of it.

   This light, so bright yet utterly harmless to us, fills us with a sort of warmth. It is a comforting feeling and it is a pleasure to sit, bathed with this warm light. Eventually, it is possible to see this light all the time, which is a wonderful feeling, but it takes time and a lot of meditation to achieve this state.

2. We are able to be in control of our lives. At the moment, most of us are like a ship that has lost its rudder and is wandering aimlessly over an ocean. Once we can start to still the mind, we find that we have control over our lives.

This control comes in the degree that we can force - persuade is a better term - our thoughts to stop and when that happens, we create a direct link between our mind and our higher self which is our version of the God spirit. So, instead of our thoughts - coming via our personality - trying to direct our lives, we have God directing our lives and God is the force that is able to control life.

Then we find absolute control of the direction that our lives take.

Let us now describe how to meditate. It is not difficult, but like all things, it requires certain actions to be carried out in a certain order.

1. A room must be selected where one can be without being disturbed by our family or any extraneous noise.

2. We must sit on a chair with our back straight. There is no need to exaggerate with this but one should not lie on a bed. Sit on a chair.

3. Calm the mind and then thank God's angels for standing guard over the meditation keeping away any unwanted interference.

4. With one's hands, describe, just outside the body, a sort of egg shape. Imagine that we are protected within a cocoon (an egg shell) of spiritual power. Once again, do not force or exaggerate.

   It suffices to describe this egg shell with one's hands and visualise it with the mind. We are now protected in the astral realms by God's angels and protected in the etheric realms by being in this eggshell of protective power.

5. Sit quietly for about 15 minutes, attempting to still the mind and pushing away the thoughts that invade our mind.

6. After about 15 minutes, send our love out to anyone we know that might be ill or has problems. Equally, we can just, with our mind, send our thoughts out to the world. This act is important. When we meditate, we receive God's power and we should always send that power onwards so that it helps others.

7. Remove, with the mind, the eggshell of protection we created. Thank God and his
   angels for having stood guard over your meditation and then return to normal and
   carry on with life.

As you can see from the above instructions, meditation is simple, but over time it will
transform your life.
Meditation enables us to break the link with the mind and create a link with the higher
self.
The mind does not know the path through life but the higher self does.
So, instead, as we said, of being like a ship with a broken rudder just drifting through life,
the higher self takes control and we are now steered by the God force.
This God force enables us to be in total control of events occurring in our lives.
This gives us confidence, assurance and enables us to proceed through life in peace, joy
and happiness.
It also enables us to link with the planes in the 4th that we have described in this book.

We will end this book here. We have attempted to describe some of the areas in the
higher 4th that affect us both in incarnation and in the spirit world.
Lastly, we have described how to meditate and we encourage all to do so. Meditation
creates a transformation from being a lost soul and enables one to take control of one's
life.

We hope that you have learnt something about life from this book and we will start
another one which will be the 9th in the series, this book being the 8th.